SITUATION MODELS AND LEVELS OF COHERENCE

Toward a Definition of Comprehension

SITUATION MODELS AND LEVELS OF COHERENCE

Toward a Definition of Comprehension

Isabelle Tapiero
University of Lyon
University of Lyon II

LAWRENCE ERLBAUM ASSOCIATES, PUBLISHERS

2007   Mahwah, New Jersey   London

Cover design by Tomai Maridou.

Lawrence Erlbaum Associates
Taylor & Francis Group
270 Madison Avenue
New York, NY 10016

Lawrence Erlbaum Associates
Taylor & Francis Group
2 Park Square
Milton Park, Abingdon
Oxon OX14 4RN

© 2007 by Taylor & Francis Group, LLC
Lawrence Erlbaum Associates is an imprint of Taylor & Francis Group, an Informa business

Printed in the United States of America on acid-free paper
10 9 8 7 6 5 4 3 2 1

International Standard Book Number-13: 978-0-8058-5550-0 (Hardcover)

Library of Congress Cataloging-in-Publication Data

Tapiero, Isabelle.
    Situation models and levels of coherence : toward a definition of comprehension / Isabelle Tapiero, Walter Kintsch.
        p. cm.
    ISBN 0-8058-5550-5 (cloth : alk. paper)

1. Comprehension. I. Kintsch, Walter, 1932- II. Title.
BF325.T37 2007   2006101919

Visit the Taylor & Francis Web site at
http://www.taylorandfrancis.com

To my mother
To the memory of my father

Contents in Brief

Contents

Foreword

Walter Kintsch
University of Colorado in Boulder

Most of us spend a good part of our days either reading or writing, so it is surprising that the psychological study of these processes is a relative latecomer. The investigation of learning processes began with memorizing lists of nonsense syllables and running rats down mazes, not with what we do everyday—reading all kinds of things. The study of thinking started with puzzles of various kinds, not with the kind of inferences that are made in reading. The reason is, of course, obvious: Investigators were put off by the daunting complexity of studying discourse comprehension. Historically, such study has been the domain of linguists, rhetoricians, and literary scholars who emphasized and reveled in the intricacies of their field. High literature and subtle issues of syntax were their topics of choice. The methods that psychologists had developed for work in their discipline were ill suited for the exacting demands of such topics.

There were, of course, a few adventurous exceptions, F. C. Bartlett above all, but for the most part, serious psychology stayed away from text and discourse until well after the start of the cognitive revolution. A hallmark of that movement in the 1950s and 1960s was an emphasis on the central role of language in cognition. Young linguists as well as psychologists eagerly devoured Chomsky's seminal *Syntactic Structure* and *Aspects* (Chomsky, 1957), only to become quickly disappointed by the master's determination to limit the study of language to syntax. Sure, syntax was crucial and fascinating, but everywhere psychologists looked, they were confronted with meaning.

In the early 1970s, a number of trends converged to give rise to the modern field of text and discourse that is the subject of this book. Several psychologists working in the area of memory endeavored to extend the study of memory from list learning paradigms to memory for sentences and memory for text. Representatives of that trend are Frederiksen (1975), Anderson & Bower (1972), and Kintsch (1970; 1974). This work was strongly influenced by linguistics, most importantly the case grammar of Fillmore (1968), the propositional analyses of Bierwisch (1969), and the microstructure–macrostructure distinction of van Dijk (1972). The importance of that early work was that it demonstrated that one could study memory for discourse within the methodological framework of experimental psychology. Of course, what was studied here was no longer high literature but simple sentences and trivial stories.

A major trend in those early years was schema theory, which had originally been developed by Bartlett (1932) and Selz (1922) but suffered neglect in the intervening years. Schema theory became very influential in the 1970s—the form of verb-frames in Fillmore (1968), propositional schemas in Kintsch (1974), and the scripts of Schank & Abelson (1977), as well as the story grammars of Mandler & Johnson (1977).

Thus, by the mid-1970s, the text and discourse area had acquired a notion of structure—the schema—that remains basic to this day. What was missing was a notion of process. How does discourse comprehension relate to the processes traditionally studied by psychologists: memory, learning, and attention? That link was formed with the publication of *Towards a Model of Text Comprehension* (Kintsch & van Dijk, 1978). We analyzed comprehension as a real-time, capacity-limited process, in accordance with current psychological knowledge about attention and short- and long-term memory.

With structure and process in place, one crucial element of text comprehension theory was still missing. That was the realization that although text comprehension starts with words, its outcome is no longer a purely linguistic object but a mental model that involves both linguistic and nonlinguistic levels of representation. Because the term *mental model* was being used in a variety of different ways for different purposes, van Dijk and I coined the term *situation model* for this purpose (van Dijk & Kintsch, 1983). As this book amply demonstrates, the notion of a situation model in text comprehension has proved to be highly productive. One effect it has had is to open the doors to the consideration of nonlinguistic representations, embodied or perceptual representations in addition to (or for some, instead of) verbal-propositional representations. It is interesting to speculate about why nonverbal representations have been relatively neglected until recent years. It was not for a lack of appreciation for their importance. The mental imagery notion has been around in psychology for many years and had found a vocal proponent in Paivio (1969). My guess is, rather, that it was the lack of a suitable notation for mental images that would allow their use in computational models. Linguists have provided psychology with workable notational schemas for words and sentences—it is easy to count words or describe their structural relations. Not so for images at this point, with the consequence that psychologists build many models for words and few for images.

Situation Models and Levels of Coherence provides a survey of the work that has been done on text and discourse in the last few decades by psychologists and cognitive scientists. Specifically, it focuses on the research based on the methodologies of experimental psychology and computational modeling. It is not, however, a review in the strict sense, but rather an integration of several decades of research and theorizing as seen by Professor Tapiero. Thus, it is an original piece of work that goes beyond the research that it summarizes. She presents research results from the literature, her own as well as that of others, clearly and objectively, but at the same time imposes her own view and perspective on the issues discussed. What emerges is not a disjointed literature review, but a fresh picture of an entire research area. Text and discourse researchers will find her views stimulating and worthwhile; students and novices will be able to obtain from this book a coherent overview that will enable them to become active participants in this exciting field.

A description of the current status of a field implicitly contains predictions for its future. What can one say about the development of text and discourse research 10 or 20 years from now, based on this volume? Its title, *Situation Models and Levels of Coherence,* indicates where Professor Tapiero thinks the field is going. The big issue, the issue that she has devoted her own research to as well as this book, is to specify and elaborate the nature and role of situation models in text comprehension. This has been the central theme in discourse research during the last decade, not only of Tapiero's research but of much of the field, but it is still unfinished business. There have been several exciting and promising new approaches in recent years that receive deserved attention in this book, such as the nature and role of nonsymbolic, perceptual representations in the formation of situation models. Another emerging research area that Tapiero favors concerns the role of emotion and self-reference in comprehension. Both of these research directions have attracted a great deal of attention in recent years and are well represented in this book. It is not too much to hope for that the results from these investigations will be incorporated into a comprehensive theory of comprehension in the coming years.

Another development that can be expected for the near future is progress in computational theories of comprehension processes. Extant theories—including my own construction-integration model—are not strictly formal, testable models. They are not as underspecified as purely verbal theories but do not meet the standards of formal models. I do not want to denounce such theories; I think they have been and still are enormously useful in providing a framework for understanding comprehension. Nevertheless, more rigorous, complete models of comprehension processes that satisfy strict standards of formal modeling are needed for the future development of text and discourse research.

What has impeded the emergence of such models in our field? We first should note that the lack of adequate formal theories characterizes all research areas in higher order cognition—concept formation, analogical reasoning, decision making, and so on. Models in all of these areas suffer from similar problems as models of discourse comprehension. I believe there is a common reason for these deficiencies. Higher order cognition is knowledge dependent. One cannot build models of higher order cognition unless one is able to model how human knowledge is structured and how it is used. Until quite recently, this just has not been possible. Researchers were forced to use hand-coded examples of knowledge structures as needed. That is the way I have operated in simulations with the CI model; that is the way other discourse researchers have operated in modeling knowledge use and structure building; that is the way researchers operate in simulating analogical problem solving: Provide the model with knowledge as needed, in the right form, and lo and behold, it works! Once again, I am not criticizing this practice, which is all theorists could do. I am just suggesting that it is time to be more ambitious. Comprehension research cannot be restricted to the laboratory in the same way many problems in experimental psychology can be. We are always interested in discourse in general, and the reader's whole person, goals, emotion, knowledge, and experience necessarily enter into the process. Tapiero describes this situation very well in these pages. One can be confident that researchers will pick up this challenge and formulate better computational models of the comprehension phenomena discussed here, made possible by modern methods of knowledge representation. In the field of discourse, as in other areas of higher order cognition, you can't start with toy models and then scale up—we have no choice but to model the whole human in all its complexity.

The reader of this book, whether an experienced text researcher, novice, or graduate student, will not only find a great deal of information about the current state of text research in these pages, but a coherent framework that will help to make sense of this rich area of research. In fact, this is not only a book for the specialist: Anyone who needs reliable information about this field can find it here, sifted and ordered by a reliable and creative author.

REFERENCES

Anderson, J. R., & Bower, G. H. (1972). *Human Associative Memory*. Washington, DC: Winston.

Bartlett, F. C. (1932). *Remembering*. Cambridge: Cambridge University Press.

Bierwisch, M. (1969). On certain problems of semantic representation. *Foundations of Language, 5*, 153–184.

Chomsky, N. (1957). *Syntactic structures*. The Hague: Mouton.

Fillmore, C. J. (1968). The case for case. In E. Black & R. T. Harms (Eds.), *Universals of linguistic theory*. New York: Holt, Rinehart and Winston.

Frederiksen, C. H. (1975). Representing logical and semantic structure acquired from discourse. *Cognitive Psychology, 7*, 371–458.

Kintsch, W. (1970). Models for free recall and recognition. In D. A. Norman (Ed.), *Models of human memory* (pp. 333–374). New York: Academic Press.

Kintsch, W. (1974). *The representation of meaning in memory*. Hillsdale, NJ: Lawrence Erlbaum Associates.

Kintsch, W., & van Dijk, T. A. (1978). Towards a model of text comprehension and production. *Psychological Review, 85*, 363–394.

Mandler, J. M., & Johnson, N. S. (1977). Remembrance of things parsed: Story structure and recall. *Cognitive Psychology, 9*, 111–151.

Paivio, A. (1969). Mental imagery in associative learning and memory. *Psychological Review, 76*, 241–263.

Schank, R. C., & Abelson, R. P. (1977). *Scripts, plans, goals, and understanding*. Hillsdale, NJ: Lawrence Erlbaum Associates.

Selz, O. (1922). *Zur Psychologie des Denkens und Irrtums*. [On the psychology of thinking and misconceptions]. Bonn: Cohen.

van Dijk, T. A. (1972). *Some aspects of text grammars*. The Hague: Mouton.

van Dijk, T. A., & Kintsch, W. (1983). *Strategies of discourse comprehension*. New York: Academic Press.

Preface

Understanding a text requires building a mental representation that is coherent. This mental representation, commonly called a *situation model* (van Dijk & Kintsch, 1983) or a *mental model* (Johnson-Laird, 1983), is the result of an interaction between the reader's prior knowledge and information in the text. One of my goals is to define what objects or entities compose the situational level of representation and what main processes are implemented by the reader to understand a text. Different types of formal models have been used to represent meaning: frames (Minsky, 1975), schemas (Schank & Abelson, 1977), propositions (Kintsch & van Dijk, 1978), scenarios (Sanford & Garrod, 1981), and cognitive categories such as states, events, and actions (François, 1991; Molinari & Tapiero, 2005; Trabasso & van den Broek, 1985; Zwaan, Langston, & Graesser, 1995). All of these entities have been proposed to define the internal structure of a reader's situation model. However, one possibility is to see the structure of the situation model as amodal (Gernsbacher, 1990) or as a structure that is analogous to that of the states of affairs it represents (Johnson-Laird, 1983). Another possibility is to view it in terms of perceptual and motor representations (Barsalou, 1993, 1999; Glenberg, 1997; Zwaan, 2004). No matter what representational format is adopted, the "internal structure" of a situation model should be the result of the reader's ability to perceive real-world situations. This gives a crucial role to the reader's knowledge in the emergence of meaning and text interpretation (see also Sanford & Garrod, 1998).

Situation models are usually defined as cognitive representations of the events, actions, individuals, and general situation evoked in a text. This definition not only implies being able to imagine individuals' properties or the linguistic relations they have, but also to understand the relationships between the facts described locally and globally in the text. In describing the different structures and processes involved in text comprehension, I present several empirical findings to show that situation models can be adequately constructed from entities in different formats, with the sole constraint that these entities be related "in a coherent way." Coherence has been shown to be a function of several dimensions that index the facts represented in the situation model: space, causation, time, intentionality, and protagonists (Zwaan, Langston, & Graesser, 1995). In this view, the reader is assumed to monitor the multiple situational dimensions that participate in the comprehension process. However, although numerous studies have investigated each of these five dimensions separately, only a few have accounted for their interrelationships. In line with this multidimensional view of the mental representation of a text, and to extend our knowledge of the contribution of situational dimensions to the situation model elaborated, I focus on two dimensions, causality and emotion, as well as on the inferential processes they trigger. It has been widely demonstrated that readers use their "naive" theories about causality to understand a text and to construct a coherent representation of what it says. There is thus no doubt that causality is a "necessary" component of situation models. However, although emotions are crucial in everyday life events and interact with cognitive activities, they have been neglected in the past by researchers working on language and text comprehension, not because of their lack of interest for this dimension, but certainly more because of the complexity of investigating them. I argue that it is necessary to more precisely define how emotion is involved in text comprehension, not only in itself, but also in relation to other situational dimensions (e.g., causality). The situation model of a text, then, would give coherence to the relevant elements of the situation described (i.e., the dimensions), and the format or nature of the entities that compose the model would simply facilitate the establishment of this coherence to a greater or lesser extent.

What kind of mental representation does the reader build? How does the reader establish coherence—or rather, levels of coherence? I assume that the reader's mental representation is composed of related entities, and that only the relevance assigned by readers to define these relations allows for the "correct" interpretation of the text, and leads to several "levels" of comprehension or coherence. This is a dynamic view of reading. In this view, the reader proceeding through the text "activates" and "retrieves" the "relevant" relations that constitute the framework of his or her representation. This representation, modified and enriched through the processing of text information, is a function of the reader's prior knowledge and the task constraints. At certain points in the processing, it reinforces some relations, whereas at other points, those relations are put into the background but still "present" (see Sanford & Garrod, 1981, 1998; van den Broek, Risden,

Fletcher, & Thurlow, 1996). This representation can thus be regarded as
the convergence of multiple sources of information, namely the reader's
prior knowledge, textual information that is being processed, and episodic
information that is no longer in working memory. Each new piece of incoming information is matched to previously processed information. The representation gradually is updated and enriched by those sources, and this
accounts for the richness of the final representation. Retrieval cues (i.e., nature and relevance) are crucial at this point. The reader's knowledge and
task requirements are what assign relevance to the structure to retrieve.

Although many studies have been conducted to gain an in-depth understanding of the cognitive processes underlying the situational level (i.e., the
mental model or situation model), we are still "groping in the dark" when it
comes to defining the internal components (or structure) of the situational
level. The main goal of the first part of this book is to present the internal
objects that emerge from the literature and that I think are fundamental for
defining the structure of the reader's situation model.

In chapter 1, a description of the two main levels of representation (semantic and situational), within a referential and causal approach (i.e., coherence), is followed by a presentation of three main theories of
comprehension: Schema Theory (Mandler & Johnson, 1977; Stein &
Glenn, 1979; Trabasso & Sperry, 1985), the Construction-Integration
Model (Kintsch, 1988, 1998), and the Landscape Model (van den Broek,
Risden, et al., 1996; van den Broek, Young, & Tzeng, & Linderholm, 1999).
These three theories are specific examples of the three generations of cognitive research that have arisen in the domain of text comprehension and
that have been described recently (see van den Broek & Gustafson, 1999;
van den Broek, Young, et al., 1999). Schema Theory exemplifies the first
generation of research. It focuses on the top-down influence of the reader's
background knowledge for interpreting text (here, stories) and on two
main types of relations between the assumed representational units in
memory: referential and causal coherence. The Construction-Integration
Model and the Landscape Model attempt to define the construction and integration of meaning by including the activation of different concept
sources (e.g., episodic or related to prior knowledge). Whereas the former
model relies mainly on the different processes that take place as the reader
processes a text and corresponds to the second generation of models, the
latter emphasizes the bidirectional relations between the process of reading
itself (online representation) and the result of the reading process (offline
representation). This dynamic view of the comprehension process corresponds to the third generation of models.

Chapter 2, the core of the first part, is devoted to the main internal components of situation models described in the literature. To my knowledge,
these "internal objects" have never been clearly identified, and this chapter

is aimed at providing a comprehensive idea of their nature. I discuss the following topics in detail: the contribution of the propositional formalization as a representational format for the units that compose the situation model (Kintsch, 1988, 1998; Kintsch & van Dijk, 1978; van Dijk & Kintsch, 1983), the assumption that propositions cannot capture meaning and are only the product of a previous interpretation (Sanford & Garrod, 1998), the discourse pointers and tokens (Glenberg & Langston, 1992; Sanford & Garrod, 1981, 1988; Zwaan & Radvansky, 1998), and the concepts of states and events (Molinari & Tapiero, in press; Zwaan, Langston, & Graesser, 1995), two crucial semantic categories that are embedded in temporocausal or hierarchical relations. I also develop the idea that the format (i.e., structure and relations) from which individuals elaborate their model guides and governs the internal characteristics of the model built (Johnson-Laird, 1983) and that people may routinely activate perceptual representations during language comprehension (Barsalou, 1993, 1999; Glenberg, 1997; Zwaan, 2004). The structure of a situation model could therefore be seen as amodal (Gernsbacher, 1990), with no particular weight to any given representational format. The situation model would be built from structures and substructures that interact with real-world situations in terms of the coherence of the dimensions implied.

Regardless of the "structure" of the situation model postulated, several cognitive mechanisms underlie the elaboration of the reader's mental representation. In the second part of this book, I describe the main processes (i.e., automatic and strategic) involved in text reading and comprehension, with an emphasis on the dynamic aspect of their occurrence (chapter 3). Then, I focus on those mechanisms assumed to be involved in elaborating and maintaining coherence in situation models (chapter 4), and I emphasize the importance of determining how top-down processes interact with more bottom-up processes. I end this chapter by discussing how these cognitive mechanisms are tied to potential "internal objects." This is the first step in defining "what the reader needs for comprehension."

My aim to define "comprehension" could not be complete without discussing the contribution of the reader's knowledge, episodic or general. One way of deeply investigating the contribution of prior knowledge is to focus on how readers establish coherence when they are engaged in a situation of discourse comprehension, which inevitably leads to a discussion of inferential processes. In Part III, I propose a description of the main theories that focus on how coherence is established in comprehension, in an automatic or strategic manner (chapter 5), by bringing to the fore the relevance of the coherence assumption of Global Models (Garrod & Sanford, 1988; Glenberg & Langston, 1992; Graesser & Clark, 1985; Graesser, Singer, & Trabasso, 1994). What does it mean to build a coherent situation model? Are the different levels of coherence a function of the level of representation built by the reader? Many empirical studies have demonstrated that a reader establishes both local and global text coherence. One assumption could be that understanding a text (i.e., building a coherent situation model) is related to the retrieval structures a reader activates in order to perform a specific task (chapter 6). This assumption refers to the idea that to build a coherent situation model, a reader needs to interrelate the events represented in the text on the basis of relations that are not explicitly stated (different from the textbase). The mechanism of coherence building with respect to the situation model should be made possible by the construction of referential relations (i.e., relations from the "possible world" described in the text or in the discourse). This section clarifies the relationship between memory and comprehension in order to define the reader's mental representation. In the last section (Part IV), I specifically consider two main categories of inferences that I think are fundamental in text or discourse comprehension: causal inferences (chapter 7) and emotional inferences (chapter 8). I then describe the main principles of the Event-Indexing Model (chapter 9) regarding the extent to which some situational dimensions are better represented than others, and I propose some arguments that could possibly lead to improving the explanatory power of this model.

In *Situation Models and Levels of Coherence*, I attempt to propose an integrated view of the various theoretical approaches to discourse comprehension, and in particular of situation-model building, as evidenced by empirical findings and computational models. My objective has been to arrive at an in-depth definition of the internal structure of situation models, and of the cognitive processes that underlie their elaboration, while articulating these two aspects of the reader's mental representations by bringing to the fore the core concept of coherence. My emphasis on the functional aspects of situation models is to demonstrate the crucial role played by the activation of readers' specific and general knowledge in the gradual emergence of a text interpretation. My aim was to approach discourse understanding in a more unified way, and bring forward all the richness, complexity, and (even so) flexibility of this highest level of representation, the situation model. This book will be useful to anyone, whether a researcher, a professor, a graduate student, or a novice, who is interested in addressing the issue of what the reader needs and utilizes for comprehension in a finer grained way.

ACKNOWLEDGMENTS

I am particularly indebted to Lori Stone, Senior Editor at Lawrence Erlbaum Associates, who supported my project, constantly encouraged me, and provided me with the best conditions for working on this book.

English editing of this book was done by Vivian Waltz, technical editor and translator. I thank her for the quality and relevance of her revisions, and for her professionalism. Without her, this volume would certainly not have had all of its "substance".

I am very grateful to my colleague Olivier Koenig, head of the Laboratory for the Study of Cognitive Mechanisms (EMc) (my research lab). I thank him for his friendly support and continuous concern regarding my progress throughout the writing process. I would certainly not have been able to complete the book if he had not provided me with financial support I needed, for which I express all my gratitude.

I warmly thank my students for our discussions and for their work, which considerably enriched the content of this volume.

Special appreciation is extended to the researchers and colleagues with whom I have been interacting or collaborating for many years: Paul van den Broek and Jose Otero for their friendship and for the projects we developed together, but also Susan Goldman, Arthur Graesser, Rolf Zwaan, Franz Schmalhofer, Charles Perfetti, Morton A. Gernsbacher, and many others who are not named here but who nevertheless contributed in a greater or lesser way to this book. My membership in the Society for Text and Discourse and my nomination as a member of the Governing Board of the Society for one term have provided me with the opportunity to reinforce my exchanges and contacts with the text comprehension community, for which I am also very grateful.

I also want to express my gratitude to Larry Erlbaum of Lawrence Erlbaum Associates. I met him for the first time at the 10th Annual Meeting of the Society for Text and Discourse, which I organized in Lyon in July 2000. His extreme kindness and strong encouragement when I told him of my intention to send him a book proposal contributed largely to making this volume come to be.

Last but certainly not least, I thank Walter Kintsch for his constant support, help, and availability. I also thank him for his essential contributions to the development of the field of discourse comprehension, for the relevance and importance of the new ideas he brings to our community. The content of this book reflects the impact his research has had and is still having on the discourse comprehension field and on my own work. I wish to express to him my respect and admiration, and to say that I am very honored and proud that he agreed to write the Foreword to this volume.

I cannot end these acknowledgments without thanking my family—Rachel and Arthur, my children, and François, my husband—for their patience and understanding while I worked on this book. Special thanks also to my sister Dominique, who always believed in me and never stopped encouraging me to finish this project.

Part I

Text Comprehension: What Kind of Mental Representation Does The Reader Build? The Internal "Objects" of Situation Models

Theoretical and Empirical Evidence for Two Main Levels of Representation: Referential and Causal Coherence

1.1. THE SEMANTIC LEVEL OF REPRESENTATION (KINTSCH & VAN DIJK, 1978)

1.1.1. Microstructure and Microprocessing

The meaning of a text can be captured by two components of the text representation: the microstructural component and the macrostructural component (Kintsch & van Dijk, 1978). These processes operate in parallel and interact without imposing any constraints on the resources of the cognitive system. A coherent textbase (i.e., microstructure) that corresponds to the meaning of the text (Kintsch, 1974) is first constructed by the reader. This textbase is defined as a list of propositions that represent the local meaning of a text. The propositional notation corresponds to the idea that the meaning of a text is represented as a well-structured list of propositions, each proposition being composed of a predicate associated with one or more arguments. The propositions are related, according to Kinstch and van Dijk (1978), by the criterion of argument repetition. Several authors have shown that the coherence of the representation built by the reader/hearer is also organized by temporal and causal relations between the states of affairs described: The reader is thought to build a causal path between the initial and final states of the text, with events and actions that describe the successive transitions between the states (Black & Bower, 1980; Schank, 1975; Trabasso & van den Broek, 1985). Still other authors have shown that referential coherence was achieved with the activity of minimal predication as the criterion for establishing coherence (Denhière, 1984; Le Ny, 1979; Tapiero, 1992). This criterion is based on the psychological activity of predication as it is described by Le Ny (1979). In general, minimal predication consists of the successive adding of new information to old information. In contrast to coreferential coherence, propositions that share arguments do not necessarily inherit a link, and propositions are only related to their own arguments (see Tapiero & Denhière, 1995).

The microstructure (i.e., micropropositions) is constructed via an automatic cycle-by-cycle process that is constrained by the reader's limited working memory capacity. Several studies have investigated the cognitive invariants that constitute the microstructure, which are representations of states, events, actions, and relations among them (see Cailliès & Tapiero, 1997; Molinari & Tapiero, 2005, in press; Tapiero, 1992; Trabasso & van den Broek, 1985; Zwaan, Langston, & Graesser, 1995), but there are only a few investigations on their respective effects on the comprehension process (see Denhière & Baudet, 1992; Graesser, Robertson, Lovelace, & Swinehart, 1980; Molinari & Tapiero, 2000, 2005, in press).

1.1.2. Macrostructure, Macroprocessing and Importance of Information

At a second, more global level of processing, the propositions of the textbase (i.e., the micropropositions) are hierarchically organized into a coherent sequence of propositions, with some propositions superordinate to others, depending on their importance. As the reader proceeds through a text, he or she builds the microstructure, step by step, by applying relations of local coherence (e.g., referential, causal, temporal). A more global kind of coherence in discourse (i.e., the macrostructure) is built by reorganizing the microstructure into a coherent global structure in terms of meaningful units that account for the gist of the text. Macroprocesses (applied by semantic condensation rules; see van Dijk, 1977) reduce textbase information and generate different types of inferences under the control of a cognitive schema that is a function of the reader's goals. Two strategies have been proposed to account for the notions of importance and hierarchical information: the leading-edge strategy (Kintsch & van Dijk, 1978), which accounts for the recency effect and the information hierarchy in terms of superordinate propositions, and the current-state strategy or the current-state strategy plus goal (Fletcher & Bloom, 1988), in which the causal structure of a text is built in a limited capacity short-term memory. The current-state strategy comes from two main theoretical approaches. The first one views comprehension as a problem-solving activity in which the reader has to discover a sequence of causal links that connect the beginning of a text to its end (or to its final outcome). Short-term memory is perceived as a bottleneck within the comprehension process. The reader keeps in working memory the last causal antecedent that maintains coherence with the subsequent sentence. When the necessary information for text understanding is no longer available in short-term memory, long-term memory is explored until the reader establishes the appropriate connection. The causal structure of a text is thus viewed as the first cause of recall (Trabasso & van den Broek, 1985). The more an event has causal connections with the rest of the text, the better its recall will be, and events that are on the causal chain are better recalled than those that are located at dead-ends (i.e., assumed to be outside the causal chain). In the second theoretical approach (see Kintsch & van Dijk, 1978), the meaning of the text is represented in memory as a network of propositions (i.e., the textbase). Two propositions are related when they share a common referent and when they co-occur in short-term memory during the comprehension process. Within each reading cycle, short-term memory is assumed to contain all propositions related to the current state plus a small number of propositions taken from the previous text. Thus, a given proposition can be maintained in short-term memory during one or more cycles. The longer a proposition is retained in short-term memory, the better the probability of its recall. The leading-edge strategy (Kinstch & van Dijk, 1978) is used to predict the content of short-term memory during each cycle.

The linking of these two theoretical views of comprehension brought complementary explanations about how the structure of text content, in interaction with the reader's background knowledge, can affect the final representation, built specifically through the probability of information recall. It also carries with it obvious implications about the cognitive operations readers carry out during the comprehension process itself. Thus, the coherence established from a text or a discourse depends not only on two structural levels, the micro- and macrostructures, but also on strategies related to the establishment of the information hierarchy and the relationships between the concepts. However, although these two approaches had a common overarching goal— that is, to predict the nature of the reader's representation at the end of the reading process—they involve clear-cut differences in the types of representational units they assume for analyzing discourse (superordinate propositional structure vs. goal hierarchies) and the types of the relations they assume between the text components (referential vs. causal).

1.2. THE SITUATIONAL LEVEL

1.2.1. Relationship Between Textual Information and the Reader's Knowledge

To account for the organizational characteristics of the semantic representation, several authors turned to units with a higher level than the propositional level, such as frame (Frederiksen, 1987; Frederiksen & Donin, 1991; Minsky, 1975; Rossi & Bert-Erboul, 1991), schema (Rumelhart & Norman, 1978), script (Schank & Abelson, 1977), and facts (Kintsch & van Dijk, 1978). During text comprehension, these units are assumed to be activated and permit specific textual information to be instantiated in empty slots or "variables." Recourse to these units was supported by several studies showing that text memory is not verbatim but is largely the product of deeper comprehension (Bartlett, 1932; Bransford, Barclay, & Franks, 1972; Thorndyke, 1977). The underlying assumption is that understanding a discourse is not intrinsic to the semantics of words but is a function of the reader's familiarity with the situations described, gained through his or her own interactions with the world (i.e., pragmatic knowledge). What is retained of a text is a model of the situation it describes rather than some propositional analog of the text itself. Such a level of representation is necessary to account for comprehension as a whole, and in particular, for inference generation. In line with this assumption, van Dijk and Kintsch (1983) defined a third level of representation, that is, the situation model, which they assumed to rely on lower levels of the micro- and macrostructures. This conceptualization replaced the notions previously stated in the 1970s and shares several aspects with the so-called "mental models" (see Johnson-Laird, 1983), although important differences in their functional and structural properties have been highlighted (see chapter 2). Thus, according to van Dijk and Kintsch (1983), text understanding is not limited to the construction of a mental representation of text content (i.e., semantic microstructure and macrostructure), but also includes the construction of a mental model of the situation evoked by the text, the latter implying integration of the information provided by the text into the reader's prior knowledge. The authors defined a situation model as the cognitive representation of the events, actions, individuals, and the situation in general evoked in a text. Specific properties have been attributed to this "higher" level of representation. First, it incorporates previous experiences, including previous textbases, about similar or identical situations. At the same time, it includes instantiations of more general knowledge of these situations; situation models are specific or episodic, unlike general knowledge structures or scripts. They represent specific objects or events at different levels of detail (Johnson-Laird, 1983). The concept of situation model allows us, first, to conceptualize the representation of the world individuals construct through experience and learning, which they activate during reading. Second, situation models provide a referential universe for utterances. In other words, understanding a text requires representing the situation it describes. If we are unable to imagine a situation in which some individuals have certain properties or experience, understanding a text itself would not be easy. And if we do not understand the textual relations between the facts or events described by the text, in a local and global fashion, we will not understand the text at all.

The concept of a situation model is particularly important because, in a sense, it separates psychology and linguistics, while simultaneously allowing us to deal with problems until then set aside by psychologists because of the lack of satisfactory theorization. This notion brought a new dynamic into the way researchers began to investigate readers' mental representations, for it stresses the role and use of background knowledge in the comprehension process itself, as well as the contextual and situational factors relevant to the situation. It is now acknowledged that understanding a discourse depends more on pragmatic knowledge than on the semantics of the words it contains. Next, I develop some of the main arguments—situational, linguistic, and psychological—in favor of using this notion.

1.2.2. Need for This Level of Representation

There are several reasons why situation models are needed to account for discourse comprehension (van Dijk & Kintsch, 1983). One of the arguments is based on the idea that a discourse may be viewed from different perspectives and different points of view, just as it may modify those perspectives or points of view. The facts, events, and situations are interpreted, described, and told by different persons, from different viewpoints, although they remain the same. The situation model, which is independent of the current discourse and of the point of view adopted, accounts for this discrepancy. The notion of situation model also accounts for the different interpretations of a text generated by two persons. It does not necessarily refer to distinct textual representations, but can correspond to differences between the concerned situation models. Using this notion leads one to dissociate the semantic content from the situational content of a text and to causes the model constructed to be dependent on the reader's prior knowledge. Indeed, under some circumstances, when the representation of the text content (i.e., semantic representation) is difficult to construct, people remember the situation model evoked by the text rather than the representation of the text itself. Conversely, there are some situations in which the text is recalled, but not the situation model, particularly for novices in a specific domain described in the text. These two distinct situations can be explained by two factors: coherence and prior knowledge. In the former, noncoherent text content may lead to difficulties in the construction of a semantic representation, although the reader may reach a certain level of coherence for the situation evoked by the text. In the latter situation, the amount of domain-specific knowledge the reader has is closely related to the level of difficulty in building a situation model. The greater the amount of knowledge about the events depicted in the text, the easier it is to elaborate a situation model.

The reordering of information is another reason why situation models are necessary. A story in which the order of events has been modified often tends to be recalled in the canonical order rather than in the actual order of the story itself (Kintsch, Mandel, & Kozminsky, 1977). This phenomenon can be explained in two ways, both of which imply recourse to the notion of a situation model. First, it is likely that during recall, the story is reconstructed from the situation model formed as the story was being told and not from the text itself. An alternative is that the text representation follows the "natural" order, despite the presentation order. However, the only way to proceed in reconstructing the story is to build a canonical situation model, and then to use that model to reorder the textbase information. In both cases, the reorganization of the events presupposes the construction of a situation model. But a text does not always lead to the construction of a new situation model. More frequently, an existing model is modified using information in the new text. This is done, for example, during the updating of knowledge from reports (van Oostendorp, 1996) or when the reader has a specific goal such as a learning goal (see Mannes & Kintsch, 1987). Some of these roles of the situation model, like those related to coherence, memory, and updating, are considered in greater detail in the following sections.

1.3. Prior Knowledge in Discourse Comprehension: From Readers' Expectations to Data-Driven Processing

Since the 1970s, researchers have focused their interest on the multiple facets of the comprehension process that are assumed to define the reader's mental representation. One particular interest has been the investigation of the defining features of what readers recall and the nature of the memory representation that results from reading. In this perspective, the reader's activation of "stereotyped" or "schema-like" knowledge is assumed to lead to the correct interpretation of a text, and the cognitive processes underlying the final representation are expectation based. The activation of these knowledge structures enables readers to reach a deep level of textual interpretation. Two sets of models were developed in this first generation of cognitive research. One set emphasized top-down effects on memory, and mainly focused on the role of text elements in the overall structure of the text. Schema Theory and the Story Grammar are instantiations of these models. The second set underlined bottom-up effects by specifically investigating the role that each text element plays in maintaining coherence with other individual elements. In that type of model, referential and causal relations are seen as core relations for building a coherent representation of various types of texts.

However, in the mid-1980s, and with the development of new technologies for measuring online activities and activations (e.g., eye-tracking techniques, probe techniques), the research interest shifted from the product of reading, that is, the memory representation, to the actual process of reading. At this point, a second generation of research was born. The goal of the models developed within this second generation was to describe the cognitive processes that take place online, and to understand the complex activities the reader must perform when he or she proceeds through the text. On one hand, he or she needs to make inferences in order to comprehend a text, and most research on this topic has focused on determining what inferences the reader makes and does not make. On the other hand, the reader has limited attentional or working memory resources available to do so, and one crucial question that arose was what elements are activated at a particular point in the reading. These two constraints, related to inference making (or the lack of it) and the allocation of attentional resources, have been accounted for by deeply investigating the process of reading. Moreover, although this second generation of models stresses the importance of prior knowledge in the construction of the reader's mental representation, the correct interpretation of a text is no longer seen as immediate or dependent on the relevant activation of prior knowledge. Rather, both relevant and irrelevant knowledge may be activated first in an automatic manner as the reader proceeds through the text —leading to a large but probably incoherent network—in order to gradually reach the correct interpretation via "flexible" but context-dependent rules. Thus, one of the strong and new arguments of this generation of models is that the "correct" meaning of a text is no longer in the "head" of the reader/hearer, but emerges from the situational context in a bottom-up fashion. The cognitive architecture developed by Kintsch (1988, 1998)—that is, the Construction-Integration Model, based on the previous theorization (Kintsch & van Dijk, 1978; van Dijk & Kintsch, 1983)—possesses these flexible properties. This model drastically changed the way researchers investigated the reading comprehension process, and part of this section is devoted to presenting its characteristics in detail. I specifically discuss how prior knowledge is activated and represented in order to achieve successful comprehension by the end of the reading process.

Although these first two generations of cognitive research still coexist and contribute to gaining important new insights into the different processes related to reading comprehension and memory, in the mid-1990s, a third generation of research developed. Its goal was to integrate the main characteristics of the first two generations, that is, the online as well as offline aspects of reading (Goldman & Varma, 1995; Langston & Trabasso, 1999; van den Broek et al., 1996). Here, the focus is on comprehension processes and memory representations as well as on the relationship between the two. This relationship has been shown to be complex and bidirectional, in the sense that (a) the representation is constantly being modified as the reader encounters and understands new textual information, and (b) the developing representation itself provides an important resource for the reader in the comprehension of subsequent events. Thus, the comprehension of new information updates the memory representation, which in turn influences subsequent comprehension. The Landscape Model developed by van den Broek et al. (1996) nicely exemplifies this view of the comprehension process. This model attempts to capture the online and offline processes that build the representation as well as its dynamic interactions. It also emphasizes the multiple sources of knowledge activation that play a role in the comprehension process. The last part of this chapter is devoted to describing the main features of this computational model.

To conclude, over the past 40 years, the focus of interest evolved and shifted from the result of the reading process to the reading process itself, and then to the interaction between the resulting representation and the processes involved in the construction of that representation. The activation of "relevant" prior knowledge as a guide for attaining the correct interpretation of a text has gradually been moved to the background to the benefit of a more bottom-up view in which the construction of meaning is context dependent and based on several sources of knowledge, in order to finally reach the point that top-down and bottom-up processes are closely interleaved.

The main features of these three main generations of investigations in reading comprehension have already been described (see van den Broek & Gustafson, 1999; van den Broek, Young, et al., 1999), with particular emphasis on each one's theoretical and empirical contributions and limits, but also their boundaries. I will shed a new light on this description, for my intention is to mainly develop the role each of the three generations has attributed to the reader's prior knowledge and expectations during the comprehension process. Indeed, although the models that came out of these three generations have underlined the importance of the activation of background knowledge on the reader's mental representation and on the construction of a coherent situation model, each one assigns a different weight and status to this activation, with strong implications on both the nature of the representation itself and the online processes involved in the elaboration of the representation. Thus, I chose to describe the properties of the three generations of investigations by exemplifying within each generation only one theory or model that I think is crucial to the study of how readers comprehend a text in relation to their prior knowledge. These models cannot be ignored by anyone who is strongly or even remotely interested in the evolution of the research on discourse comprehension. My choice was influenced by their large explanatory power in the cognitive activities related to text understanding.

1.3.1. First Generation of Cognitive Research in Reading Comprehension. Meaning Is "In the Head": The Concept of Schema

The first generation of models emphasized the mental representation of texts (the product of the reading process) and was mainly based on the properties of these mental representations. This generation gave substantial weight to the reader's prior knowledge and expectations in text interpretation. Schema Theory and, more specifically, Story Grammars (Mandler & Johnson, 1977; Stein & Glenn, 1979; Thorndyke, 1977) are central in the theoretical approach developed in the first generation. Story Grammars (i.e., rewrite rules defining story components) are aimed at providing a theoretical model of the conventional knowledge individuals have about stories, and therefore mainly emphasized top-down influences on memory and the importance of text elements in the general text structure. Several studies have shown that readers have an ideal internal schema representating the different parts of a story and the relations between those parts. Such schemas have been shown to guide the storage and retrieval of information. During storage, a story schema helps orientate the reader's attention to certain aspects of the input (setting). It also helps the reader keep track of what preceded and informs him or her about which parts of the story are complete and which parts are not. This generation of cognitive research also described the role that each textual element plays in maintaining coherence with every other element (resulting from the reader's limited processing capacity), and the reader's mental representation is viewed as coherent with the story's referential (Kintsch & van Dijk, 1978) and causal structures (Graesser & Clark, 1985; Trabasso, Secco, & van den Broek, 1984). Here, the main assumption is that the reader is capable of identifying connections between textual information via higher level processes, and that the creation of these connections lends coherence to the mental representation. In other words, the construction of a coherent text representation is thought to provide the basis for inferences that identify semantic relations between textual elements and enable the reader to relate the different parts of the text to each other.

Referential relations (i.e., argument repetition) have been described as one of the most crucial types of relations for the construction of a coherent mental representation (see Gernsbacher, 1990). Cognitive functioning is based on the activation of knowledge such as schemas and propositions (Kintsch 1988, 1998; Kintsch & van Dijk, 1978; van Dijk & Kintsch, 1983). The reader is perceived as a cognitive processing system in which working memory is a crucial structure in that it determines the number of elements the reader can retain in order to maintain coherence while processing a text. Coherence is established by the criterion of coreference and by co-oc-currence in working memory. The process that selects relevant units (such as propositions) in working memory is the result of the leading-edge strat-egy, with recency and the level of the hierarchy built during each cycle as the two main characteristics. Propositions that are not maintained in working memory are kept in long-term memory or lost, depending on their impor-tance. If referential coherence between propositions cannot be established, a search in long-term memory is initiated in order to find a previous propo-sition that makes the connection. If such a proposition exists, it is reintro-duced into working memory, and if not, an inferential process takes place. The main implication is that the recall probability depends on the number of cycles during which a given proposition is maintained in working mem-ory. However, although the psychological importance of shared reference among propositions has been repeatedly demonstrated (Haviland & Clark, 1974; Kintsch & Keenan, 1973), coherence cannot be regarded simply in terms of argument repetition (van Dijk & Kintsch, 1983), and other rela-tions, such as causal relations, have been shown to be crucial in the estab-lishment of a coherent mental representation. Within this "causal" view, comprehension is conceived of as a problem-solving activity (Black & Bower, 1980; Trabasso & van den Broek, 1985): The reader has to discover a sequence of causal links that connect a series of statements (from the be-ginning to the end). Several empirical findings support this view. For exam-ple, data on reading time have shown first, that causally related events are read faster than other types of related events (temporal, and/or argument repetition; see Haberlandt & Bingham, 1978), and second, that reading time increases with the number of inferential steps required to causally con-nect two sentences (Bower, Black, & Turner, 1979; Keenan, Baillet, & Brown, 1984). Other experiments using free and cued recall tasks (Black & Bern, 1981) have shown that two causally related sentences are recalled better than sentences related temporally or referentially (i.e., argument repetition). Moreover, Omanson (1982) and Black and Bower (1980) pro-vided evidence of the fact that readers use their causal knowledge to assign importance to semantic information, and to introduce coherence into their representations. In their study, an event that belonged to the causal path re-lating the beginning of a text to its end was rated as more important than other textual events or states. Research on story grammars has also shown that applying causal reasoning when processing a text is a necessary condition for establishing coherence between events and for reaching a "correct" representation of what is read. Thus, all these findings point to the idea that meaning achieves its full coherence via interpropositional relations, and any two events causally related in the world should be causally related in the representation. The reader constructs a representation to explain a possible world, and readers must establish relations of causality between the facts of this world in order to build a coherent mental representation of a narrative (Black & Bower, 1980; Omanson, 1982; Trabasso et al, 1984; Trabasso & van den Broek, 1985; van den Broek & Lorch, 1993). They use their naive theories about causality to understand a text and to construct a coherent interpretation of what is said in it. As stories are goal-directed in nature (Thorndyke, 1977), the reader must identify not only adjacent relations between events but also distant relations (including adjacent relations) to capture the causal structure of a text (Black & Bower, 1980; Trabasso, 1991; Trabasso & van den Broek, 1985). Two main theories of this process have emerged: the Linear Causal Chain Theory and Causal Network Theory, both of which capture the coherence of the reader's mental representation (see Black & Bower, 1980; Bloom, Fletcher, van den Broek, Reitz, & Shapiro, 1990; Fletcher & Bloom, 1988; Trabasso et al., 1984; Trabasso & Sperry, 1985; van den Broek & Lorch, 1993; van den Broek, Trabasso, & Thurlow, 1990; van Dijk & Kintsch, 1983). I discuss the importance and main properties of these two ways of approaching the causal structure of a text in Part III (chapter 5) because they allow us to make strong predictions about the kinds of inferences that can be generated online (Magliano, 1999).

Thus, first-generation studies showed that text comprehension requires the construction of a coherent representation in memory. This representation may be described as a network of events, states, and facts connected by semantic relations of different natures. The relations introduced by the reader throughout the reading process are a function of his or her coherence criteria, but most of the data point to the fundamental role of referential and causal relations.

The findings of the preceding studies led to a greater interest in the processes that underlie the construction of a mental representation during reading. From a theoretical point of view, greater importance has been given to the assumption that readers have limited attentional resources that constrain cognitive processing. From a methodological point of view, the development of new technologies led researchers to examine and measure the activities carried out during the reading process, including the inferences the reader does and does not make. In the framework of text understanding, the limited capacity of working memory and attentional resources leads to the assumption that readers cannot keep all discursive information active and consequently must select the relevant elements that permit text understanding. Thus, studies conducted in the first generation were aimed at examining the different elements activated during each processing cycle, which roughly corresponds to one sentence. The main results indicate that the information available to a reader at a particular point in a text can come from three potential sources. The first source is the text itself. In each processing cycle, the information currently being processed is activated and maintained in working memory. In parallel, it is assumed that elements associated to those actually processed are also activated. They may correspond either to previous discursive information that is present within the episodic representation of the text or to the reader's prior knowledge stored in semantic memory. Finally, the inferences generated during reading are the third potential source of activation. The results of first-generation studies showed that understanding a text implies the construction of a coherent representation containing interconnected nodes within a network. For this reason, the reader has to infer relations of different natures (e.g., referential, causal, spatial, instrumental, etc.) between the text elements he or she encounters. It seems that most, but not all, of these inferences are generated during the reading process itself. This led to studies on the nature of which inferences are generated and which are not, as well as on the factors that influence or affect the inferential processes carried out, such as the spreading of activation from the basic inferences made during the reading process. The main findings indicated that although the reader activates the necessary information for the generation of referential and causal inferences in a quite straightforward way, the probability that the reader will infer relations of other natures should be a function of their role in establishing the level of coherence the reader wants to attain. Accordingly, the second generation focused on the reading process itself, and most researchers became interested in the kinds of information readers activate while processing a text. In the studies conducted in this second generation of investigations, prior knowledge is assumed to play a crucial role, but the way it influences and guides the reading comprehension process is much more flexible than stated here in my discussion of the first generation.

1.3.2. The Emergence of Meaning: "Fluctuation" Between Bottom-Up and Top-Down Processes

1.3.2.1. Second Generation of Research on Text Understanding: The Construction-Integration Model (Kintsch, 1988, 1998)

As I stated previously, several authors have demonstrated the relevance of using higher level organizational units than propositions, such as schemata or frames. In this approach, developed in the framework of cognitive models, psychological processes are explained in terms of symbols and rules interpreted in a sequential manner. Connectionist models, on the contrary, use subsymbolic units that have no meaning per se, but that can be related dynamically to each other. In these kinds of models, each unit is seen as representing a hypothesis, and each relation represents some constraints on those hypotheses (see Andler, 1991). For instance, in the Parallel Distributed Processing Model (PDP; Rumelhart, McClelland, & The PDP Research Group,1986), there is no schematic representation in the sense of permanent units stored in long-term memory. What is stored is a set of connection strengths which, once activated, have the implicit capacity to generate states that correspond to schema instantiations. These schemata constitute the emergent structures that result from the interaction of a large number of simple units working together. Schemata are implicit entities created by the environment they tend to interpret. Given that the network is reorganized for each stimulation as a function of the structure of its input, it can provide output that is more or less adapted to the schematic structures. Compared with traditional views of the representational format, this schema-based conception is more flexible and more fluid, for it is capable of matching the input data (Rumelhart, McClelland, & the PDP Research Group, 1986, chapter 14). It is these principles that guided the Construction-Integration Model proposed by Kintsch in 1988. Scripts and traditional frames cannot be used: If they are too powerful, they are too rigid; if they are too general, they fail (Kintsch, 1988).

The approach developed in the Construction-Integration Model (Kinstch, 1988, 1998) consists of providing an "intelligent" system (i.e., a production system) in which the rules need to be just powerful enough to have the "right" elements be present among others, which may be neither appropriate nor relevant. A process of integration is then used to reinforce the contextually appropriate elements and inhibit all the others. One of the main characteristics of this cognitive architecture is that it accounts for the prior knowledge readers activate and use while understanding a text (Kintsch & Welsch, 1991). Knowledge is organized in a minimal way; that is, if no structure is stored in a permanent way, it can be produced in the context of the task for which it is necessary. It is represented as an associative network, a highly interconnected set of nodes corresponding to concepts and propositions (see Kintsch, 1988, 1998; Tapiero, 1992, 2003; Tapiero & Otero, 1999). The connections between nodes have a positive, negative, or zero value, varying from +1 to –1, and the nodes are equivalent to the propositions used to represent texts (Kintsch, 1974).

First, there is a construction phase with symbolic features, which involves building the textbase using linguistic signs and the reader's prior knowledge. This phase is followed by an integration phase with connectionist features, in which the textbase is integrated as a coherent whole to generate the final interpretation of the text (assumed to be coherent). The construction process functions as a production system output from a former production system (Dellarosa, 1986; Kintsch & Greeno, 1985) with rules acting at different levels (surface, semantic, and situational). The rules do not need to be "smart" to ensure that only the right interpretation is generated, but can be weak, producing a network in which relevant information as well as redundant, inappropriate, and even contradictory information may be activated. Examples of such rules are ones that interconnect propositions in the network or ones that activate knowledge. The process ends with a very rich textbase, albeit sometimes incoherent, which is generated from textual information and the reader's knowledge. The nodes in the network (concepts and propositions) are interconnected by links. Link strength between propositions may be chosen to be all equal or to vary according to theoretical considerations (see Arocha & Patel, 1995; Kintsch, Welsch, Schmalhofer, & Zimny, 1990; Tapiero, 2000, 2003; Tapiero & Otero, 1999), and different versions of the model may be obtained to empirically evaluate their adequacy. Also, propositions may be indirectly or directly related, or one proposition may be subordinated to another. A negative link may be assigned between two alternative propositions that are formed from the same sentence or phrase. As I mentioned earlier, the resulting network at the end of the construction process involves nodes from the reader's knowledge net. The basic mechanism for knowledge activation is assumed to be associative. Items in working memory activate neighboring nodes in the knowledge net with probabilities proportional to the strengths with which they are linked. Although this mechanism may be modeled formally, sometimes a more informal approach, which the Construction-Integration Model allows, is more suitable. Thus, at this stage of the process, the network (textual propositions, inferences, and elaborations produced by the reader) does not yet correspond to an appropriate representation of the text. At the different levels of representation, the components associated with the textual elements have been included, but there is no reference to the context and some of its components may be inappropriate.

An integration process takes place in order to eliminate irrelevant information and to strengthen relevant elements. This second phase involves a spreading activation process that strengthens contextually appropriate elements and inhibits others. At the end of the second phase, the resulting structure (i.e., an associative network) takes on the form of a coherent textbase via some connectionist relaxation procedures (Rumelhart, McClelland, & the PDP Research Group, 1986). This hybrid model thus uses a production system and connectionist procedures. Although the elements from which the knowledge network and the textbase are constructed are the same, the textbase and the knowledge network correspond to separate structures with their own properties. The concepts are not defined in the knowledge network, but their meaning can be constructed from their network location. The most highly associated elements and the semantic neighbors of a particular node constitute the node's "central" meaning. However, the complete and global meaning can be obtained only by exploring its relations with all the other nodes in the network. To summarize, meaning has to be constructed. However, it is unlikely to construct meaning by using a complete knowledge network. At each moment, only one part of the network can be activated, and only the activated propositions can modify the meaning of a given concept. Thus, the meaning of a concept is always situation-specific and context-dependent, and it is necessarily unstable and incomplete.

Because a reader cannot psychologically construct and integrate the text representation of a long text, the model assumes that text understanding is a cyclical process (Kintsch & van Dijk, 1978; van Dijk & Kintsch, 1983). Within each cycle, a new network is constructed. It includes all information stored in short-term memory. This produces overlap among the sentence elements, and coherence is obtained via the reprocessing of propositions. In terms of the Construction-Integration Model, this operation is described as a constraint-satisfaction process. The activation value of the nodes in the network (the activation vector) is successively multiplied using a matrix indicating connectivity among nodes (the connectivity matrix) until the activation vector stabilizes, that is, until no activation value changes by more than some cutoff value, for example, .0001. The integration process is assumed to occur without much effort, and its outcome is the fully contextually integrated representation in long-term memory of the meaning of the text. This model has been successful in predicting the mental representations constructed by readers after processing texts of various structures and different tasks, such as recognition (Kintsch et al., 1990), free and cued recall (Arocha & Patel, 1995; Tapiero & Denhière, 1995; Tapiero & Otero, 1999), detection of scientific text contradiction (Otero & Kintsch, 1992; Tapiero & Otero, 1999), expertise in medicine (Arocha & Patel, 1995) or other domains (Tapiero, 2003), and problem solving (Kinstch, 1998).

One important aspect of this model is that it gives a powerful role to the reader's prior knowledge during the comprehension process, not in a top-down predictive manner but throughout the process itself. In a recent study (Tapiero, 2003), I investigated the contribution of prior knowledge by comparing predictions of the Construction-Integration Model when appropriate knowledge is added to the associative input networks, with cued recall data in text learning and comprehension (Cailliès & Tapiero, 1997; Tapiero & Cailliès, 1995). Most studies dealing with the role of prior knowledge in text learning and text comprehension have contrasted novices to experts (Arocha & Patel, 1995; Britton & Tesser, 1982; Chiesi, Spilich, &

Voss, 1979; Kintsch & Kintsch, 1995; Tapiero, 1991) and have shown that prior knowledge facilitates the encoding and recall of new information (Graesser & Clark, 1985; Spilich, Vesonder, Chiesi, & Voss, 1979). Moreover, several studies indicate that novices tend to organize information linearly and causally, whereas experts use higher goal–subgoal relations. From these two sets of data, an interesting question that arises concerns the kind of changes that occur in the knowledge-base of a novice who is acquiring information and gradually developing expertise. This question has been approached by studying expertise as a continuum, that is, with intermediate levels. Whereas many authors have found a recall function that increases monotonically with domain-specific expertise, as in chess (Chase & Simon, 1973), others working on medical expertise have found evidence of a counterintuitive effect (the "intermediate effect"), demonstrating more accurate recall by intermediates than by novices or experts (Patel & Groen, 1991; Schmidt & Boshuizen, 1993). Groen and Patel (1988) explained this paradox by arguing that the experts' situation model allows them to "filter out" irrelevant information and to extract only relevant information, which leads them to recall less information than persons with less advanced levels of expertise. Schmidt and Bozhuizen (1993) provided another explanation for this phenomenon in terms of a bottom-up process underlying the notion of knowledge encapsulation: Lower level propositions activated during text processing are thought to be encapsulated into higher level concepts (see also Potts & Peterson, 1985; Potts, St. John, & Kirson, 1989). In a previous study, Cailliès and Tapiero (1997; see also Tapiero & Cailliès, 1995) replicated the so-called "intermediate effect" (see Arocha & Patel, 1995; Schmidt & Boshuizen, 1993) by investigating the organization of the mental representation of a complex system (i.e., the text editor Microsoft Word) in subjects with different levels of expertise (novices, intermediates, and experts). The main assumption of the authors was that the type of text structure (causal/ hierarchical) affects memory and learning in the specific domain in accordance with the reader's level of expertise. Three main functions of the text editor (i.e., "Select," "Cut," and "Paste") were described by the units that compose it, and by relations between those units in terms of adjacent (causal) and nonadjacent (hierarchical) relations. The graphic representation of the three functions (i.e., domains) is given in Figure 1.1 (for the temporal-causal structure) and in Figure 1.2 (for the hierachical structure).

Two types of learning text were constructed from the preceding framework. One text described the system with temporal-causal relations, and the other described the functions in terms of goal-subgoal relations. Each knowledge group was assigned to the reading of only one type of text (causal or hierarchical), and each text was characterized by its semantic coherence: local for the text with causal coherence, and global for the text

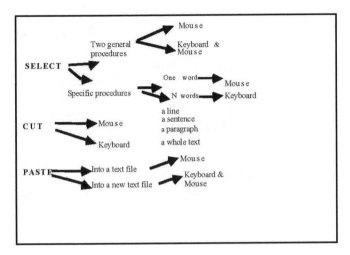

FIGURE 1.1.   Graphic representation of the temporal-causal structure of the three functions of the text editor (from Tapiero, 2003).

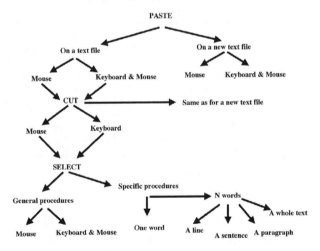

FIGURE 1.2.   Graphic representation of the hierarchical structure of the three functions of the text editor (from Tapiero, 2003).

with hierarchical coherence. Events from the causal structure were described by a causal path; in the hierarchical structure, the superordinate goal was presented first, followed by subordinate goals. Thus, the two types of text contained the same information, but they differed in their text structure. They had some identical statements that were irrelevant to the textual organization, and some different statements, which were important parts of the text structure. Table 1.1 gives the first 12 (identical and different) statements in the causal text and Table 1.2 presents these statements for the hierarchical text.

Immediately after reading the experimental text, each subject performed a cued recall task: "Recall everything you remember of the Edit menu." The texts and each recall protocol were propositionalized (Kintsch, 1988, 1998; Tapiero, 1992; Tapiero & Otero, 1999) with concepts (e.g., P1: CONCEPT) and propositions (e.g., P2: PREDICATE [CONCEPT]) as nodes in an associative network. Protocol analyses confirmed the existence of an "intermediate effect" on recall, in a domain other than clinical expertise. As predicted, novices and intermediates recalled more information after studying the causal text than the hierarchical text, whereas experts recalled more information from the hierarchical text than from the causal text (see Caillies & Tapiero, 1997).

TABLE 1.1

Examples of Identical (i) and Different (d) Statements
in the Causal Text (From Tapiero, 2003)

(1 d) To select one or n words in a text file, (2 i) put the cursor at the end of one or n words to be selected by pressing the mouse button, (3 i) and then (4 i) either drag the selection to the other end and release the mouse button, (5 i) or press and hold the finger on the "shift" key of the keyboard and put the cursor at the other end by pressing the mouse button. (6 d) These two general procedures allow you to select one or n words. (7 i) Put the cursor on the word and press the mouse button twice. (8 d) The word is now selected. (9 i) Put the cursor at the left end of the line and press the mouse button when the diagonal arrow appears. (10 d) The line is now selected. (11 i) Put the cursor on the sentence and press simultaneously on the "apple" key and the mouse button. (12 d) The sentence is now selected.

TABLE 1.2

Examples of Identical (i) and Different (d) Statements in the Hierarchical
Text (From Tapiero, 2003)

(1 d) To paste one or n words into an existing text file, (2 i) put the cursor at the insert point you choose by clicking on the mouse, (3 i) and then (4 i) either you use only the mouse, (5 i) which requires (6 i) putting the cursor on the "Edit" menu by pressing and holding the finger on the mouse button, (7 i) selecting the "Paste" command and releasing the button, (8 i) or you use only the keyboard by simultaneously pressing the "apple" and "v" keys. (9 d) To paste one or n words into a new text file, (10 i) put the cursor on the "File" menu by pressing and holding the finger on the mouse button, (11 i) select the "New" command and release the button. (12 i) A new file appears on the screen.

Thus, an interesting challenge was to test whether predictions from Kinstch's model are consistent with these data. I assumed that using different networks as input, each one corresponding to knowledge presumably activated by the three knowledge groups (novices, intermediates, and experts), would match the recall data for the causal text. This would provide evidence of the intermediate effect (see Caillies & Tapiero, 1997).

I performed different types of simulations (see Tapiero, 2003) derived from both theoretical hypotheses and empirical findings. The simulations were based on the framework developed by Kintsch in 1988 (i.e., the Construction-Integration Model) and extended to the cognitive architecture in 1998. They were performed by Mross and Robert's program (Mross & Roberts, 1992) . The propositions corresponding to the information subjects would ideally recall served as input (i.e., the textbase network) for the simulations. Three simulations were performed, one for each level of expertise (novices, intermediates, and experts). For each simulation, a network corresponding to the knowledge level subjects were assumed to have (i.e., the situation model network) was integrated into the textbase network. For all three simulations, one main principle was to relate the propositions of each situation model network (novice, intermediate, and expert) to the textbase network, as if the reader processed the text online. Indeed, insofar as Kintsch's model implies that bottom-up processes are at play rather than processes driven by contextual expectations, situational information was introduced as input to a given cycle in order to account for the emergence of the representation; on the other hand, schematic information was assumed to guide the comprehension process at the beginning of the processing. Thus, only propositions from each specific situation model network that were assumed to be activated while reading a sentence were related to the textbase network (see Tapiero, 1992; Tapiero & Otero, 1999). For the three simulations, the text was processed sentence by sentence, while keeping the most activated proposition in each cycle. This proposition was reintroduced into the next cycle except when more than one proposition reached the maximum value. Once a sentence was processed, the representation of that portion of text was integrated into the text representation in long-term memory. Whenever a proposition was used in more than one cycle, its representation in long-term memory was updated at the end. Relations between propositions were established using the criterion of referential overlap (Le Ny, 1979; Tapiero, 1992; Tapiero & Denhière, 1995) rather than argument overlap (Kintsch, 1974; Kintsch & van Dijk, 1978). This was done to control the number of links relating to the propositions in the networks and to avoid nonelicited relations. At the end of all cycles, the final activation values of the whole network in long-term memory were obtained by adding the long-term-memory activation values of the situation-model propositions to those of the textbase propositions related to the model.

This procedure increased the activation values of some textbase propositions (those related to situation-model propositions) compared to their initial long-term memory activation levels (i.e., without adding the activation value of situation-model propositions). The resulting activation values of the textbase propositions were compared to the recall data collected for those propositions.

An "Ideal" Situation Model.   In order to construct the situation model for the three expertise groups (novices, intermediates, and experts) and to integrate it into the textbase network, 10 expert users of Microsoft Word (who did not otherwise participate to the experiment) were asked to perform a knowledge-assessment task. They were asked to state everything they knew about the Edit menu, without having read the causal text beforehand. From these protocols, concepts and predicates that systematically occurred in the recall (i.e., common knowledge) were selected to serve as the "ideal" situation model. This model was a network composed of eight nodes: EDIT MENU, SELECT, CUT, PASTE, CLICK, KEYBOARD, MOUSE, and CURSOR, plus two other propositions referring to text-editor functions that can be done directly on the keyboard (i.e., CUT and PASTE). Thus, the situation model network had a total of 10 nodes. This set of concepts—the "ideal" situation model—was assumed to be activated when a person (with good prior knowledge) read something about the Microsoft Word Edit menu. A graphic representation of the "ideal" situation model network is shown in Figure 1.3.

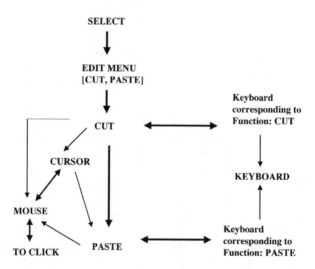

FIGURE 1.3.   Graphic representation of the "ideal" situation-model net (from Tapiero, 2003).

A strength value of 2 was assigned to the main links that relate the propositions of this network to each other. This was done to increase the weight of the macro-units in the model assumed to be the main knowledge of good users. Thus, SELECT was related to EDIT MENU [CUT, PASTE], EDIT MENU [CUT, PASTE] was related to CUT, and CUT was related to PASTE with a link strength of 2. A value of 1 was assigned to relations between these nodes and other concepts or propositions in the situation-model networks, and to all other links in the network (e.g., the relation between MOUSE and CUT). Some two-directional links were also introduced into this network such as between CURSOR and MOUSE, or between MOUSE and CLICK. Finally, the links between the situation-model propositions and the text-base propositions were also set at 1. This network was used as a framework for implementing the three levels of expertise (novice, intermediate, and expert). Whereas all the network units were used in the expert simulation, only some were activated for simulating the other two expertise levels (intermediate and novice). Thus, a second main principle was to keep the same situation model for simulating the three expertise groups but to selectively activate or differently relate the propositions in the situation model to those in the textbase, depending on the level of expertise. The specific principles applied to the simulations for each level of expertise follow.

Experts Situation Model. The situation model of experts was assumed to be close to the one constructed from the interviews described earlier (see Figure 1.3). Portions of the network, as it is shown in Figure 1.3, were activated whenever they were relevant to the text being read in a particular processing cycle. Because the topic of the first three cycles of the text was rather general and not specifically related to knowledge about editing, none of the knowledge nodes were added to the textbase for these first three processing cycles. However, on the fourth cycle, six nodes from the situation model network (i.e., EDIT MENU, CUT, the node referring to the keyboard function for "to cut," CLICK, MOUSE, and KEYBOARD) were activated. Four of these six nodes were related to the corresponding textbase propositions: EDIT MENU, CUT, MOUSE, and KEYBOARD. The same rules were applied for all remaining cycles, and by the end of the simulation, all nodes of the "ideal" situation model network had been activated at least once.

Intermediates Situation Model. Intermediates had experience with a PC but had never used a Macintosh before. Hence, all knowledge nodes in the "ideal" situation model that were closely linked to Macintosh functions were deleted from the situation model of the intermediates. At the end of the simulation, then, only six of the ten nodes were activated: SELECT, EDIT MENU, CUT, PASTE, KEYBOARD, and MOUSE. It was assumed that experts activate knowledge only when it is specifically called for. Intermediates, on the other hand, have less knowledge but are more likely to activate it, even when not specifically called for. Therefore, knowledge activation for intermediates started on the first cycle, and more links between text propositions and knowledge nodes were established than for experts, resulting in a more broadly interconnected network. Moreover, to account for the greater reliance of intermediates on semantic information, textbase nodes were assigned a self-strength of 2 (rather than 1 like all other nodes in the network).

Novices Situation Model.   The knowledge network for novices contained only nodes that represented general knowledge but nothing specific to text editors, with which novices have no experience. Thus, only four nodes remained activated in the novice situation model: SELECT, EDIT MENU, CUT, and PASTE. Otherwise, the simulation for the novices was the same as for the intermediates. Thus, four series of simulations were performed: a simulation that involved only the textbase network, without any additional knowledge (i.e., textbase) and three simulations that combined the textbase with the characteristic knowledge of experts, intermediates, and novices, respectively. To illustrate, the correlations between the recall data collected for the causal text and predictions based on the Construction-Integration Model are presented in Table 1.3. Table 1.3 compares the results of the four simulations (activation values of the text propositions) with empirical data.

Simulations based on the comprehension of the text by itself (textbase only), without taking the reader's knowledge into account, were generally unsuccessful, which points out the importance of dealing explicitly with the reader's situation model. Furthermore, any situation model will not do: The situation model must fit with the reader's knowledge level. When comprehension was simulated by adding a novice knowledge net to the textbase (column 2), the results correlated the best with the novice data. Similarly, when a knowledge net for intermediates was added (column 3), the correlation was the highest with the intermediate data (boldface in Table 1.3). Finally, an expert knowledge net (column 4) yielded the best correlation with the expert data (boldface in Table 1.3). On the other hand, the predictions for intermediates were closer to the novice data than the predictions for novices were, which probably means that the novices' knowledge was underestimated. Thus, the recall data reported here were predicted quite well by Kintsch's model (1988), provided the appropriate domain knowledge was included in the simulation. Kintsch's Construction-Integration Model was also tested via a series of multiple regression analyses. The recall probability for the three knowledge levels based on the criterion variables and the three simulations based on the reader's knowledge were the predictor variables. Table 1.4 presents the beta weights from the multiple regression analyses.

TABLE 1.3

Correlations Between Recall Data and Predictions of the Model
(From Tapiero, 2003)

Data	Only TB	TB & N	TB & I	TB & E
		Predictions		
Novices	.22	**.43**	.63	.28
Intermediates	.19	.37	**.72**	.41
Experts	.19	.24	.51	**.62**

Note. Legend: TB = Textbase, N = Novices, I = Intermediates, E = Experts (Correlations greater than .22 were statistically significant at the .05 level).

TABLE 1.4

Beta Weights From the Multiple Regression Analyses of the Recall
Probability for the Three Expertise Groups (From Tapiero, 2003)

Predictors	Novice	Intermediate	Expert
		Data	
TB & N	**.21***	.09	.009
TB & I	**.55****	**.63****	**.29***
TB & E	−.02	.11	**.49****
R2	.43	.54	.45

Note. Legend: TB = Textbase, N = Novices, I = Intermediates, E = Experts (* $p < .01$; ** $p < .001$).

The simulations with novice and intermediate knowledge were reliable predictors of the recall data for novices, but adding a knowledge net characteristic of intermediates had a highly significant effect (boldface in column 1). Only intermediate knowledge was a reliable predictor of the intermediate data (boldface in column 2). Also, the simulations with the knowledge of intermediates and experts were reliable predictors of the recall data for experts, with the knowledge net characteristic of experts having a highly significant effect (boldface in column 3). These findings emphasize the necessity of adding information that fits with the appropriate situation model in order to allow the model to predict data for each level of expertise. Moreover, and in line with my assumption, these results show that the knowledge added to the situation model for intermediates was a good predictor for all three of our expertise groups. This suggests that the intermediate level is the best model, as it is close to novices but is also on the way to becoming an expert.

The empirical data reported here show that predictions based on Kintsch's model fit quite well with the recall data obtained. They illustrate how subjects use their knowledge when reading, and stress one of the main principles of the Construction-Integration Model: Knowledge structures are not prestored, but generated in the context of the task for which they are needed. I applied this principle to the simulations performed by gradually activating appropriate prior knowledge, whenever it was relevant to the current processing cycle.

Thus, the Construction-Integration Model is a significant example of the models developed in the second generation of research. It offers a new way of investigating the contribution of knowledge to the reading comprehension process, and allows for a step-by-step study of how a reader's mental representation evolves. It also shows that several sources of information are activated during the reading comprehension process, inducing fluctuations in the activation of concepts, propositions, and relations throughout the comprehension process, until the network reaches a "stable" state assumed to correspond to the mental representation. These two properties (i.e., fluctuation and various sources of activation) are two characteristics of the Landscape Model (van den Broek et al., 1996) that illustrate the transition from the second generation of research to the third. One interesting property of the third generation is that it emphasizes the interaction between the reading process and the product of the representation. In this type of model, multiple sources of knowledge may contribute to the elaboration of the mental representation during reading. The goal is to investigate the activation of multiple text elements as well as inference making throughout the reading process. The Landscape Model (van den Broek et al., 1996) not only integrates these notions, but also accounts for the dynamic aspect of the reading comprehension process. This model is described next.

1.3.2.2. The Third Generation of Research: The Landscape Model (van den Broek et al., 1996)

As previously discussed, the third generation of models attempts to integrate the online and offline aspects of reading brought to the fore by the first two generations. The reading process postulated in this kind of model differs in several respects from the one postulated in the second generation. First, the comprehension process is defined as a continuous and dynamic fluctuation of activation patterns. This dynamic aspect of reading leads to the assumption that discursive elements and inferences are not activated in an all-or-none way but that activation patterns occur at different degrees. Moreover, the idea that attentional resources are limited led second-generation researchers to postulate the existence of a fixed attentional buffer with a limited number of inputs. The third generation denies this hypothesis for a fixed but distributed number of activations.

Most models consider the text currently being processed and the residual activation of the preceding cycle to be the principal source of activation. The Landscape Model developed by van den Broek et al. (1996) involves four potential sources of activation within each processing cycle: the text currently being processed, the information output from the preceding cycle, the elements of the episodic representation in memory, and the reader's prior knowledge assumed to be stored in his or her long-term memory. Concerning the first source of activation, concepts that are explicitly mentioned in the sentence currently being processed become activated and strongly associated to explicit concepts in semantic memory (Kintsch, 1988). In the second source, the information that was activated in a preceding reading cycle becomes available and can be either completely or partially activated. This source may require some elaboration from the reader in order to relate information. Among the concepts, those that are likely to remain active are those that were explicitly mentioned in the preceding sentence (Kintsch, 1988), those that are referentially coherent (leading-edge strategy; Kintsch & van Dijk, 1978), and those that are causally coherent (Fletcher & Bloom, 1988). In this model, causal and referential coherence are the two main criteria for the establishment of coherence, automatically generated by the reader, although other levels of coherence (e.g., linguistic markers) have been noted for expository texts (see van den Broek, Virtue, Everson, Tzeng, & Sung, 2002). The third source of activation corresponds to information from prior reading cycles. If the information activated in the current cycle is not sufficiently coherent, then the reader may reinstate information that was activated in a preceding cycle, insofar as this information was explicitly mentioned in the text or was originally activated from any of the other sources such as background knowledge (van den Broek et al., 1996). Finally, and in line with other views of the comprehension process (Kinstch, 1988), readers are assumed to activate background knowledge (often automatically) when they process textual information. This activation involves access to and retrieval from semantic memory (the activation of knowledge is further discussed in Parts III and IV of this book).

Crucial to this model is the idea that the activation levels of elements explicitly mentioned in the text or inferred from it (i.e., from these four sources) fluctuate during the reading process. These fluctuations describe a "landscape" of activations, and their dynamic properties are captured in a computational model (see van den Broek et al., 1996).

The nature of the activation constitutes a central point in the model. On one hand, concepts may be activated to different degrees, and on the other, the reader is assumed to have a limited pool of activation that can be distributed over the various concepts. Thus, during reading, the accumulation of information is thought to motivate the reader to selectively allocate his or her attention to certain elements. The construction of a coherent representation implies that during reading, the information that is not mentioned in the current sentence is retrieved by the reader from the emerging text representation or from his or her prior knowledge. Two types of mechanisms are involved in reinstatements and in background-knowledge activation. First, a concept (i.e., directly taken from the textual input) is retrieved via the activation of the cohort associated with its processing; in other words, the activation of a concept triggers the activation of other elements with which it is associated (its cohort). The amount of activation allocated to a retrieved concept is a function of the strength of its relations to the concept initially retrieved and the amount of activation received from it (i.e., the context). Moreover, the amount of activation of a secondarily retrieved concept is dependent on the cohort parameter that defines the extent to which the activation of the initially retrieved concept is transferred to other concepts in the cohort (the activation value ranges from 0 to 1). Cohort activation is assumed to be a fast and passive process (see Myers & O'Brien, 1998) and to be identical for both episodic and semantic memory (Linderholm, Virtue, Tzeng, & van den Broek, 2004). Thus, the cohort of a concept, and the activations that result from its processing, differ from one point in the text to another. The mental representation elaborated thus evolves as the reader processes the text, which implies the constant creation of new nodes and new connections within the network. Finally, like the other members of the cohort, the probability of activation of a concept in the subsequent processing cycles depends on its degree of activation in the preceding cycle and on its self-connection within the network (i.e., node strength). Consequently, a concept with a high self-connection strength has a higher probability of remaining activated in memory than does a concept with a low self-connection strength. The second type of mechanism for reinstating information or for activating background knowledge is coherence-based retrieval. This retrieval mechanism is assumed to be strategic and deliberate, and its main function is to create coherence by accessing the episodic memory representation or the reader's knowledge base. In both cases, processing is effortful and slow.

In the Landscape Model, the four sources of activation combined determine the activation patterns (i.e., the activation vectors) at each point in the reading process. The activation vectors dynamically and gradually construct the episodic representation of the text. Changes in the activation vectors are captured by the mental representation, which, gradually emerging, encodes (via directional and asymmetrical connections) the order of the associations between the concepts of a text and their levels of activation. Changes in the strengths of connections between concepts are guided by an asymptotic (modified delta) learning rule. According to this rule, if the level of activation of a concept is easily predictable by the existing representation, no major change occurs. By contrast, if the activation level of a concept is not anticipated, the connections within the network have to change to account for the dynamics of the activation vectors. Connections between concepts also affect the current representation due to a principle called *cohort competition*: There is competition between concepts for predicting the activation of another concept. This competition has deep effects on the representation built during each consecutive processing cycle and serves to represent the dynamics of the text in an efficient way. For instance, if a concept is already highly activated by an associated concept, the probability that a third concept is activated in the same cycle becomes low. If Concept A predicts Concept B at the beginning of a text, and, if at the end of the text, Concept A always co-occurs with Concept C, then a kind of competition occurs that tends to not associate B with C. In a similar way, when a group of concepts (ABC) tends to predict the activation of Concept D, then the strength of the association with Concept D is distributed over Concepts A, B, and C. Finally, the online updating of concepts, and connections strengths between them, depends on the cohort of the concept that partially orients the activation vector generated by the new input, but also on the cohort competition and asymptotic learning that are responsible for the extent to which the activation vector changes. Thus, the backward direction of this process guarantees the involvement of the complete representation during updating. Within each processing cycle, the online activation of concepts triggers the reconstruction or reconfiguration of the entire representation.

One crucial notion in this model is the existence of a reciprocal relationship between the episodic memory representation and the activation patterns. The representation in episodic memory is conceived of as a network of interconnected nodes. The nodes and connections in the network differ in memory strength. In the present architecture, the activation vectors represent the concepts activated for each processing cycle. These vectors help the reader gradually build the text representation during the reading process. For each new cycle, new nodes and connections are updated in the reader's representation. Connections already present in the network change strengths. The extent of the changes in the representation is a function of the new activation vector. In other words, the more activated a node, the greater the change in the connections among the concepts in the memory representation. However, the change is asymptotic because it depends on the strengths of the nodes or connections that preceded the current cycle. The strengths of the nodes and connections in the network influence the subsequent activation vectors by providing a basis for the activation cohort. Thus, the Landscape Model allows dynamic and reciprocal relations between the activation vectors and the episodic memory representation of the text. It is assumed that the sequence of activation patterns observed during the reading process gradually leads to the construction of a complete representation of what has been read. Moreover, information from the sentence currently being processed may reactivate information from the preceding cycles (episodic representation), which would in turn cause the activation of other associated information. The reactivated elements of the episodic representation are part of the process of understanding the current sentence. In this perspective, the interpretation of a new sentence by the reader is partly determined by his or her interpretation of the text as a whole.

The Landscape Model has been successful in predicting several processes that readers carry out during comprehension. In one study, van den Broek et al. (1996) compared the Landscape Model's predictions with human participants' recall and ratings. The authors' goal was to find out whether the Landscape Model could successfully predict the online (ratings) and offline (recall) components of activation fluctuations during reading. They obtained strong correlations between the model's predictions and the empirical data. The strength of a concept within the representation was found to predict not only the probability of recall of that concept but also the order in which the elements are recalled. The first concepts to be recalled are those that receive a large amount of activation on all processing cycles. The probability of subsequent recall depends on the strength of the relationships between the concepts because readers tend to recall the element in the representation that is the closest to an initial concept. Finally, if two concepts are related in an equal way to the last concept recalled, then the concept with the highest node strength tends to be recalled. More recently, Linderholm et al. (2004) tested the predictions of the Landscape Model on the availability of elements in two different reading situations: reading purpose in the context of expository text, and detection of textual inconsistencies in stories. In both situations, the predictions of the Landscape Model fit human performance quite well. In the first test of the validity of the model (i.e., reading purpose expository text), the simulations captured the dynamic representation the reader was assumed to build based on causal and referential coherence, and on other types of coherence as well (i.e., logical and contrastive relations). In the second test (i.e., detection of inconsistencies in stories), the authors showed that to detect inconsistencies, readers need to keep contradictory information activated in the developing episodic memory representation of the text (see Linderholm et al., 2004).

Thus, this model accounts for the fluctuation of activations as the reader proceeds through the text, as well as his or her interactions with the resulting final representation of the text. It provides an account of the dynamic construction of the text representation, and of the bidirectional relations between the online and offline representations. This computational model nicely combines relevant aspects of theories on text comprehension and on the accessibility of information, both of which contribute to a deeper understanding of the readers' mental representation. What I have described here shows that this architecture accounts for a wide range of phenomena occurring in a text-reading situation and allows for combining several factors (e.g., types of relations, standards of coherence). These factors may vary according to theoretical or empirical assumptions, and they can be adjusted according to the assumptions to be tested.

As the authors mentioned, this model would benefit from several extensions (see Linderholm et al., 2004). I focus in particular on two limitations of this model that are not discussed by the authors: the contribution of background knowledge, and the nature of the input. Although the Landscape Model can predict the accessibility of knowledge in episodic memory, and it can simulate the concepts that are inferred during reading, there is no evidence of how prior knowledge activated in semantic memory contributes to the reading comprehension process, nor of how it interacts with prior knowledge in episodic memory to influence the distribution of activation. Also, whereas background knowledge for stories may be quite easy to activate, this is not the case for knowledge from expository texts (and even less so for scientific texts). As argued by van den Broek et al. (2002), inferences are relatively difficult to make in expository texts, for they depend on the reader's prior knowledge. Secondly, and in line with this first point, it is not clear what kind of information serves as input in the Landscape Model: Concepts, propositions, and sentences are all treated in the same way. This last remark questions the validity of the model for distinguishing between the multiple situational dimensions the reader is assumed to monitor, and for predicting their interaction. How are the different dimensions specified in the Landscape Model? How are they separated? Are there some semantic rules that stipulate how to do so? These are some of the questions that could challenge the Landscape Model in future research. However, despite these limitations, this model has been shown to be powerful enough to predict a wide range of behavioral data. It elegantly describes how bottom-up and top-down processes interact during the reading comprehension process.

Situation Models as Integrated Representations: What Kind of Model Does the Reader Build?

There is a large consensus on the idea that discourse comprehension involves three levels of the reader's mental representation in memory[1] (Graesser et al., 1994; Johnson-Laird, 1983; Just & Carpenter, 1987; Kintsch, 1988; Schmalhofer & Glavanov, 1986; van Dijk & Kintsch, 1983): surface, textbase, and situation model. The surface representation corresponds to the exact wording and syntax of the text. Although this surface structure may be initially available in memory, this level of representation has been shown to decay rapidly (Kintsch et al., 1990; Sachs, 1967). The textbase representation captures the meaning conveyed by the text, independently of its surface formulation, but remains closely tied to the text's formulation. The situation model or referential representation of discourse is "the reader's representation of the world the text refers to" (Just & Carpenter, 1987, p. 195) or "the cognitive representation of the events, actions, persons, and in general the situation a text is about" (van Dijk & Kintsch, 1983, pp. 11–12). It is based on a construction of the events or situation a text is about in episodic memory, that is, a subjective representation of a fragment of reality in the reader's mind. Johnson-Laird (1983) and other researchers have used the term *mental model* to refer to analogous representations of situations and world events that fulfill different roles in comprehension and reasoning. Throughout this book, I use both terms interchangeably to refer to the reader's mental repre-

---

[1]Although some theories refer only to a perceptual level and a mental model level (see Barsalou, 1993, 1999; Johnson-Laird, 1983).

sentation, although each of these constructs has different structural and functional characteristics.

2.1. THE INTERNAL "OBJECTS" OF SITUATION MODELS

Any representational system relates two elements to each other: a represented world and a representing world (Rumelhart & Norman, 1988). Both of these worlds may be conceptualized as consisting of a set of objects, and of relations among the objects in it. Situation models are one kind of representational system, given that they are commonly defined as consisting of entities and of relations between those entities. However, more is known about the role of situation models and the mechanisms underlying their construction than about the objects and relations that constitute them (van Dijk, 1995). Until now, there is still no clear evidence for one specific type of entity. Langston, Kramer, and Glenberg (1998) point out the same problem:

> A mental model is a representation of what the language or text is about, rather than a representation of the language itself. Apart from this essence there is little agreement as to how to characterize a mental model. Is it an image? A schema? A set of propositions? (p. 247)

In addition, it is likely that situation models reflect properties and relations of the perceived world. This is consistent with the idea that perception is intrinsically linked to cognition. In this chapter, I review some theoretical and empirical arguments that shed light on the nature of the objects in situation models and on the relations among them.

2.1.1. The Predicate-Argument Schema (Kintsch, 1988, 1998)

The construction of meaning (concepts and semantic relations) is central for understanding the nature of the objects in situation models. Different kinds of formalisms have been used to represent meaning, including feature systems, frames, schemata, scripts, propositions, and networks (associative and semantic), but only a few have been considered as objects or entities in situation models. Schemata (Schank & Abelson, 1977) are defined as fixed, complex mental structures that are retrieved from memory when needed and used to organize experienced events. The specificity and context-sensitive nature of situation models led to a revision of the initial conception of these mental structures, for it lacked flexibility in accounting for human-experience events. Schemas then

> came to be thought of not as fixed structures to be pulled from memory upon demand, but as recipes for generating organizational structures in a particular task context. Context-sensitive generation ensures that the structure that is generated is always adapted to the particular context of use. (Kintsch, 1998, p. 37)

The predicate-argument schema—"the proposition"—has been regarded as a basic unit of language and has been widely proposed as a compound unit of situation models. A notation system in terms of atomic propositions (Kintsch, 1974) was followed by notation in terms of complex propositions (Kintsch & van Dijk, 1978) for the purposes of improving representation. Atomic propositions consist of a relational term, the predicate, and one or more arguments. The predicate determines the number and kinds of arguments that may fill argument slots, that is, the semantic role (e.g., agent and object). Complex propositions are compounds composed of several atomic propositions that are subordinated to a core propositional meaning. Not all expressions in the surface structure are represented in this notation, and the choice of which sentence properties to represent in the propositional notation is pragmatic and depends on one's theoretical and experimental goals. According to Kintsch (1998), the predicate-argument representation of meaning has advantages over the other forms of representation (e.g., schemata) because it is flexible enough to subsume alternative systems. Schemas, associative networks, and production rules can be expressed in this notation. Therefore, the author argues, the propositional representation is capable of expressing of a wide variety of structures at different levels and hence can account for the content of situation models. He postulates the construction of a situation model in which textbase and knowledge-based propositions are related to form the situation model evoked by the text. He also assumes that a flexible process of multiple constraint satisfaction may supply a good mechanism through which such an interpretation can emerge.

In Kintsch et al.'s (1990) studies, situation models are based on scripts (daily life events) or on schemata (computer procedures), but are made up of units translated into propositions and connections between propositions, just like the representational units that form the semantic level of representation (i.e., the textbase). However, substantial evidence for the importance of nonpropositional representations (i.e., linear or spatial) in cognition has been found, and in 1988, Kintsch evoked the case of nonpropositional situation models, such as cognitive maps like those assumed to be involved by Perrig and Kintsch (1985). In 1998, Kintsch modeled spatial-image processing using a cognitive architecture called the Construction-Integration Model (Kintsch, 1988). His main assumption was that imagery and linear strings can be translated into propositional format by maintaining the unique properties of the analogous representations. For instance, representational properties such as perspective or framing effects, which are characteristic of imagery but not of verbal or propositional information, can be represented in propositional format, with the use of spatial predicates: "...some spatial information can be translated into a propositional format by using spatial predicates and thus becomes an integral part of the text representation" (Kintsch, 1998, p.46). How, then, can spatial information be translated into a propositional format? Kintsch (1998) gives the example of the sentence "John traveled by car from the bridge to the house on the hill" in which several concepts, JOHN, CAR, BRIDGE, HOUSE, and HILL, and several propositions are involved: TRAVEL[agent: JOHN, instrument: CAR, source: BRIDGE, goal: HOUSE, modifier: ON[HOUSE, HILL]. Given the visual image that comes to mind after reading this sentence, the author assumes that verbal and imagery information are in part redundant—*The house is on the hill.*—but not entirely, as imagery information may be richer because it may add information such as, *John's car might be on the road*, and *A river might be under the bridge.* However, in some cases, verbal information is richer: *John travels.* Kintsch represents the verbal propositional information derived from the sentence, and the propositional translation of the image, in a propositional network, that is, a set of interconnected nodes (i.e., concepts and propositions). Two networks are thus constructed, one dealing with concepts and propositions built from the propositional representation, and the other dealing with concepts and propositions related to the visual representation: *bridge, road, river, between,* and *under.* In each network, the concepts and propositions are related. The main merit of this representation concerns the existence of connections between concepts and propositions from the two networks: *road* (imagery net also related to *between*) is related to *on* (propositional net), and *between* (imagery net also related to *bridge*) is related to *house* (propositional net). This resulting net accounts for the imagery representation "... not in a fully satisfactory manner, but there is at least some way to deal with imagery by modeling comprehension processes" (Kintsch, 1998, p. 47). However, Kintsch himself points out that the predicate-argument format invites a verbal bias, and theorists must be aware of this limitation when representing nonverbal properties.

Building a situation model requires the contribution and use of prior knowledge as well. In Kintsch's theory (1988, 1998), knowledge is also represented as a propositional network (i.e., associative net). The network's nodes can refer to propositions, schemata, frames, scripts, or production rules, which can all be formally written based on the predicate-argument schema. This unique format makes the task easier when knowledge and text representations are integrated into the situational level of representation (see Kintsch, 1988, 1998). The knowledge net is based on perception and experience, and can be constructed from scripts and other types of schemata. According to Kintsch (1988, 1998), these structures are always built in the context of their use and are defined as *emergent structures.* This view differs from the more traditional script-based approach in which scripts refer to fixed, fully elaborated preexisting knowledge structures that need to be retrieved for use. Thus, in the Construction-Integration Theory (Kintsch,

1988, 1998), knowledge contribution is inherent to the processing itself, and this model therefore accounts for both forms of representation: propositional and situational. As discussed in the first chapter, the application of weak, noncontextual rules (i.e., during the rule-based construction phase) allows the knowledge net (and the propositional net) to emerge, and the resulting representation may be irrelevant. The integration phase, which follows the construction phase, occurs without much effort through spreading activation, and leads to a contextually integrated representation of the text's meaning in long-term memory. At this point, the representation, as the product of the construction and integration processes, or integrated textbase, is viewed as a "kind of situation model" (Kintsch, 1988, p. 180). Because this representation is propositional, the situation model under consideration here is propositional as well.

In a recent study, Otero and I (Tapiero & Otero, 1999) conducted a comparison, both experimentally and by predictions from the Construction-Integration Model (Kintsch, 1988), of the construction of the semantic- and situation-model levels of representation in relation to the elaboration and tagging hypotheses of enhanced memory for inconsistent information. We assumed that whereas elaborations should cause inconsistencies to be integrated into the rest of the text and should lead to an updated model of the situation described in the text, tagging should be conceptualized as a textbase phenomenon that allows readers to form a correct semantic representation but not to update their situation model. Propositions, concepts, and their interrelationships (Kintsch, 1988, 1998; van Dijk & Kintsch, 1983) were used as network input in the simulations. The comparison between the behavioral data and the model's predictions supported Tapiero and Otero's findings: Inconsistencies had different effects at the textbase- and situation-model levels, depending on task requirements (text-based and situation-based). When relevant knowledge was introduced via propositional networks, we showed that the model could account for the differential effect of prior knowledge on the memorability of inconsistent information. This was done in two ways: first, by incorporating propositions from the situation model in case the reader had the opportunity to elaborate on the inconsistencies; second, when elaborations were impossible, the model's predictions fit the empirical data better when the negative effect of an inhibitory link between inconsistent propositions and the positive effect of a tag for inconsistencies were combined at the textbase level. In this way, introducing a tagging node in the Construction-Integration Model's textbase network seemed to be a natural way to account for the positive effects that contradictions or inconsistencies may have on memory. Thus, the model allowed us to nicely predict empirical data and to test crucial hypotheses about knowledge readers apply in a text-comprehension situation. Propositions were used as basic units in the networks.

The psychological relevance of using the propositional format for describing readers' mental representations has been widely demonstrated with various experimental paradigms (Goetz, Anderson, & Schallert, 1981; Ratcliff & McKoon, 1978; van Dijk & Kintsch, 1983). In this sense, the propositional system has shown its "massive explanatory power" (Stanfield & Zwaan, 2001). However, although situation models have sometimes been represented propositionally (Haenggi, Kintsch, & Gernsbacher, 1995; Kintsch et al., 1990; Tapiero & Otero, 1999), Kintsch himself pointed out the weakness of this format, as the text and knowledge propositional networks have to be constructed by hand. Although this limitation has no serious implications for small texts, it is a real obstacle when one has to deal with large corpora. One way to overcome this problem is to represent propositions not as nodes in a network, but as vectors in a multidimensional space. With a technique called Latent Semantic Analysis (LSA), knowledge in a large corpus can be represented (see Foltz, 1996; Landauer & Dumais, 1997). Loosely described, the meanings of words, sentences, and whole texts are represented in LSA as vectors in a multidimensional semantic space. New words and documents can be added to this space and compared with one another by a measure of relatedness between vectors (i.e., the cosine between vectors in the dimensional space). One of the main advantages of using LSA vectors is that there is no limit on the size of the to-be-analyzed texts. In addition, it does not require defining or specifying the individual features of vectors, and the multidimensional LSA vector can objectively and automatically represent the meaning of various verbal units. Kintsch combined this alternative knowledge representation method with the Construction-Integration Model in order to describe various aspects of discourse comprehension, and this technique has been shown to offer new perspectives in theories of comprehension (for a detailed description of the use of this technique, see Kintsch, 1998).

Thus, the propositional system, which is part of the more widely called amodal symbol systems, has the ability to describe semantic processing and knowledge in a "satisfactory" manner. However, although a great deal of procedural information can be successfully modeled using this type of representational system, other relevant formats have been proposed to represent meaning and knowledge. For instance, meaning representation has also been described in terms of semantic categories such as events, states, and actions (see Molinari & Tapiero, in press; Zwaan, Langston, & Graesser, 1995). Also regarding knowledge, Sanford and Garrod (1981) developed a theory that underlines the crucial role of knowledge activation in interpreting discourse. In this theory, although the forming of propositions is an important part of a future reasoning process, propositional units are not viewed as a precursor in discourse interpretation, but are seen as the outcome of an interpretation. This approach leads one to regard situation models as the result of a mapping between explicitly stated information, defined in terms of tokens, and implicit information activated from a script-based structure (i.e., scenario). This mapping relies on discourse pointers that relate the two types of information. Another way of defining situation models involves accounting for the analogical relationship between the representing world and the represented world. Gernsbacher (1990) pointed out that the reader's mental representation should reflect the way he or she envisions real-world situations, but did not make any statements about the definition of specific units in the reader's mental representation. Similarly, Johnson-Laird's (1983) mental-models theory emphasized the analogical relation between the represented and representing worlds, and argued that the propositional representation is not sufficient for representing mental models because they are elaborated from perception. However, and in line with Kintsch's and Sanford and Garrod's theories, he also argued that readers' prior knowledge contributes to model interpretation and hence made three main assumptions relevant to his theory (Johnson-Laird, 1983). First, each entity is represented by a corresponding element in the mental model. Secondly, the properties of entities are represented by the properties of their elements. Finally, relations between entities are represented by the relations between their elements. Consequently, it is not the subjective experience of the model that matters because the model may not be conscious, but rather the structure of the model: Entities are represented by elements, their properties are represented by the properties of the elements, and the relations between them are represented by the relations between the elements (Johnson-Laird, 1983). These three hypotheses make mental models different from other representational formats such as semantic nets and propositional representations.

Thus, although I have shown that propositions can sometimes adequately represent nonpropositional information (e.g., spatial predicates; see Kintsch, 1988, present section), this format cannot underlie a full theory of knowledge, mainly because the analogical relationship between the referent (i.e., the objects) and the mental representation (i.e., the symbols) is not maintained as it is arbitrary (Barsalou, 1999; Glenberg, 1997; Stanfield & Zwaan, 2001). More broadly, the very existence of the amodal symbol in the cognitive system has been questioned. In line with this last argument, other formalisms have been developed that account for a wide range of cognitive activities, including language processes, given that the mental representation of the reader/listener relies on the structural identity of the represented and representing worlds. Therefore, how individuals perceive real-world situations should have a large effect on word interpretation (Johnson-Laird, 1983). In this vein, a new approach in cognitive science, with strong implications on language understanding, has provided some relevant insights for defining the potential nature of representational units. Here, situation models are viewed as experiential (perception and action) simulations of the described situation (Barsalou, 1999; Zwaan, 2004) in which affordances derived from sensory-motor simulations are essential for semantic processing. Zwaan (1999a,b) also stressed the role in defining situation models of vicarious experiences in narrative comprehension, and recent empirical evidence converges in suggesting that the comprehender can be viewed as an immersed experiencer: Readers experience information as if they were participating in the corresponding activity (Zwaan, 1999a,1999b, 2004; Zwaan & Rapp, in press). Understanding discourse is viewed as a complex and dynamic activity and, for the reader, implies accounting for many properties of the entities evoked in a text in an "experiential way," and for the relations that connect them as well. This view of cognition, and in particular of language understanding and meaning construction, puts strong emphasis on the general assumption that cognition is inherently perceptual, with a common representational system for perception and cognition (Barsalou, 1993; Glenberg, 1997; Miller & Johnson-Laird, 1976). In contrast to the symbolic approach to language representation (i.e., the propositional format), these systems are inherently perceptual, with modal and nonarbitrary symbols (see Barsalou, 1999).

Let us now discuss models based on representational units other than propositional units.

2.1.2. States, Events, and Actions Are the Core Elements of Situation Models (Molinari & Tapiero, in press; Tapiero, 1992; Zwaan, Langston, & Graesser, 1995)

If a situation model is the cognitive representation of the events, actions, persons, and situations a text is about, then the representation the reader constructs while reading a text should revolve around these conceptual categories. They should allow the reader to organize representations of the world, and to construct the situation model evoked by the text as it is being read (van Dijk & Kintsch, 1983). Cognitive semantics has isolated these conceptual categories and provided a description of the fundamental categories that structure mental and linguistic representations in terms of states, events, and actions (Baudet, 1990). According to Baudet (1990), states can be seen as "snapshots" in time of the properties of a system's components and the stative relationships (e.g., spatial relations) among those components; events are defined as changes in the states of the system's components. These conceptual categories are retrieved from long-term memory during text comprehension, and a subset of this information is instantiated, just as inferences can be activated in situation models (Graesser & Zwaan, 1995).

The differential effect of the state and event categories on the comprehension process has been demonstrated. Graesser et al. (1980) showed that readers of familiar stories have more difficulty inferring states than events. Molinari and Tapiero (2000), who investigated the influence of states and events on the reader's mental representation, presented high and low prior-knowledge subjects with a text about a scientific domain (i.e., the neuron) described in terms of states (e.g., the unequal distribution of electric charges on the two sides of the neuron membrane) and events (e.g., the opening of sodium channels in response to depolarization). Before the reading phase, both knowledge groups had to study an outline designed to provide them with concepts related to the text domain. The task subjects had to perform just after studying the outline induced the activation of either a semantic representation (summary task) or a situation model (diagram drawing) of the outline. The main results indicated that beginners focused more on states than did experts, although the two groups did not differ in the processing of events. The authors also found that the summary task facilitated subsequent event information processing (i.e., activation of a semantic representation), whereas new states were better integrated into long-term memory when subjects had to draw a diagram (i.e., activation of a situation model).

Thus, it seems likely that semantic categories are among the determinants of the representation elaborated by readers. Individuals, states, events, and actions are key concepts for categorizing mental representations and for understanding the internal structure of situation models. Moreover, not only are these categories able to describe the domains of expository or scientific texts, they also adequately represent story content and particular stories' causal structure, defined in terms of causal chains and causal networks (see Black & Bower, 1980; Bloom, Fletcher, van den Broek, Reitz, & Shapiro, 1990; Fletcher & Bloom, 1988; Trabasso, Secco, & van den Broek, 1984; Trabasso & Sperry, 1985; van den Broek & Lorch, 1993). Finally, Zwaan, Langston, and Graesser (1995) recently developed the Event-Indexing Model in which events and characters' intentional actions are the focal points of situation models. In their model, as each incoming story event or action is comprehended (denoted by a verb), the reader monitors and updates the current situation model by defining five indices: temporality, spatiality, protagonist, causality, and intentionality. Each story event is then indexed on each of these five dimensions, and the reader monitors whether incoming story events require updating of the index on any of these five situational dimensions. Incoming events are easier to integrate into the evolving situation model to the extent that they share indexes with the current state of the model. Zwaan and Radvansky (1998) proposed a more sophisticated version of the Event-Indexing Model that distinguished three characteristics of situation models: the situational framework, situational relations, and situational content. The situational framework is a spatial-temporal framework, and the authors assume that establishing the situational framework is a necessary step in the construction of a situation model. Situational relations are relations along the five situational dimensions previously defined in the Event-Indexing Model (see Zwaan, Langston, & Graesser, 1995). The situational framework and situational relations differ and are therefore not redundant. For instance, spatial-temporal framework information establishes when and where the situation occurs, whereas spatial-temporal relations denote the spatial and temporal interrelationships among entities at that location or time. Second, whereas the situational framework is necessary, situational relations are optional. Finally, situational content "includes information such as entities (i.e., protagonist and object) and their properties (e.g., physical and mental attributes). These entities are represented as tokens in a situation model" (Zwaan & Radvansky, 1998, p. 180). Each token is associated with properties of the entity (e.g., physical appearance or state, intentions or goals, emotions). Like relations, entities and properties are optional because they are included in the situation model only when they are crucial to understanding the situation, except of course for the protagonist, which is a mandatory part of the representation. However, there are some cases where situation models can become very complex, and not all information can be stored in the token or by way of properties. To solve this problem, the authors added pointers, as part of the token, that refer to more general information about an entity. Whenever more information is necessary for the situation model, references to the general information are made via the pointers. This is consistent with Sanford and Garrod's (1981) and Glenberg and Langston's (1992) views of situation models, which are defined as the result of a mapping between tokens in explicit focus and the scenario (i.e., knowledge-based script) in implicit focus, via the use of discourse pointers.

2.1.3. Situation Models Result in an Automatic Mapping Between Linguistic Input and an Activated Knowledge Structure Called the Scenario (Sanford & Garrod, 1981)

The theory proposed by Sanford and Garrod (1981) brings us complementary information about the objects that constitute situation models and is aimed at explaining how knowledge is used when readers interpret texts. According to these authors, propositions cannot capture meaning unless one first attributes an interpretation to them. Interpretation is crucial, because it is the basis of the situation model or mental model. Therefore, the situation model can be thought of as the manner in which the propositions that constitute the discourse are interpreted in order to form a representation that is not only coherent but also that corresponds to some possible world. Thus, Sanford and Garrod's theory gives propositions the status of a product of interpretation, not a precursor. In this theory, propositions (predicates and arguments) are minimal discourse interpretations, and are simply interpreted at the level of thematic cases or roles. The roles are only assigned once previous access to prior knowledge occurs. Thus, Sanford and Garrod (1981) argued that the situation model built needs to be coherent and requires knowledge activation. What is remembered of a text is a knowledge-based model of the situation, rather than some propositional analog of the text itself.

According to Kintsch's Construction-Integration Theory, the reader's mental representation of a text corresponds to an integrated propositional network generated by the concatenation of a text-based network and a knowledge-based network. In Sanford and Garrod's theory, knowledge also plays a crucial role in the construction of the mental representation, and human understanding is script-based (Sanford, 1987; Schank & Abelson, 1977). When faced with a text, the reader first has to identify an appropriate reference domain (i.e., setting and situation) that loosely corresponds to what the text is about, and then has to use the identified domain to interpret the subsequent text. This approach is supported by evidence of scenario matching (Sanford & Garrod, 1981) because knowledge of settings and situations constitutes the interpretative scenario for a text.

According to Sanford and Garrod's theory, the construction of the interpretation of a text occurs in several steps. First, readers map entities mentioned in a linguistic input to a script-based structure in long-term memory (i.e., a scenario) as soon as they have enough information to do so. Explicitly mentioned entities are represented with respect to a certain role that constrains the behavioral expectations of the entities in that scenario. Second, representations in the scenario involving individuals that are not explicitly stated in the text but which form a normal part of the episode and situation are activated. Thus, linguistic input is interpreted via two sources: scenario information (which is implicit) called up from long-term memory, and newly input text information (which is explicit). Two situations might arise when readers interpret texts. In the case where a scenario is available and selected, it is used as an interpreter to incoming text that maps into the role slot and action representations. This mapping or interpretation process is rapid and automatic. However, if no current scenario is available, or if the current one is inappropriate for interpreting a new input, then a search for a new or more appropriate scenario, more time consuming, has to take place. Thus, the initial problem for a reader is not to match textual information and propositional elements, but rather to find out how linguistic input is related to knowledge (i.e., the previous situation). This first level of interpretation allows the reader to build a mental representation (i.e., a situation model) that can vary in complexity.

In line with a dynamic view of reading, Sanford and Garrod (1981) also assume that as the text unfolds, certain information is of central importance whereas other information is not. Not only explicit information, but also scenarios themselves may shift in and out of attentional focus, the accessibility of scenario-dependent entities being affected by whether the scenario is currently foregrounded. Thus, only a relatively small subset of information will be accessible at a particular point in the reading process. Sanford and Garrod (1981) introduced the notion of focus to describe the active state of a scenario. If a scenario is active, it will be in "focus" and will be available to the processing system. In addition, at any given point in the reading, there will be a limited number of foregrounded items explicitly mentioned in the text in conjunction with a particular scenario. Sanford and Garrod (1981) refer to entities mentioned in the text as being in explicit focus as long as they are represented in working memory. In contrast, information provided by the current scenario is described as being in implicit focus. These two types of focus (explicit and implicit) represent different partitions of working memory (see chapter 3 for a description of these partitions), and both serve to provide a retrieval domain that incorporates the current "topic" of the text.

Explicit and implicit focus have different properties. Explicit focus is regarded as a short-term store with a limited capacity. It is structured in a simple way, for it only consists of memory representations of entities and objects mentioned in the discourse, called "tokens." By contrast, implicit focus contains current scenario information and is more complex structurally. The scenario representations are composed of slots and default specifications. When a search for implicit focus occurs, there will be no token corresponding to its partial description, but there will be a slot corresponding to it in the scenario. Whenever implicit focus is implicated in a search procedure, there is a mapping between a token in explicit focus and the scenario itself. Glenberg and Langston (1992) defined tokens as representational elements of situation models that are maintained in focus. According to the authors, when a new entity is mentioned in a text, a corresponding token is constructed in explicit focus. These tokens serve as discourse pointers to information no longer active in memory, and they prime contextually relevant information in long-term memory in an automatic manner. In addition, because implicit focus is not limited in terms of memory capacity, some "filters" are necessary to guide the implicit focus search.

Thus, in this approach to the comprehension process, the mental representation of a text consists of entities and scenario tokens, plus a number of pointers that specify the roles of entities in the various scenarios. Scenario content is not directly represented in explicit focus, but is connected to it when necessary. Part of what is remembered will have its origin in the prior explicit-focus contents, whereas another part will reflect the original implicit-focus contents, being reconstructed from general knowledge. When an incoming text is integrated with information in focus, contextually relevant information in long-term memory is also connected to new information. In this way, new information is mapped onto relevant information in both active memory and long-term memory. As Glenberg and Langston (1992) pointed out, such a mechanism is quite powerful because it allows the reader to check and maintain coherence at both a local level (against information in focus) and a global level (against relevant information in long-term memory). The occurrences maintained in explicit focus serve as pointers and prime relevant information from the scenario in implicit focus. When new information is matched with occurrences in explicit focus, the reader evaluates the new information as a function of information of the relevant scenario through discourse pointers. In other words, items in explicit focus serve as pointers to the relevant elements in long-term memory (Albrecht & Myers, 1998; Cook, Halleran, & O'Brien, 1998; Sanford & Garrod, 1998). Relations between these pointers are significant, as mental models can be updated by introducing new pointers or by rearranging existing ones to reflect the situation evoked in the text. When an existing pointer is moved or a new pointer is introduced, the reader's attention is oriented toward this pointer.

In conclusion, Sanford and Garrod underlined the importance of entities or events called tokens in discourse interpretation. These tokens (via discursive pointers) allow for fast and automatic matching between information that is currently being processed and knowledge that readers have about the situation evoked in the text. Situation models thus result in "script-based" knowledge activation in relation to text information.

This theory has several advantages and provides an interesting definition of situation models. First, mental representation is viewed as the product of meaning construction (in explicit focus) involving retrieval of relevant information (in implicit focus) via pointers. Second, it stresses the dynamic aspect of the comprehension process by introducing the concept of focus: At any given point in the reading process, some information is moved into the background, although still accessible, while other information is highlighted. This conception emphasizes how memory, in relation to theories of comprehension, contributes to deepening our understanding of discourse interpretation. Last, the knowledge readers activate (and retrieve) about the situation evoked in the text guides and orients their assignments of relevance throughout the reading process. Relevance can be conceived of as a property of the information made current through discourse pointers, which play the role of retrieval cues and make connections with information in long-term memory. Therefore, the situational representation is intrinsically distinct from the semantic representation proper, and propositions cannot adequately capture different levels of discourse interpretation. In the next paragraphs, I present other models that assume that propositional format cannot adequately represent situation models because such models reflect the way individuals perceive the world. Here, the perceptual component of the representation is highlighted (in contrast to the more traditional approach using propositions), along with the analogy in entities and relations between the represented and representing worlds. Some crucial aspects of these theories are discussed next.

2.1.4. Situation Models as Amodal Structures: From Propositional Symbols to a More Analogical Relation Between Symbols and Referents (Gernsbacher, 1990; Johnson-Laird, 1983)

In the Structure Building Framework, Gernsbacher (1990) assumes that the goal of comprehension is to build coherent mental structures and substructures (i.e., representations). Comprehenders' success at building such mental structures depends on their ability to envision real-world situations. In this model, representations are introduced at two levels: the micro- and macrolevels. At the microlevel, representations are memory cells, conceptualized quasi-neurologically as individual cells with a base activation level. At the macrolevel, there are abstract structures and substructures that represent episodes, sentences, and clauses. In Gernsbacher's approach, the mental-structure medium must handle both linguistic and nonlinguistic input, and an intermediate level of representation such as the propositional representation is not adopted. This theory has the advantage of proposing a variety of compatible representational media, and although the author states that van Dijk and Kintsch's (1983) and Johnson-Laird's (1983) theories could account for this variety, she does not give any clues about the potential similarity between the structures defined in her model and the mental or situational models assumed by Johnson-Laird and van Dijk and Kintsch. According to van Dijk and Kintsch (1983; see also Kintsch, 1988, 1998), and as I discussed extensively earlier, information is represented as propositional networks at the semantic and situational levels, and the propositional system is a good candidate for representing structures. In contrast, in Johnson-Laird's (1983) theory, propositional format is not sufficient to represent mental models, mainly because the organization of elements (i.e., individuals, objects, abstract notions, and various relations) in mental models is governed by the principle of structural identity: The structure of the model is identical to that of the state of affairs it represents. Thus, for a particular text, the structure of the model reflects the structure of the situation described in the text.

Consistent with Johnson-Laird's main assumptions on the internal structure of mental models, Gernsbacher (1990) assumes that comprehenders mentally represent physical situations expressed by language, and develop relatively iconic representations of the physical situations conveyed by texts. In other words, readers build mental representations on the basis of structural identity between the represented and representing worlds, or on their perceptions of daily events.

Therefore, regardless of the structure of the assumed model and the representational units postulated for defining the reader's mental representation, understanding a text means interpreting the world denoted by the text. Although it is likely that some aspects of situation models can be represented propositionally, the sole use of this format "makes the task of distinguishing between the textbase and the situation model fairly difficult" (Fletcher, 1994, p. 598), due to its inability to account for the analogical character of situation models. This last property stresses the crucial role of the reader's knowledge as a guide for interpreting discourse, and points out the importance of developing an integrated theory of knowledge. In Kintsch's theory, knowledge is represented in terms of propositional nodes in an associative network, and the mental representation emerges from the context of use of interconnected nodes. By representing situation models in terms of events, states, and actions, mental representations denote the knowledge readers have about objects, categories in the world, and the relations between them. In Sanford and Garrod's theory, knowledge is mapped into explicit entities represented in the text, and its activation leads to discourse interpretation. Finally, in Gernsbacher's theory, knowledge of real-world situations has to be called on in order to give coherence to the structure. Therefore, there is a relatively strong consensus on the contribution of knowledge to building the reader's mental representation, although the intrinsic nature of this activation is still under debate.[2] However, beyond this difference, coherence in the reader's mental representation should closely approach coherence he or she attributes to real world-events. This conception inevitably leads to reducing the "cognitive" distance between cognition and perception.

2.1.5. Situation Models as an Analogical Mapping Between Symbols and Referents (Barsalou, 1993, 1999; Glenberg, 1997; Johnson-Laird, 1983; Zwaan, 2004)

Assuming that knowledge representation requires storing the analogical relationship between symbols and referents, at least in some situations, certain theorists developed another framework based on a perceptual theory of knowledge. Proponents of this approach (Barsalou, 1993, 1999;

---

[2] For some authors, knowledge activation is conceived of as an automatic process (Kintsch, 1988, 1998; Sanford & Garrod, 1998), whereas others view it as a strategic process (Gernsbacher, 1990; Zwaan & Radvansky, 1998).

Glenberg, 1997) assume that cognition is grounded in perception and action. In this theoretical framework, cognition relies on the use of perceptual and motor representations, rather than on abstract, amodal, arbitrary representations such as the propositional format (Barsalou, 1999; Glenberg, 1997). This view is supported by empirical data mainly collected for visual and spatial representations, and also by recent findings in the neurosciences showing that perceptual and motor representations activate previous traces stored in specific brain areas (see Damasio, 1989). Because this theory of perceptual symbol systems is described as being involved in a wide variety of cognitive functions, it should provide a fruitful framework for studying—among various other areas of cognitive science—situation-model construction in text comprehension (Barsalou, 1999; Glenberg & Robertson, 2000; Zwaan, 1999a, 1999b, 2004).

One crucial hypothesis in perceptual symbol systems relies on the existence of an analogical correspondence between symbols and referents. Johnson-Laird (1983) was one of the first to assume that the way we interact with and observe our environment underlies our understanding of verbal materials, and that situation models built from reading and comprehending texts are derived from how we build situation models of our environment:

> Mental models play a central and unifying role in representing objects, states of affairs, sequences of events, the way the world is, and the social and psychological actions of daily life. They enable individuals to make inferences and predictions, to understand phenomena, to decide what action to take and to control its execution, ... they allow language to be used to create representations comparable to those deriving from direct acquaintance with the world, and they relate words to the world by way of conception and perception. (p. 397)

This analogy between perception and cognition has strong implications for defining the nature of the reader's mental representation and leads to specific predictions with respect to the perception-based approach. First, each referent has a perceptual representation that is created from a series of perceptual symbols. The symbols have features (e.g., shape, color, orientation, etc.) that define the referent (i.e., those relevant for comprehension). Once combined, the features constitute the unified representation of the object, which is called its *simulation* (Barsalou, 1999; Glenberg, 1997). Thus, any change in one component of the referent should cause a change in the perceptual symbol specific to it, and should therefore have an effect on the representation. The perceptual symbol framework also predicts an interaction between the mental representation (i.e., the simulation) and the referents due to object affordances. Any transformation the referent undergoes can cause an analogous transformation in the simulation. For example, if the referent is an object (say a pencil) and if the orientation of the referent is changing, so too is the representation. Stanfield and Zwaan (2001) went one step further in this assumption and argued that if any change in the referent produces similar modifications in the simulation, an alteration in the simulation should have implications for the interpretation of the referent. These relations should be established without too much effort, that is, a few inferential steps, and lead to the building of a rich situation model (Zwaan & Rapp, in press).

According to Barsalou (1999), perceptual symbols are related in long-term memory and may become organized into a simulator. This allows the cognitive system to construct specific simulations (i.e., representations) of an entity or event. In this theory, a simulator (i.e., a concept) can produce an infinite number of simulations of a given kind, each simulation providing a different conceptualization of it. For instance, the simulator for "chair" can simulate many different chairs under many different circumstances, each one offering a different conceptualization of the category (Barsalou, 1999). Simulators bear important similarities with other constructs, such as schemata, and contain two levels of structure: (a) an underlying frame that integrates perceptual symbols across category instances (i.e., generating mechanisms)—this is an unconscious level of structure—and (b) the potentially infinite number of simulations that can be constructed from the frame—this is a conscious level of structure. Together, a frame and the simulations it produces constitute a simulator.

Barsalou (1999) also argued that mental models (Johnson-Laird, 1983) are related to simulators but are not identical because they are roughly equivalent to the surface level, namely, simulations of specific entities and events. "Mental models tend not to address underlying generative mechanisms that produce a family of related simulations, and are only constructed from the frame" (Barsalou, 1999, p. 586).

Among the various kinds of representations assumed to be involved in readers' mental representations, spatial representations have been shown to make a clear distinction between "analog" and "propositional" models. Two events or objects spatially near each other in the represented world may be located farther apart in the surface or textbase representation. However, they are expected to be near each other if the situation model is an analogical representation. In the domain of space representation, there is considerable interest in mental models of spatial environments constructed from verbal descriptions. It has been widely shown that representations constructed from descriptive texts reflect the spatial properties of the environment described in those texts. When coherent and complete descriptions are made, the mental model that gets built retains information about the spatial relations among the objects of the environment described. In particular, information on distances may be efficiently stored (Denis &

de Vega, 1993). When subjects have to memorize the location of different objects in a complex environment, for instance, accessibility of objects tends to decrease as their distance from the location of the protagonist whose movement must be followed increases (Morrow, Greenspan, & Bower, 1987). Also, when subjects mentally explore distances between objects whose location has been specified by a verbal description, mental exploration time appears to be longer as the distance between the objects increases (Denis & Cocude, 1992). However, one cannot reduce spatial models to a single or simple view of the described environment. They may be situated at a more abstract level and may code a "multiperspective" rather than separate scenes from a single point of view. It is this assumption that Taylor and Tversky (1992) tested by comparing two texts that described the same spatial environment from two different perspectives: route and survey. The participants' task was to make inference judgments about the spatial layout. The results showed that judgments were equally fast and correct, regardless not only of the perspective adopted by the subject for judging inferences but also of the reading perspective. Thus, spatial models are not "biased" by the particular perspective adopted during reading (see also de Vega, 1991). They are just general, abstract, and flexible enough to allow for the adoption of different perspectives. They are equivalent to a "structural description," that is, an abstract representation that specifies relations between different parts of an object (Tversky, 1991).

The way people canonically perceive the world influences their comprehension of spatial terms (Levelt, 1984) and this provides evidence of the construction by the reader of a spatial framework. In order to test this analogy, Franklin and Tversky (1990) attempted to determine which spatial dimensions were best represented. Participants had to process texts that described a set of objects located in an environmental space (i.e., front/back, left/right, up/down). When they had to retrieve the location of each object from memory, not all of the spatial dimensions were as easy to access, and some dominated others, such as the vertical dimension (see also Hayward & Tarr, 1995). The subjects rapidly found information about the position of objects located above or below them that was consistent with the description they had memorized. Second, although the front–back dimension appeared to be strongly asymmetric, the left–right dimension did not show any asymmetry and was the most difficult to represent. Thus, spatial mental models are "biased" by knowledge and perceptual-motor experience, which makes some spatial dimensions more difficult to access than others. Location on the vertical dimension is the easiest to discriminate because it implies two strong sources of asymmetry: gravity and the canonical position of the body. The front–back dimension is also well-discriminated because perceptual and motor activities involving objects are strongly affected by their position on the given dimension. Finally, discriminations between left and right are the most difficult to represent because no salient differential cues are available. Thus, mental models of tridimensional environments are more than just simple figurative representations of texts describing the environments. They are a "working space" in which subjects make calculations on relations that are not direcly mentioned in the text and are required to generate it (Tversky, 1991).

Finally, spatial descriptions also contain statements that locate objects with respect to a frame of reference (Taylor & Tversky, 1996). A frame of reference includes an origin, a coordinate system, a point of view, reference terms, and a reference object. Three kinds of frames of reference have been distinguished as a function of their origin: viewer-centered, object-centered, and environment-centered. Experimental investigations on these frames have emphasized the importance of situational factors in how they are defined (Bryant, Tversky, & Franklin, 1992).

What I have reported here points out the importance of knowledge and perceptual-motor experience in the construction of a spatial mental model. However, this process has been shown to be highly dependent on the subject's goals and strategies. Gray-Wilson, Rinck, McNamara, Bower, and Morrow (1993, Experiment 3) showed that participants built detailed spatial situation models only when specific task requirements asked them to focus on spatial information during reading. This reflects the relative complexity of spatial models, or stated differently, the possibility for situation models to include different levels of complexity (see Johnson-Laird, 1983). Whereas all individuals create a spatial model of a described situation, each person's model is highly specific, more or less complex, and clearly focuses on some information, and only active information processing allows the reader to build an "ideal" situation model, that is, one that perfectly fits the situation described. Denis and Cocude (1992) showed that the more a text is read, and thus processed, the more precise the representation built from metric spatial information is, leading to a greater resolution of the representation after several processings of the text. However, Zwaan and van Oostendorp (1994) found opposite results by showing that, with normal reading instructions, the number of readings did not affect the quality of the spatial model built. In their study, spatial information was processed more rapidly than nonspatial information during the first reading, and the difference increased during the second reading. This indicates that the second reading was not used to build a more precise spatial or nonspatial representation, and that after the first reading, the subjects judged their situational representation to be just rich enough. In addition, data collected from an inference judgment task showed that subjects who read the text twice did not have more precise spatial or nonspatial information compared to those who read the text only once.

Thus, there is no doubt that people create spatial models of situations conveyed in texts. However, whether or not they represent all of the entities in the environment and their relations that may evolve over time seems to be strongly dependent on the focus of subjects' attention on specific parts of the text, for example, entities and relations (see Zwaan & Radvansky, 1998), and on the relevance they give to some spatial relations that take into account their prior knowledge, perceptual experience, goals and strategies, or self-estimates of the comprehension level of the situation. Perceptual symbol systems allow for representing spatial knowledge by assuming an analogical relation between symbols and referents. This provides more complete information about the referent than do amodal symbols, and the findings presented here about how spatial information is represented underline this point. However, and as Barsalou himself pointed out, a perceptual-based approach has many common properties with propositional systems, and the author argues that the former type of system exhibits propositional features (see Barsalou, 1999; Zwaan, 1999a,1999b):

> Perceptual symbol systems produce type-token mappings that provide a wealth of inferences about construed individuals. They produce alternative construals of the same scene, either by selecting different aspects of the scene to simulate, or by simulating the same aspects in different ways. They represent complex hierarchical propositions by constructing simulations productively and then mapping these complex simulations into scenes. They represent the gist of sentences with simulations that can be paraphrased later with different utterances. Finally, they represent false and negative propositions through failed and absent mappings between simulations and scenes. (Barsalou, 1999, pp. 596–597)

Therefore, the perceptual symbol theory is considered a valid theory for representing various types of knowledge, in addition to the fact that it also contains all the features of amodal systems.

Based on the different formalisms proposed to represent knowledge and its use, several characteristics of the internal structure of situation models emerge. First, and in line with most researchers interested in understanding language processes, situation models are made of entities and objects and of relations among them. Moreover, although it is likely that the nature of the entities postulated has an effect on the representation built, a more crucial aspect seems to be their intrinsic properties, and one such property is that the analogy between the represented world and the representing world must be maintained. To fully succeed, this analogy requires the activation and retrieval of specific and general knowledge from the reader's memory. In this sense, further investigations of the nature and function of the postulated discourse pointers (see Glenberg & Langston, 1992; Sanford & Garrod, 1981, 1998) should help deepen our understanding of the structure of situation models. In addition, objects in situation models appear to be related to their affordances, and mental representations also involve experiential traces issued from real-life events. Accordingly, the way readers represent discourse entities is closely related to how they envision real-world situations. In particular, how readers interpret discourse is closely tied to their perception of real-life events and to how they act in these situations as well. This is true not only for the elaboration of a spatial model of a situation, but also for other dimensions (e.g., causality and emotion). Finally, as a well-defined structure is often assigned to these entities, objects in situation models should also reflect that structure. In other words, the internal structure of situation models may be a reflection of how individuals perceive and relate entities in the world.

The definition of entities and objects in situation models is also dependent on the situational context. The specificity of the situational context may facilitate or impair how readers attribute a role to objects or entities in their situation models (see Sanford & Garrod, 1981). Given this characteristic, not all properties that define the content of situation models can be ideally called on when readers interpret oral or written discourse. Rather, depending on the situation evoked in the text, on task constraints, and on the activation of the reader's prior knowledge, only some of these properties may be activated, leading to a more or less elaborate situation model. Thus, for some situations, certain characteristics described earlier are brought into the foreground, whereas others are left in the background, and a different pattern can be expected for each specific situational context. In this view, a situation model can be regarded as a "mental space," with its internal structure being as dependent on the properties of the situation as on the objects that compose it. Accordingly, for readers' mental representations to attain their richness and complexity, the internal structure of situation models should necessarily be conceived of in more than one representational format. This implies incorporating the main features of the objects, the relationships among them, and affordances with the world, along with the experiential relationship between the reader and the world evoked in the text. Although fictitious, this world is assumed to share many characteristics with the real-world situations experienced by readers.

Is there a preferential system that defines "ideal" units or entities in situation models? This question cannot be answered in a simple way. However, in order to best capture the complexity of what we define as the deepest level of representation, that is, the situation model, an integrated theory of comprehension should account for a combination of systems or formats that would be called on in a dynamic and "contextual" way, depending on situational factors and the reader's prior knowledge.

Part II

What Cognitive Mechanisms Are Involved in the Elaboration of a Situation Model?

Although the internal structure of situation models and the nature of the knowledge that readers call on when interpreting discourse are still under debate, a large consensus exists among researchers interested in text comprehension regarding the assumption that the mental representation readers construct must be coherent. This coherence has been noted in the study of the various cognitive activities that readers engage in when processing linguistic as well as nonlinguistic information. Many cognitive mechanisms have been shown to be involved in the comprehension process, although I do not provide a detailed account of all of them. Rather, my aim is to highlight some of the processes that I think are crucial to the establishment of coherence. In this section, I show that in a coherent mental-representation building, specific and general knowledge activation and how it accounts for the integration of situational and contextual information play a major role. In particular, I assume that retrieval components and the updating process are fundamental to the elaboration of a coherent representation; together, they constitute the "skeleton" for developing a valid theory of what "comprehension" means in terms of coherence. In chapter 3, I describe the main ideas proposed in the literature about the cognitive operations readers carry out when processing a text. I highlight not only their similarities and differences, but also their strengths and limitations. Then, in chapter 4, I present how coherence is perceived within these theoretical frameworks and how accounting for it contributes to defining the reader's mental representations in a more comprehensive way.

Current Theories of Comprehension: The Main Processes Involved in Mental-Representation Building by the Reader

3.1. MEANING CONSTRUCTION, SELECTION, AND INTEGRATION: FROM WORD IDENTIFICATION TO TEXT UNDERSTANDING (KINTSCH & MROSS, 1985; TILL, MROSS, & KINTSCH, 1988)

The preceding chapters presented the main principles of the Construction-Integration Model (Kintsch, 1988, 1998), a hybrid architecture devoted to describing and modeling knowledge use in text comprehension. This model has two phases: a construction phase and an integration phase. During the construction phase, a large and complex associative propositional network is built. It results from the association of two propositional nets: the textbase network, directly built from the linguistic input, and the knowledge network, in which each textbase proposition serves as an independent retrieval cue for all close associates in the knowledge net. Although the construction of this last net leads to certain elaborations, another step requires generating bridging inferences and macropropositions. Finally, connection strengths are assigned to all of the element pairs that have been created, depending on theoretical and empirical considerations. One of the main differences between this model and previous models of text comprehension is that "weak" and "dumb" rules allow for the construction of this large associative network, assumed to be built during each processing cycle. Thus, at the end of the construction process, the propositional net is rich, but some of the propositions or concepts with their interrelationships, also part of this network, are irrelevant or even contradictory. The integration phase rapidly reinforces contextually appropriate elements while it inhibits those that are irrelevant or contradictory. This is done via an automatic spreading activation process using connectionist procedures. This second phase, which is automatic and not resource consuming, provides an integrated mental representation that corresponds to "a kind of situation model" (Kinstch, 1988, p. 180). Thus, consistent with a bottom-up view of the comprehension process, the construction of a propositional network is the raw material for understanding a text. However, it is not sufficient for attaining a deep level of textual interpretation, and relevant information has to be integrated into the resulting net while irrelevant information has to be deleted from the reader's representation (i.e., the propositional net). In essence, these two phases describe two crucial mechanisms involved in the reading comprehension process: knowledge activation, which is independent of contextual relevance, and knowledge integration, which is dependent on the situational context. The integration process (i.e., integration phase) involves the updating of the representation, which brings into play several mechanisms such as information retrieval, inhibition of irrelevant or contradictory information, and reinforcement of relevant information. Updating reinforces relevant elements and inhibits those that are irrelevant and will be removed from long-term memory.

However, text understanding involves a complex chain of cognitive activities, starting with access to word meanings and ending with a fully integrated representation. This extensive model is powerful enough to explain and predict the main processes involved in the wide range of comprehension activities. In line with this assumption, Kinstch and collaborators (Kintsch & Mross, 1985; Till, Mross, & Kintsch, 1988) assumed that understanding a text involves three main phases: activation, selection, and elaboration. These phases tell us what processes the reader engages in as he or she processes linguistic input, and also inform us about their order of occurrence. Applied to homonym identification (see Kintsch, 1988; Kintsch & Mross, 1985; Till et al., 1988), the first "Sense-Activation" phase is the word meaning activation phase, which occurs independently of its initial context. All potential lexeme or grapheme meanings are activated, at least for a short period. This first step in meaning construction fits with the idea of activation of nodes in a semantic network (i.e., lexical items) and with spreading activation toward the closest neighboring nodes. In particular, each concept evoked in a text activates its own mnemonic trace and the traces of all its orthographic, phonological, and morphological associates, regardless of their contextual relevance. This phase corresponds to the construction stage described in the Construction-Integration Model (see Kintsch, 1988). In the second phase, the selection of appropriate meanings occurs as a function of the discursive and situational contexts in which the words are inserted: Only contextually relevant associates remain activated, whereas associated concepts that are incompatible with the context are deactivated. This "Sense-Selection" process gradually stabilizes the initial representation but only provides a schematic version. Finally, in the third and last phase, the elaboration of a more complete contextual meaning occurs. The reader builds an integrated meaning by making several types of inferences that are guided by the context. These three phases, Activation-Selection-Integration, give rise to the distinction stipulated by Kintsch between lexical and textual priming, which underlie the occurrence of two different causal mechanisms. The first mechanism is responsible for lexical priming and is defined as an automatic, uncontrolled, and irrepressible activation process. It is a contextually independent mechanism that occurs during the Sense-Activation phase. The second mechanism, responsible for textual priming, is defined as an inference- or elaboration-generation process that occurs during the selection and integration phases. Information selection and elaboration are context-dependent: Relevant meanings are reinforced, whereas irrelevant ones are deactivated. According to Kintsch, textual priming plays only a minimal role in comprehension. Without any associative relations between prime and target words, textual priming will be observed if there is enough time for more complete processing of the prime word in its discursive context.

The cognitive plausibility of these two causal mechanisms has been demonstrated empirically in several experiments (see Kintsch & Mross, 1985; Till et al., 1988). In Till et al. (1988), the authors investigated the temporal course of the processes underlying lexical access and meaning construction, and two main questions were raised: (a) Does the context play a role in the initial phase of lexical access by guiding access to the appropriate meaning? and (b) When are the inferences needed for meaning elaboration generated?

To answer these two questions, the authors designed three experiments in which 28 sentence pairs containing a prime (a homonym) were constructed. The two sentences in each pair were assumed to induce two different meanings of the prime homonym, as in the following example:

(a) "The townspeople were amazed to find that all the buildings had collapsed except the *mint*."

(b) "Thinking of the amount of garlic in his dinner, the guest asked for *mint*."

In this example, the first sentence stresses the "bank" meaning of the word "mint," whereas the second sentence orientates the reader toward the "herb" meaning of the word "mint."

To answer the first question, the authors used target letter strings that referred either to pseudowords or to words highly associated to one or the other meaning of the ambiguous word (e.g., the targets "money" and "candy" were associated to the prime "mint"). The primes were introduced in a contextual sentence that orientated the participant toward one or the other meaning with contextually appropriate or inappropriate targets. To answer the second question, the authors had the targets refer to words that were related to potential inferences induced by the discourse context. For instance, in the first sentence, the appropriate inferential target was "earthquake," whereas "breath" served as the control word for the inappropriate inference.

The participants were asked to read the sentences for understanding, and had to perform a lexical decision task on the target letter strings. The time interval that separated the onset of the prime display from the onset of the target display (SOA) varied across experiments: 333 or 1,000 milliseconds in Experiment 1; 200, 300, 400, 500, 1,000, and 1,500 milliseconds in Experiment 2; and 200 and 300 milliseconds in Experiment 3. The contextual sentences were presented using the PVSR procedure, and the target was displayed on the screen with asterisks on either side (****money****) to make identification easier.

The main results indicated that when the target was related to the prime and the SOA duration was no longer than 300 milliseconds, the lexical decisions were facilitated as compared to the control condition, whether the target meanings were contextually appropriate or inappropriate. Beyond 300 milliseconds, the lexical decisions were faster for appropriate targets. When the SOA duration was less than or equal to 500 milliseconds, there was no difference between the target response times on appropriate inferences and unrelated words. It was not until 1,000 milliseconds that the responses were faster for appropriate inferences. From these data, the authors concluded that initial meaning activation takes place regardless of the context. The effect of discourse context thus occurs in a phase that follows lexical access, either during Sense-Selection, where it eliminates irrelevant associations, or during Elaboration, where it leads to inferences generation.

These findings are consistent with Kintsch's Construction-Integration Model: Word-meaning access is achieved in a bottom-up fashion, without any contextual constraints. Specifically, the authors provided evidence of the existence of a short period (Sense-Activation phase) in which an initial, automatic, and irrepressible activation of the multiple meanings of a homonym takes place. Then an "integration" process (see Kintsch, 1988) allows for the selection of appropriate word meanings. At this point, inappropriate meanings have to be eliminated or inhibited. This last mechanism is crucial for maintaining coherence in the representation; I discuss the nature of this mechanism in the next chapter. Finally, the elaboration process requires time because readers need to construct meaning and to integrate it into their representation as well. Therefore, gaining access to a word's meaning and integrating it into a coherent whole necessitates "... an intricate interplay between the construction and integration phases: the textbase construction and the context-free, associative knowledge elaboration during the first 350 milliseconds of the processing; the establishment of a coherent textbase, which is assumed to be complete by 400 milliseconds; and finally an inference phase, involving new construction and new integration and requiring more than 500 milliseconds of processing" (Kintsch, 1988, p. 173).

3.2. BUILDING FOUNDATIONS FOR STRUCTURES, MAPPING, AND SHIFTING TO A NEW STRUCTURE (GERNSBACHER, 1990)

The Structure Building Framework Model (Gernsbacher, 1990) has much in common with the Construction-Integration Model (Kintsch, 1988, 1998). I have already discussed the type of units postulated by Gernsbacher's model (see chapter 2), so I focus here on the main processes readers are assumed to carry out during reading comprehension, although the author conceives of these processes as nonspecific to language activities.

According to Gernsbacher (1990), understanding a text requires building structures or substructures, and three main steps or processes are involved in this construction: laying foundations for the structures or representations (i.e., construction process), mapping information onto a foundation (incoming information needs to be coherent with the previous information), and shifting to the building of a new substructure. The shifting process takes place when the information that is being processed is unrelated or has only a few relationships with the information that belongs to the existing foundations. The structures and substructures that result from the mental representations built correspond to memory nodes that are activated by incoming stimuli. Primary activation of these nodes is the basis for the foundations. Several data supported this first step of the comprehension process (Aaronson & Ferres, 1984; Carreiras, Gernsbacher, & Villa, 1995; Cirilo, 1981; Gernsbacher & Hargreaves, 1988, 1992; Haberland & Graesser, 1985). Once memory nodes are activated and foundations are laid, the textual information read is integrated (i.e., mapped) into the structure being elaborated. The mapping process is a function of the degree of overlap between new and previous information (i.e., second step in the construction process). The more coherent the incoming information is with information already present in memory nodes, the higher the activation level of the nodes. Consequently, the greater the degree of overlap, the greater the mapping. This process results in the activation of similar memory nodes, and coherent information is represented in the same structure or substructure. On the other hand, if the incoming information is unrelated to the preceding information, node activation decreases. Incoherent information initiates the activation of new nodes in memory and thus provides the foundation for a new structure (i.e., third step in the construction process). Several empirical findings support this last phase. For instance, readers have easier access to information represented in the structure being developed (e.g., after a change) and tend to more rapidly forget the information that is at the boundary of two structures.

Activation of the first nodes in memory increases or decreases the activation level of other nodes that are memorized. This is done by transmission of certain processing signals. Spreading activation and fluctuations of activation during the matching (i.e., updating and shifting processes) via other memory nodes are modulated by two general mechanisms, reinforcement and suppression. In her model, Gernsbacher attributes a crucial role to these mechanisms because they modulate memory-node activation triggered by the processing of new incoming information. Consequently, these two processes are assumed to be critical in maintaining coherence. Reinforcement increases node activation when the information the nodes represent is relevant to the structure currently being developed. Suppression decreases node activation when the information the nodes represent is no longer necessary for structure elaboration.

Both Kintsch's and Gernsbacher's frameworks approach comprehension in a comprehensive manner inasmuch as they describe the processes involved in understanding discourse in detail. In addition, they share assumptions because both postulate the occurrence of two stages: the construction (or activation) of mental representations that might not be coherent at first, and the mapping (or integration) of the information being processed to previously processed information. However, they also have contrasted assumptions regarding the strategies readers use to process linguistic information. On one hand, Kintsch argues that the comprehension process occurs in a bottom-up fashion and the construction and integration processes are automatic. As the result, this architecture does not involve an active "search for coherence", but the system automatically finds the most relevant configuration for the representation that emerges, depending on the specificity of the situations. We will see (§3.2.2., this chapter) that this is done throughout reading via a retrieval process that keeps the necessary elements available for integration. On the other hand, and unlike Kinstch, Gernsbacher assumes that readers actively participate in the mapping and shifting processes, suppressing or reinforcing inconsistent or consistent information, respectively, in an active way that depends on how they interpret coherence signals coming from five postulated sources: referential, temporal, spatial, causal, and structural. In a recent study, Gernsbacher and Faust (1991) provided evidence of the intervention of an active suppression process by showing that activation decreased for inappropriate meanings. Participants read sentences in which concepts with multiple associated meanings (homonyms) were presented. Then they had to perform a lexical decision task that immediately followed the presentation of the target word. The probe items corresponded to a pseudoword, a word related to one or the other of the meanings of the target word, or a neutral word (related to any of the meanings of the critical word). The authors varied the presentation duration of the probe words from rapid (16.7 milliseconds per letter) to slow (50 milliseconds per letter). This was done to test for the activation of all potential meanings right after the processing of the homonym (rapid presentation) and after a more elaborated processing guided by the contextual constraints assumed to be involved (slow presentation). The main results indicated that the activation level of appropriate meanings did not vary as a function of the presentation duration, whereas a decrease in the activation level occurred for inappropriate meanings when the display time increased. Moreover, the activation decay for inappropriate meanings did not lead to an activation increase for appropriate meanings. Finally, the lack of a difference between the activation levels of the neutral words on rapid and slow presentations suggested that the activation decrease of unselected meanings does not correspond to a single activation decay. Gernsbacher and Faust (1991) interpreted these results in terms of the control function of the reinforcement and suppression mechanisms. According to these authors, the activation decrease of an inappropriate meaning triggers an active suppression mechanism guided by contextual information, and is solely an activation decay. In addition, the reinforcement mechanism maintains the activation level for contextually appropriate meanings.

What I have reported here shows that although Kinstch and Gernsbacher assume opposite reader strategies for the integration process (mapping), they both attribute a crucial role to the mechanisms of reinforcement and inhibition (or suppression in Gernsbacher's model) in its occurrence. This strongly emphasizes the importance of retrieval during the comprehension stages. According to Kintsch, mapping is dependent on an automatic retrieval process and is not guided by coherence signals. By contrast, for Gernsbacher, it is based on strategic processes and relies on linguistic signals.

3.3. RETRIEVAL AND UPDATING PROCESSES

3.3.1. Implicit and Explicit Focus: The Processes of Foregrounding and Backgrounding Information (Sanford & Garrod, 1981, 1998)

In the model developed by Sanford and Garrod (1981, 1998), called the Scenario-Mapping and Focus Theory, crucial importance is granted to the updating and retrieval processes through the concepts of foregrounding and backgrounding. This theoretical approach is based on a memory-based framework, which assumes that retrieval of information is achieved via a passive resonance process (Garrod, O'Brien, Morris, & Rayner, 1990). This model gives a preponderant role to the explanatory power of memory theories for interpreting discourse. According to Sanford and Garrod (1981), taking reference resolution into account clearly allows one to examine the relationships between comprehension and memory. In this perspective, the authors specifically account for the way text information is integrated into the reader's prior knowledge, and assume that the reader's task is to relate, as soon as possible, the currently processed information to his or her assumptions and prior knowledge, the latter being formalized in terms of scripts or scenarios (for a description of scenarios, see chapter 2). Access to a scenario relies on a dynamic view of the reading process in which some concepts are moved into the foreground and others are moved into the background. In other words, at each point in the reading process, the reader accesses foregrounded information faster and more easily than backgrounded information. Thus, not all previously processed text elements (e.g., protagonists, actions, or events) are equally accessible.

In line with these ideas, the reader's focal attention might be concentrated on one or two nodes that are part of the discursive representation, like a camera that zooms in on certain information (e.g., protagonists, objects, or events), and this would put any other entities out of focus (Graesser, Millis, & Zwaan, 1997). When reading a story, the reader has to keep track of the foregrounded entities (i.e., protagonists), in addition to creating relations among them and relating those entities with other parts of the text (Sanford & Garrod, 1998).

Based on this assumption, Sanford and Garrod (1998) divided memory into dynamic and static partitions and assumed that the reader analyzes a text in reference to these memory parts. To characterize the different parts, two main distinctions must be made. The first concerns which elements are in focus and which are not. Easily accessible information belongs to the dynamic memory partitions and corresponds to the representations built from recent text input. General knowledge and long-term memory representations are part of the static part of memory (static memory partitions). These partitions are defined as more permanent than the dynamic ones. The second distinction concerns memory representations that come from the direct interpretation of the text (explicit focus) and knowledge from other sources (implicit focus). Explicit focus only involves representations of elements mentioned in the text (entities and events) whereas implicit focus involves representations based on the current scenario (a subset of the reader's general knowledge). Table 3.1 illustrates the four memory partitions postulated by Sanford and Garrod (1998).

TABLE 3.1

Memory Partitions Based on the Scenario-Mapping and Focus Theory
(Revised From Sanford & Garrod, 1998)

	Text-Based	*Knowledge-Based*
Dynamic	Explicit Focus	Implicit Focus
Relatively Static	Episodic Representation of the Text	General Knowledge (Scenarios)

As already discussed in chapter 2, Garrod and Sanford (1988) assume that readers keep the protagonist and the events explicitly mentioned in the text in explicit focus, whereas information relevant to the scenario, like the protagonist's characteristics, are held in implicit focus. Because explicit focus has a limited memory capacity, occurrences that represent entities in explicit focus are matched to information maintained in implicit focus (i.e., dynamic memory partitions). When the occurrences are no longer in explicit focus, their implicit-focus relationships are also removed. Thus, this model captures changes in the activation of discursive entities and also changes related to the availability of relevant discursive information in long-term memory (Garrod, 1995; van den Broek et al., 1996).

In terms of memory, the authors postulate that the comprehension process (i.e., reference resolution) can be conceived of as the retrieval of appropriate information and the construction of a unique text representation. Three variables are thought to specify the retrieval process (equivalent to the mapping process): (a) the restrictive domain to be searched (explicit focus), (b) a given partial description of information to be found (semantic specification of information), and (c) the type of information to be returned (a unique concept to be found in explicit focus, or a role description in implicit focus). In addition to the retrieval process, the construction process that produces the representation of the content of the text's content is also specified by three variables: (a) the domain of memory where the construction is recorded, (b) a description of the information to be incorporated, and (c) the type of resulting structure. These two operations—"Retrieve" and "Construct"—occur in relation to focus, and the information retrieved has to be combined into a coherent structure in the memory partitions described earlier (see Sanford & Garrod, 1981, 1998).

Thus, the Scenario-Mapping and Focus Theory developed by Sanford and Garrod (1981) provides a framework in which the reader is assumed to integrate the most relevant information (i.e., highly foregrounded entities) in order to understand the text. The information being processed is related to information in short-term memory (explicit focus) but also to information that is relevant to the currently activated scenario (implicit focus). This activation occurs via a bottom-up process through passive resonance (see chapter 4). This framework stresses the relationship between traces in short-term memory and corresponding cues in long-term memory. However, it is now widely acknowledged that more information is brought into short-term memory than the cue resonating in long-term memory, and other pieces of information from the earlier part of the text and world knowledge are reactivated as well. Thus, one important aspect of the retrieval process is how much associated information in long-term memory is also activated. It is likely that retrieval depends on the relationship between memory traces and other information in long-term memory. Next I present some arguments that are consistent with this approach to the retrieval process.

3.3.2. Updating Requires Fast Information Retrieval and Efficient Integration of New Information (Ericsson & Kintsch, 1995; Zwaan & Radvansky, 1998)

Ericsson and Kintsch (1995) looked specifically at how much information is activated in long-term memory during the retrieval process when they analyzed the role of the retrieval structures needed to create coherence in text comprehension. These authors suggested a mechanism for global coherence by postulating a modification of long-term memory (LTM). In particular, they assumed that aspects of LTM might be easily accessible from working memory under certain circumstances, and called this extended part of memory long-term working memory (LT-WM). According to the authors, LT-WM is different from short-term working memory (ST-WM), the more or less passive storage buffer that is routinely adopted in theories of working memory. It acts as an extension of short-term memory (STM) for activities that correspond to skilled performance in particular domains. Consequently, readers can quickly access information from LTM that is triggered by the content of STM.

Ericsson and Kintsch's (1995) proposal is based on experimental evidence of skilled memory and also on some unexplained phenomena in text processing. Readers maintain, in long-term memory, a multilevel representation of the text being read. Relevant parts of this representation remain accessible in order to be related to information being processed at a given moment. Traditionally, this relating process has been explained in terms of working-memory operation: Certain information from previously read sentences is kept in a working-memory buffer. Reading proceeds smoothly as long as the currently processed information can be related to the previous information in the buffer. If this is impossible, a time-consuming search in LTM has to be initiated. This account implies that any reading disruption that prevents paying attention to working-memory content leads to a loss of information in the buffer. This, in turn, would impair comprehension of subsequent text information. However, Glanzer and colleagues (Fischer & Glanzer, 1986; Glanzer, Dorfman, & Kaplan, 1981; Glanzer, Fischer, & Dorfman, 1984) reported that when subjects are prevented from using the working memory buffer to link propositions from successive learning cycles, it does not have the expected disrupting effects on comprehension. How are readers in this situation able to connect propositions from one processing cycle to the representation of the previous text? Ericsson and Kintsch (1995) argued that this is done through LT-WM. Readers keep their attentional focus on a series of propositions that correspond to the sentence being processed at a certain moment. Some of the propositions in ST-WM are linked to other propositions from previous processing cycles stored in long-term memory, and serve as cues to retrieve other integrated information that forms a retrieval structure. Propositions that belong to this retrieval structure are easily accessed in a time interval of about 400 milliseconds. Thus, LT-WM is the portion of long-term memory that is readily available while a text is being processed.

The concept of LT-WM, together with some extensions of the Event-Indexing Model (see Zwaan, Langston, & Graesser, 1995), enabled Zwaan and Radvansky (1998) to propose different stages of situation model elaboration for narrative texts and for establishing coherence in the corresponding representation. According to these authors, three models can explain the different steps involved in the comprehension process: (a) the current model, which corresponds to the model constructed while a person reads a particular clause or sentence; (b) the integrated model, which corresponds to the global model constructed by integrating the previously constructed models, one at a time (i.e., the current models); and (c) the complete model, which is the model stored in LTM after all textual input has been processed. These three models are based on three theoretical frameworks: Ericsson and Kintsch's (1995) distinction between ST-WM and LT-WM, Garrod and Sanford's (1990) distinction between implicit and explicit focus, and the Event-Indexing Model proposed by Zwaan, Langston, and Graesser (1995). Together, these three models provide an extensive description of the updating process, as Zwaan and Radvansky's (1998) framework shows.

Ericsson and Kintsch (1995) proposed that the capacity of ST-WM can be extended via efficient storage of information in LTM (by way of relevant retrieval cues accessible from ST-WM). This extension, called LT-WM, allows for fast retrieval of information and efficient integration of information across sentences. According to Zwaan and Radvansky (1998), and consistent with Ericsson and Kintsch's proposal, the reader keeps the integrated situation model in LT-WM while the current model is constructed in ST-WM. During the construction process, activation spreads from ST-WM to the retrieval cues, to parts of the integrated model. Updating is done by forming links between the current model and the retrieved elements of the integrated model. At this point, the current model has been integrated and the integrated model has been updated, leading to the construction in ST-WM of a new current model. This process continues until the complete model is stored in LTM.

One crucial characteristic of Garrod and Sanford's (1990) view of the comprehension process relies on the distinction between implicit and explicit focus. Explicit focus involves tokens corresponding to the protagonists currently introduced into the discourse world, whereas implicit focus involves a representation of the currently relevant aspects of the scenes portrayed. This distinction is part of Zwaan and Radvansky's model because these authors assume that relevant aspects of the integrated model are in implicit focus, whereas the current model is in explicit focus. Finally, in the Event-Indexing Model (Zwaan, Langston, & Graesser, 1995), connections between the current model and relevant aspects of the integrated model in LT-WM are triggered by five situational dimensions: temporality, spatiality, causality, intentionality, and protagonist. Different criteria for each dimension, such as what constitutes a relevant part of the integrated model, are necessary. The next chapter further develops the notion of "relevance," which is tied to the concept of foregrounding (see also Sanford & Garrod, 1981, 1998) and may be triggered by several cues (e.g., world knowledge).

3.4. MATCHING NEW TEXTUAL INFORMATION AND UPDATING: THE ONLINE AND BACKWARD HYPOTHESES

From the previous sections, we can see that there is a large consensus among psychology researchers in discourse processing about the idea that the situation model of a text is activated at the beginning of reading and is then completed by incoming textual information and inferences made by the reader (Gernsbacher, 1990; Graesser, Singer, & Trabasso, 1994; Johnson-Laird, 1983; Kintsch, 1988; van Dijk & Kintsch, 1983). The situation model the reader builds evolves and is enriched as he or she proceeds through the text; this highlights the dynamic aspect of the comprehension process. Readers map incoming textual information with information previously encountered, and this process, which leads to a coherent mental representation, is called the updating process. However, although researchers commonly agree about the existence of this mapping process, they differ in their assumptions about when it occurs. Some authors assume that it occurs online, that is, during comprehension; others hypothesize that it does not take place until the end of the comprehension process (i.e., a backward process). My goal is to demonstrate that this distinction regarding the occurrence of this process is an experimental artifact because both temporal components are involved in updating. The next section discusses the main arguments supporting those two views of the temporal occurrence of updating, in an attempt to provide a more integrated view of its occurrence.

3.4.1. Updating as an Online Process

The online hypothesis is supported by those researchers who postulate the online integration of incoming text information into the situation model (Ericsson & Kintsch, 1995; Garrod & Sanford, 1988, 1990; Gillund & Shiffrin, 1984; Glenberg & Langston, 1992; Hintzman, 1986; Sanford & Garrod, 1981; Zwaan & Radvansky, 1998). The integration process is assumed to be improved by a subset of information that is selected and maintained in working memory. Sanford and Garrod (1981; Garrod & Sanford, 1988, 1990) initially proposed that this subset of information is held in explicit focus (i.e., active memory), whereas other information relevant to the described situation is held in implicit focus. In their view, incoming information is mapped to information currently held in both explicit and implicit focus. This perspective was extended by Glenberg and Langston (1992), who postulated that representational elements that are brought to the foreground promote the online integration of new incoming information. These elements serve as discourse pointers that make direct links to information that is no longer active in working memory. The online hypothesis also fits with the modeling approach of text comprehension proposed by Zwaan and Radvansky (1998; see §3.3.2., this chapter). Indeed, in their theoretical framework, updating is described as occurring online, that is, when links are established between information currently being processed (i.e., the current model) and information previously processed and maintained in LT-WM (i.e., the integrated model). These links lead to the repeated integration of new information into the integrated model until a complete model of the described situation is stored in LTM.

The idea that updating occurs online was first tested empirically by Morrow, Greenspan, and Bower (1987). In their experiments, participants had to keep track of a main protagonist moving in a layout that was just learned. The authors specifically tested whether the accessibility of the main protagonist's surroundings varied as a function of the protagonist's goals. A probe composed of pairs of objects from the layout was presented during text reading, after a protagonist's movement had been mentioned (e.g., *Wilbur walked from the repair shop into the experiment room*). At the point in the narrative when the probe occurred, the participants had to judge whether the two objects presented were located in the same room in the layout. Objects were located either in the protagonist's goal room (e.g., *clock, speakers*), source room (e.g., *plywood, cart*), or in the path room (e.g., *television, ping-pong table*). It was hypothesized that if readers integrate the protagonist's movement online, objects located in the goal room would be more accessible than those located in the path and source rooms. This is, in fact, what Morrow et al. (1987) showed with the spatial judgment task they used. They concluded that participants adopt the protagonist perspective; in other words, they construct and update their spatial situation model online by taking into account explicit information and inferences relevant to the protagonist's point of view (see also Morrow, Bower, & Greenspan, 1989).

3.4.2. Updating as a Backward Process

De Vega (1995) also examined the ability of participants to track the protagonist's position and surroundings, but using ordinary comprehension conditions (i.e., continuous reading). After demonstrating that readers were sensitive to the objects surrounding the protagonist (Experiment 1), the author used recognition probe words to test the accessibility of objects that were either consistent or inconsistent with the protagonist's location. The results indicated that the readers did not update their model when no target objects were mentioned again in the last sentence, which was assumed to reactivate the participant's interest in the protagonist's surroundings (Experiments 2 and 3). However, the readers updated their model when they had to resolve the antecedent to an ambiguous pronoun (Experiments 4 and 5). From these results, de Vega (1995) drew three main conclusions. First, readers can update a complex spatial situation model that contains several objects at different locations. Second, updating should not be considered as an automatic process because it occurs only when it is relevant to the reader's comprehension goals. Finally, updating is a backward process, that is, it is never done in advance. According to de Vega, then, updating is a backward or delayed process that is rarely executed online because readers do not update their spatial model when processing new incoming information. However, when the task stresses the relevance of tracking the protagonist's location, and when the layout does not involve too many objects and spatial relations, it is likely that readers attempt to compute all of the inferences (de Vega, 1995).

Thus, the various models of comprehension differ in their assumptions about the occurrence of the updating process, and empirical data have not brought clear-cut evidence for one or the other of these alternatives.

3.4.3. An Integrated View of the Updating Process

Blanc and Tapiero (2001) went one step beyond the theoretical and empirical positions previously discussed (de Vega, 1995; Garrod & Sanford, 1988, 1990; Glenberg & Langston, 1992; Morrow, Bower, & Greenspan, 1989; Morrow, Greenspan, & Bower, 1987; Sanford & Garrod, 1981; Zwaan &

Radvansky, 1998), arguing that the updating process should involve two temporal components, the first occurring online and the second occurring after a certain delay and under specific circumstances. According to these authors, although incoming information may be mapped to the existing mental representation in an online manner, its final integration into the situation model should depend on a backward updating process whose occurrence is a function of the reader's prior knowledge and the task demands. First, the reader's prior knowledge should play a role in updating because it has a major influence on the construction process in general, and on inference making in particular (Graesser, Singer, & Trabasso, 1994; Johnson-Laird, 1983; Kintsch, 1988; van Dijk & Kintsch, 1983). The impact of this factor on the time course of the updating process might explain why Morrow et al. (1987, 1989) and de Vega (1995) did not obtain compatible results. Whereas in Morrow et al.'s (1987, 1989) studies, participants were provided with background knowledge of the layout in which the protagonist moved in the story, in de Vega's (1995) study, they did not know the protagonist's surroundings beforehand. The account that the reader's knowledge plays a role in the updating process is also strengthened by Ericsson and Kintsch's (1995) theory and by Zwaan and Radvansky's (1998) theoretical framework. Consistent with Ericsson and Kintsch's theory (1995), Blanc and Tapiero (2001) assumed that the extension of working memory allows readers to maintain more new information and to delay its integration into long-term memory (i.e., delayed updating) as a function of its relevance to the rest of the text. In Zwaan and Radvansky's framework (1998), delayed updating takes place between the elaboration of the integrated and complete models, and prior knowledge is required for this delayed process to occur. Thus, information stored in the integrated model should be mapped to the complete model only when it is relevant to subsequent text information and only when the reader has sufficient knowledge of the described situation. Consequently, the delayed component of updating is more sensitive to the reader's prior knowledge than the online component, the former depending more on memory capacities.

Moreover, it is now widely accepted that task demands have to be carefully analyzed in discourse processing studies because they constrain the inferences readers can make (Graesser et al., 1994; see also, Zwaan & van Oostendorp, 1993). Gray-Wilson et al., (1993) investigated the crucial role of performing an orienting task. In their study, they demonstrated that the occurrence of the effect reported by Morrow et al., (i.e., the spatial separation effect; 1987, 1989) was a function of the demands of the spatial judgment task the participants had to perform. After reading the following critical sentence—Wilbur walked from the *repair shop into the experiment room.*—participants had to judge either probe pairs composed of two objects that had locations whose narrative stories differed (i.e., goal, path, source, or different rooms) or probe pairs composed of the protagonist's name and an object name (e.g., *Wilbur, speakers*). Gray-Wilson et al. (1993) suggested that readers do not follow the protagonist's movements in the layout previously learned unless they encounter this latter kind of probe pair. The validity of this assumption was supported by their results: Objects located in the protagonist's goal room were more accessible only when the protagonist was named in the pairs (i.e., same findings as Morrow et al., 1987, 1989). Thus, from these results, it appears that participants draw certain types of online inferences about how the situation evolves mainly when the task demands stress their relevance.

Blanc and Tapiero (2001) empirically tested the assumption that the reader's prior knowledge and the task demands determine the time course and the quality of the updating process, and that two temporal components are involved in this process. In their study, participants had to read a text (divided into two parts) that described three characters and their spatial surroundings. The text described a play that took place on a theater stage, and the scene was composed of a living room and a dining room. Each sentence was distinguished on the basis of the topic to which it referred, that is, either to the scene or to the characters. In the first part of the text, the scene sentences located 16 objects (e.g., *A mirror is placed above the mantelpiece on which there is a candlestick*). The second part described the movement of four of the previously located objects (e.g., *The candlestick now lights up the glass and the letter located on the dining room table*). The presentation order of the text sentences was such that a character sentence was given first (e.g., *Marie, seated on the sofa, takes the book placed on the coffee table*) and was then followed by a scene sentence (e.g., *The armchair, facing the large chimney, is perpendicular to the living room sofa*). The sentences alternated in this way until the end of the text.

Participants could study one of three introductory texts to gain either specific (more specific or less specific) or general prior knowledge about the layout described in the experimental text (i.e., between factor). The first text was highly specific and described all of the props on the stage that corresponded to the layout of the experimental text (i.e., fixed and moved objects) (e.g., *The living room, on the left side, is furnished with a sofa, an armchair, and a coffee table*). The second text was not as specific and only mentioned the location of objects that were never moved by a character (i.e., fixed objects; e.g., *The coffee table is halfway between the armchair and the sofa*). Finally, the third text was general and dealt with the layout of a theater (e.g., *The theater is composed of a lobby, a seating area for the audience and a stage*). After studying one of these three introductory passages, subjects had to read the first part of the experimental text in order to build a model of the situation described. Then they read the second part, which was aimed at integrating new information into the situation model initially built.

The time course of the updating process was studied through two different tasks that differed in their temporal occurrence but assessed the same information. One task was proposed as the second part of the text was being read. It was an online spatial judgment task similar to the one used by Morrow et al. (1987, 1989), and was aimed at testing whether participants were able to integrate incoming information as they were processing it. This task was composed of 48 pairs of words naming objects in the scene. Each time the reading was interrupted (i.e., every two sentences), participants had to decide whether the pairs of objects presented were located in the character's goal room. The location (i.e., goal, source, or different rooms) and status (i.e., fixed or moved) of the objects in the pairs were manipulated. To correctly judge the object pairs presented, the participants had to keep track not only of the characters moving in the layout, but also of the objects moved by a character. For example, after each sentence that described a character's movement (e.g., *John, holding the candlestick, discovers Marie hidden behind the sofa and drags her into the dining room*), six pairs of words were presented one after another. The two objects in each pair were located either in the source room from which the character moved (20 pairs, e.g., *armchair–mantelpiece*), in the goal room where the character went (20 pairs, e.g., *piano–sideboard*), or in two different rooms in the layout (eight mixed pairs, e.g., *armchair–sideboard*).

The reading of the second part of the text was followed by an inference task that dealt with the same information as the online probe. (e.g., *John is sitting in the dining room whereas Juliete finds Marie in the living room.* [true]). This was aimed at testing the delayed component of the updating process. Finally, to find out whether the time course of the updating process was determined by an intermediate task, the authors proposed an initial testing phase, between the reading of the two parts of the text, during which half of the participants had to perform a preliminary inference task and the other half had to answer a visuospatial imagery questionnaire.

First, the results provided evidence that readers' prior knowledge determines the time course and the quality of the updating process (see Table 3.2).

The data for the online task (first row) indicated a greater number of correct responses in the more-specific condition ($M = .81$) than in the less-specific and general conditions, $F(1, 66) = 5.33$, $p < .05$; these last two conditions did not differ significantly ($M = .73$ and $M = .69$, respectively). The results for the inference task (second row) also showed that readers' prior knowledge determined the accuracy of the updated situation model, $F(2, 66) = 4.8$, $p < .05$. As shown in Table 3.2, accuracy scores were significantly higher in the more-specific condition than in the less-specific and general conditions, with means of .73, .68, and .62, respectively, $F(1, 66) = 6.74$, $p < .05$.

TABLE 3.2

Participants' Performance (Correct Responses) as a Function of Prior
Knowledge (Revised From Blanc & Tapiero, 2001)

	More Specific	Less Specific	General
Online Task	.81	.73	.69
Inferences	.73	.68	.62
Online Task	.68	.67	.65
Compared to Inferences	.75	.55	.49

To test whether new incoming information encountered and probed
during the reading of the second part of the text had been incorporated
into the final model (i.e., the complete model defined by Zwaan &
Radvansky, 1998), the correct responses to the moved-object pairs in the
probe task were compared with those obtained for the statements dealing
with the movement of those objects from the second inference task. Participants' performance on these two tasks (last two rows in Table 3.2) confirmed the hypothesis that readers' prior knowledge determines the time
course and the quality of the updating process, and that this factor has a
stronger effect on delayed integration than on online integration. As Table
3.2 indicates, all online participants incorporated new incoming information into their situation model (probe task), but the backward retrieval of
this piece of information only occurred for those who had more specific
prior knowledge (inference task). Whereas for participants with more-specific prior knowledge, performance improved between the first and second
tasks (.68 and .75, respectively), it decreased for those with less-specific
knowledge (.67 and .55) or general knowledge (.65 and .49, respectively).
Thus, new incoming information was incorporated online into the integrated model (see Zwaan & Radvansky, 1998), but its backward integration
into the complete model did not occur unless there was highly specific
knowledge. One possible interpretation is that readers maintain more incoming information about the situation in LT-WM and delay their integration as a function of its relevance to the rest of the text (see Ericsson &
Kintsch, 1995). Without highly specific prior knowledge, participants were
unable to correctly maintain more incoming information long enough to
evaluate its relevance, and then failed to incorporate it backward into the
complete model. In addition, the quality of updating may account for the
differential performance observed on the three knowledge conditions of
the later inference task: participants with less-specific or general prior
knowledge integrated the moving of objects in a temporary way, whereas

those with more-specific prior knowledge incorporated it permanently. Thus, the reader's prior knowledge not only determines when updating occurs but also its quality or duration.

Second, and as predicted by the authors, the intermediate task also differentially affected updating (see Table 3.3). An analysis performed only on correct responses to scene inferences indicated that the participants who took the inference task (first row of Table 3.3) performed less well compared to those who answered the visuospatial imagery questionnaire ($M = .63$ and $M = .71$, respectively), $F(1, 66) = 4.73$. Finally, updating preferentially occurred online when the subjects had previously taken the first inference task. Probably, this task allowed them to strengthen their layout representation, which was more readily available to them than to those who had been given the imagery questionnaire.

TABLE 3.3

Participants' Performance as a Function of the Intermediate Task Performed (Revised From Blanc & Tapiero, 2001)

	Imagery Questionnaire	Inference Task
Inferences	.71*	.63*
Online task	.63	.71
Compared to Inferences	.65	.54

Note. (*): Data obtained from an analysis of scene inferences only.

In conclusion, these findings indicate that updating should be regarded as a process that occurs in an online and delayed way. In particular, two main factors appear to determine the temporal occurrence of the updating process: the reader's prior knowledge and task demands. Participants with highly specific prior knowledge of the situation can maintain more new incoming information and delay its integration, depending on its relevance to the rest of the text (Ericsson & Kintsch, 1995). Without prior knowledge, readers can only integrate new incoming information in an online and thus temporary way. Moreover, task demands also affect the way readers integrate new incoming information. These results thus have direct implications for theories of text comprehension (Ericsson & Kintsch, 1995; Zwaan & Radvansky, 1998).

3.5. Conditions That Have to Be Met in Order for The Updating Process to Occur

In several studies, van Oostendorp (1996) examined the conditions under which readers modify and consequently update the situation model they initially built. His studies were inspired by the work originally done by

Wilkes and Leatherbarrow (1988) as well as Johnson and Seifert (1993, 1994): Participants were instructed to read short, simple messages about fictitious events in which a fact told at the beginning of the story was denied afterwards. Wilkes and Leatherbarrow (1988) showed that the effect of old, obsolete information could not be fully removed even if that information was denied. Similar conclusions were obtained by Johnson and Seifert (1993, 1994). However, these authors underlined that correcting an incorrect fact told earlier was more successful when a causal explanation of the correction was provided. In order to further understand these findings, van Oostendorp (1996) asked participants to study a text (a newspaper article) dealing with the situation in Somalia during operation "Restore Hope." The experimental text was followed by a second text that contained transformations of facts mentioned in the first text. After studying each text, participants had to perform an inference verification task. Correct updating of the situation model required replacing the old information with the new information. The author's goal was to find out whether the transformations were incorporated into the reader's situation model after the reading of the second text, and to investigate the influence of five factors on the updating process: (a) the reading instructions (read carefully or read at a normal speed), (b) the time between the first and second text presentations (immediate or one day later), (c) the reader's interest in the situation in Somalia (low and high), and (d) the degree of item relevance. The fifth factor referred to the strength of the model initially built (low or high) and was measured with the inference verification task performed after the reading of the first text.

The main results indicated that updating performance was in general very low, and that only the strength of the situation model built had a significant effect on its updating. Moreover, information with a low level of relevance was transformed better than information with a high level. Van Oostendorp (1996) proposed two possible interpretations for the latter result. The first is that the reader might adopt a rejection strategy when the changes that have to be made concern important elements of the situation model initially built. The second relies on the idea that new information is stored in a shallow way because the reader thinks he or she already knows it. To test this alternative, van Oostendorp (1996) carried out a second study and examined the influence of an alternative causal explanation on the updating of the situation model. He used the same procedure that Johnson and Seifert (1993, 1994) did. Three experimental conditions were tested. In the first condition, a possible cause of the event was mentioned and then denied. In the second condition, the negation of this cause was confirmed. With only one negation of the event's possible cause, the impact on the reader for updating his or her situation model was assumed to be very low (i.e., Condition 1). In a similar way, the possibility of shallow processing would be less likely if, even after confirmation of the negation by its repetition, the wrong information still had an influence (i.e., Condition 2). This effect would be due to the fact that readers actively refuse to update their situation model by rejecting the negation. Finally, in the third condition, a possible cause of the event was mentioned, then denied, and the negation of the cause was followed by an alternative causal explanation. This last condition was aimed at replicating the results already obtained by Johnson and Seifert (1993, 1994). Van Oostendorp (1996) used several texts, each one referring to a fictitious event, and the participants' task was to read each text at a normal speed, knowing that they could not return to the beginning of the text. Then they had to answer two types of questions: one type dealt with information explicitly mentioned in the text, and other type was based on inferential processing. The main results provided evidence of a rejection process: The influence of old information was difficult to neutralize because in all three conditions, the subjects introduced old information more often than new information.

In order to support the argument that task requirements have an impact on the updating process, Tapiero and Otero (1999) also investigated situation-model updating ease by looking at the textbase and situation-model levels in terms of how inconsistencies in text information are represented. According to the authors, inconsistencies may merely result in the creation of a "tag" in the textbase, or alternatively, in the elaboration of the situation model. Both of these operations should improve the reader's memory of the contradictory information. We tested these two explanatory hypotheses and postulated that different mechanisms are operating in each case. Elaborations should lead to the integration of inconsistencies to the rest of the text and to an updated model of the situation described by the text. This should facilitate memory tasks that involve this model (such as a comprehension questionaire). By contrast, tagging is regarded as a textbase phenomenon: It may allow readers to form a correct semantic representation but it should not lead to updating of the situation model. Consequently, readers will rely more on the information that precedes the inconsistency (old information) than on the information that deals with it. Thus, the tagging explanation for the memorability of inconsistent information should be valid only for memory tasks (e.g., recall), but not for tasks that require inference making, like answering comprehension questions.

The relative contributions of elaborative inferences versus the tagging node on the textbase versus situation model levels of text representation was tested with two types of tasks[1]: free and cued recall, and questions involving inferential processes.

---

[1] A recognition task was also performed but the procedure and results are not presented here (for more details, see Tapiero & Otero, 1999).

The participants were provided with six passages to read on a computer screen. Two of them, "Satellites" and "Cavitation," involved explicit contradictions between the third sentence and the last (fifth) sentence. A control (noncontradictory) version of the two experimental passages was written by replacing the contradictory information in the second sentence by a neutral statement. The contradictory and control versions of the Satellites paragraph are presented in Table 3.4.

TABLE 3.4

Satellites Passages (From Tapiero & Otero, 1999)

---

1. There are surveillance satellites in orbit at different heights

2. They have telescopes and sensors in order to detect radiation.

3. Contradictory Condition: 3. The telescope of a surveillance satellite is able to distinguish buildings.

Control Condition: 3. The telescope of a surveillance satellite is able to distinguish cities.

4. The capacity to distinguish depends on the optical sensitivity of the instrument.

5. The telescope of a surveillance satellite is not able to distinguish buildings.

We propositionalized the Satellites and Cavitation passages (contradictory and control) using Kintsch's (1988) procedure, with concepts and propositions as the network's units. The propositions and concepts corresponding to the two contradictory sentences for the Satellites text (Sentences 3 and 5) were the following: P19 ABLEDISTINGUISH [P10,P18]; P29 UNABLEDISTINGUISH [P10,P18] with P10 Telescope, and P18 Building.

The participants were randomly assigned to one of the four testing conditions (CE, CNE, NCE, NCNE) depending on the existence of the contradiction in the two target texts (C: both texts contradictory; NC: both texts noncontradictory version) and the possibility of elaborating the target information (E: enough time to elaborate in both texts; NE: not enough time to elaborate in either text). The passages were displayed on a video monitor and the words appeared from left to right, one word every 350 milliseconds until the sentence was completed. Once the sentence was completed, the words in the next sentence were displayed in a similar way. The reading of each passage ended with a comprehension question probing the acquisition of the target information (contradictory in the contradictory conditions). The comprehension question for the Satellites passage is given in Table 3.5.

Once this testing session was completed, two sheets of paper were provided with the following instructions: "Write everything that you remember

TABLE 3.5

Comprehension Question at the End of the Satellites Passage
(From Tapiero & Otero, 1999)

Would it be possible for a surveillance satellite like those described in the text to distinguish the Science Building or the Polytechnic School of the University of Alcala through its telescope?

a. Yes

b. No

c. Satellites are not equipped with telescopes

d. One cannot tell from the paragraph

---

from the 'Satellites' paragraph about the capacity of telescopes in surveillance satellites to distinguish things." A similar question was asked for the other contradictory paragraph. After this, participants were given two pages informing them of the contradictions in the paragraphs and asking them if they had detected them while reading. If they had noticed the contradiction, they were asked to write what they had thought about it.

Elaboration was manipulated by introducing an interrupting message about data saving after the two target paragraphs. In the E conditions, the whole sentence stayed on the screen for 4,000 ms after the onset of the last word that created the contradiction (i.e., "buildings" in the Satellite paragraph), and then the warning message about data saving was displayed. In the NE condition, elaboration was prevented by displaying the warning message immediately upon the disappearance of the last word in the sentence. The interrupting message stayed on the screen for 3,000 ms and then the testing procedure followed as usual. Assuming tagging is a process that takes place in a much shorter time than needed for elaboration, tagging would be the only mechanism operating in the condition where the warning message was presented immediately after the contradictory sentence. Tagging effects were compared to elaboration effects and to the control situation in which the same target sentence was presented but there was no contradiction.

The analysis of the recall protocols of those subjects who detected the contradiction showed that although overall recall was disrupted by the contradiction, recall of the target propositions was better in both the CE and CNE conditions than in the respective NC conditions. Table 3.6 presents the proportion of subjects (detectors in the contradictory conditions) who recalled the target propositions in the Satellites paragraph. Propositions P19 and P29 are the two contradictory statements (located in Sentences 3 and 5). Proposition P30 is the contradictory statement transformed into a neutral statement in the NC conditions (a different label was given in the

NC version, because an additional argument [BUILDINGS] had to be introduced).

First, the values presented in Table 3.6 indicate that the second contradictory proposition (P29) was recalled less well than the first (P19). This result is consistent with the idea that a textbase representation was created by detectors of the contradiction in which the first contradictory proposition (old information) was more salient than the second (new information). This finding is also in agreement with the recall patterns obtained for detectors in previous experiments using the same type of texts (see Otero & Kintsch, 1992). Second, the existence of a contradiction had a positive effect on the recall of contradictory information in both the CE and CNE conditions. This contrasts to the effect observed for the global recall of information: Subjects recalled less information in the contradictory conditions.

TABLE 3.6

Proportion of Detectors Recalling Either the First Contradictory
Proposition (P19), the Second Contradictory Proposition (P29),
Both Propositions, or None of the Propositions in the Satellites Passage.
The Proportion of Participants Recalling the Target Propositions (P19, P30)
in the NC Version are also Provided (From Tapiero & Otero, 1999)

	CE	CNE	NCE	NCNE
Only P19	0.45	0.50	0.25	0.38
Only P29/P30	0.18	0.33	0.25	0.08
P19 & P29/P30	0.36	0.17	0.33	0.31
None	0.00	0.00	0.17	0.23

Finally, the participants' answers to the end-of-paragraph questions provided information about the relative weight of the two contradictory propositions in the situation model they built after reading the texts. Table 3.7 shows the proportion of subjects who answered the comprehension question for the Satellites paragraph by agreeing with the first contradictory proposition, by agreeing with the second contradictory proposition, or by saying they could not decide.

These proportions showed that the subjects' answers to the end-of-paragraph questions are at variance with recall data. More subjects in the CE condition agreed with the new information than with the old information. This is consistent with the idea that the recall task only tested semantic text content without taking the situation model into account. Old information was more salient than new information in the textbase representation but not in the situation model. Subjects in the CE condition updated their situation model using this updated version when the task required doing so—when they needed to apply this knowledge to answer a question. This inter-

TABLE 3.7

Proportion of Responses to End-of-Passage Questions
(Only Detectors in C Conditions; From Tapiero & Otero, 1999)

	CE	CNE	NCE	NCNE
Agreement with old information (P19)	.11	.50	.27	.30
Agreement with new information (P29)	.67	.00	.73	.50
Impossible to decide	.22	.50	.00	.20

pretation is also consistent with the fact that more agreement with old information was found than with new information in the CNE condition. It was more difficult to update the situation model in this case because of a lack of time. Also, the rates for "impossible to decide" were lower in the CE condition than in the CNE condition. A lower rate of impossible-to-decide answers in the CE condition was expected: subjects may "fix" the contradiction when given time to elaborate, as already shown in other studies (Baker, 1979; Otero & Campanario, 1990).

Thus, the relative facility with which subjects in this study updated their situation model is at odds with findings about the difficulty of discrediting old information by corrections presented later in a text (Johnson & Seifert, 1994; van Oostendorp, 1996; van Oostendorp & Bonebakker, 1996; Wilkes & Leatherbarrow, 1988). A possible explanation of this discrepancy may lie in the different types of texts used: narratives in the experiments just described, and expository-scientific in Tapiero and Otero's work. Campanario and van Oostendorp (1996) found similar results showing the importance of new information in situation-model updating, when subjects read scientific texts, even with clear-cut contradictions like the ones in our paragraphs.

These findings indicate that updating depends on the task the subjects have to perform and on the level of processing they apply to linguistic input. Old information was more salient than new information in the textbase representation, which guides recall. However, new information took precedence in the situation model of the text used by subjects to answer comprehension questions. This was interpreted as indicating a different effect of elaboration on the two text representation levels, textbase and situation model. Although the situation model was updated by subjects when given time to elaborate, updating did not have an effect on the recall protocols. In the nonelaboration condition, old information prevailed in the recall task and also in the participants' answers to comprehension questions. This suggests that tagging is a textbase-level process that does not affect the situation-model level: The readers did not have time to update their situation model with the new information but only to add a tag to the textbase.

3.6. CONCLUSION: WHAT ARE THE MAIN PROCESSES INVOLVED IN THE ELABORATION OF A SITUATION MODEL AND ARE THERE SOME FUNDAMENTAL PROCESSES IN THAT CONSTRUCTION?

One major conclusion that arises from what has been presented here is that activation is a first and necessary step in the reading comprehension process. However, it is important to keep in mind that comprehension is not just activation but is also a product of two-way relationships between the activation and integration of meanings. The activation process is commonly viewed as being rapid and automatic, and may often lead to a rich representation that is sometimes irrelevant to the discursive context (Gernsbacher, 1990; Kinstch, 1988, 1998). However, it is widely acknowledged that understanding a text requires more than just activating units and relations, which grants the integration process a crucial role in explaining how the reader's mental representations are elaborated. The integration process can be viewed as a core mechanism in situation-model construction because it allows readers to achieve a coherent situational representation. Next, I describe some of the main characteristics of this process and emphasize how theories that focus on understanding the reader's discourse representation have approached both its nature and its functioning.

What does integration mean? Why does integration occur? In order to build a coherent representation, readers have to integrate text units and their relationships in interaction with episodic knowledge and general knowledge related to them, these two sets of knowledge being activated during reading. In other words, understanding text information requires readers to combine their current text representation with their knowledge. I have attempted to show that this assumption necessitates accounting for the occurrence of a matching process, not only between the information currently being processed and what has already been processed, but also between the reader's prior episodic and semantic knowledge. This matching process is assumed to result in a coherent mental representation. Two conditions of coherence might arise. In the case where these two sets of information have several common properties, and are therefore related in some ways, existing connections are reinforced and this strengthens coherence. In this situation, reading comprehension is not disrupted and readers continue to process the text in a smooth way. The theories and related empirical findings described earlier provide evidence of this mapping process. Nonetheless, the nature of this process is still under debate, and whereas some authors view it as automatic (Kintsch, 1988, 1998; Sanford & Garrod, 1981, 1998), others argue that in order to attain a level of coherence that allows the representation to be fully integrated, mapping may be under the control of the reader's strategies (Gernsbacher, 1990; Zwaan & Radvansky,

1998), in which case coherence mainly relies on signals readers search for while processing text information. Thus, the idea that coherence is achieved automatically or in a strategic way would depend on the nature of the information processed and on the level of processing used by the reader. In the other coherence condition, the mapping process does not occur so smoothly due to a large discrepancy between currently processed information and information already processed, in which case readers would suppress or inhibit inconsistent information from their representation. Here, coherence would be a function of mechanisms that reinforce or inhibit potential relations between elements.

We have seen that situation models are activated and then enriched by incoming information being processed. New textual information is matched to previous information stored in episodic or semantic memory. The matching process is a function of the connections between the two sets of information: The more connections there are, the greater the match. Integration occurs when the mapping is successful, and updating is the result of the integration. Thus, the mapping process could not be properly assigned a crucial role without emphasizing the relationships between theories of comprehension and the principles of memory theories. In other words, mapping the information currently being processed to previous information requires taking into account the retrieval mechanisms highlighted in most theories. Consistent with this argument, Ericsson and Kintsch's approach to the retrieval process and Garrod and Sanford's view of the availability of discursive information are two core theories that exhibit some commonalities. For example, both theories assume that comprehension results in the automatic retrieval of appropriate information. The notion of "appropriate" is an important one and is further discussed later. However, whereas in Ericsson and Kintsch's theory no clear arguments are provided to explain how relevance is attributed to information, Sanford and Garrod assume that the relevance or appropriateness of information is included in discourse pointers that make the connection between explicit and implicit focus (see also Glenberg & Langston, 1992).

Zwaan and Radvansky (1998) developed an "integrated" framework based on similar theoretical principles, and they account for the different steps in the elaboration of situation models. These authors provided an interesting definition of the updating process. In particular, they distinguished three models, based on Sanford and Garrod's (1981) concepts of explicit and implicit focus, Ericsson and Kintsch's (1995) concept of LT-WM in relation to STWM, and Zwaan, Langston, and Graesser's (1995) Event-Indexing Model. In their framework, explicit focus corresponds to the concept of ST-WM and implicit focus to the concept of LT-WM. This theory is of interest because it not only highlights the influence of memory principles throughout the comprehension stages, but also combines the automatic and strategic aspects of situation-model elaboration as well. Accordingly, the current model is built and information is activated automatically and in an online way, whereas the integrated model depends on coherence signals that readers rely on while reading the text. Thus, to deeply define what comprehension means, and to develop a valid theory of comprehension, one cannot ignore the "power" of relevant aspects of memory retrieval and the automatic and strategic aspects they involve.

Although the principles of these theories are well defined, some of their features are still unclear. One question that should lead to further investigation concerns the way relevance is attributed, and two main questions that arise concern the nature of retrieval cues and how relevance is triggered. On the hand, it seems worthwhile to look at whether the nature of the retrieval cues facilitates (or disrupts) the link between information in explicit and implicit focus (or between units in ST-WM and those in LT-WM). This question is closely related to the concept of relevance or appropriateness widely used to define how integration occurs. It is also closely tied to the coherence signals readers are assumed to rely on when processing a text. The concept of relevance and how and when it is attributed by readers is another important question. Is relevance assigned automatically and rapidly, as the reader maps textual information to previous information? Or does it require a certain amount of time that allows the reader to use strategies based on linguistic, semantic, and situational cues? In the next chapter, I attempt to provide some answers to these questions and to show how relevance can affect retrieval.

Finally, I have shown that the reader's prior knowledge and the task demands have a reliable effect on the quality and temporal course of the updating process. It seems likely that these two factors also influence relevance in a top-down fashion by guiding the retrieval process. As I mentioned earlier in this conclusion, comprehension is more than the mere activation or passive reactivation of retrieval structures; rather, it is the product of the "active" interaction between bottom-up and top-down processes.

Chapter 4

Current Theories
of Text Comprehension:
What About Coherence?

Understanding a text requires building a coherent representation of the situation evoked in the text (Tapiero, 2000; Tapiero & Otero, 1999; van Dijk & Kintsch, 1983), and several models have attempted to describe the mechanisms involved in elaborating this coherence (Gernsbacher, 1990, 1991, 1996; Kintsch, 1988, 1998; Myers & O'Brien, 1998; van den Broek et al., 1996; Zwaan, Langston, & Graesser, 1995). At the same time, the recent proposal in psycholinguistics of connectionist models (McClelland & Elman, 1986; Rumelhart & McClelland, 1986) led researchers to assume that language activities are underlain by the activation and inhibition of related units. The repeated use of the priming paradigm to study language in its various aspects, such as comprehension and production, has also participated in supporting this assumption (for a review, see McKoon & Ratcliff, 1992) for units ranging from words to texts (Gernsbacher, 1991, 1996), and findings using this experimental paradigm have provided evidence of recourse to theories involving both of these mechanisms.

With the merging of these two sets of data, researchers were able to investigate comprehension by using the explanatory power of activation and inhibition, assuming that both participated in the establishment of coherence when readers were processing a text. In particular, although activation is seen as a mandatory phase when readers process any kind of text information, inhibition is assumed to occur only when a reader is faced with irrelevant information or inconsistencies (Gernsbacher, 1989; Gernsbacher &

85

Faust, 1991; Kinstch & Mross, 1985; O'Brien, Albrecht, Hakala, & Rizzella, 1995; Otero & Kintsch, 1992; Stevenson, 1986; Till et al., 1988). However, no clear interpretation of how readers maintain coherence and presumably eliminate irrelevant meanings from their representation has been proposed, and there is still no consensus on the exact features that define the cognitive mechanisms at play in this situation. In particular, although several authors have evidenced inhibition of irrelevant information based on an automatic inhibition process (Hasher & Zacks, 1988; Kintsch, 1988, 1998), others have suggested either its active suppression (i.e., suppression mechanism) (Gernsbacher, 1990, 1991, 1996) or have not explicitly addressed this question (Zwaan, Langston, & Graesser, 1995). Still others have suggested that both kinds of information (i.e., relevant and irrelevant) are maintained in memory (van den Broek et al., 1996). In this chapter, my goal is to provide an overview—while referring to the various theoretical frameworks presented in chapter 3—of how coherence is tied to the underlying processes readers carry out when they encounter inconsistencies or irrelevant information. First, I describe some of the empirical studies that have found evidence of two crucial mechanisms for maintaining coherence, namely automatic inhibition and active suppression, based respectively on Kintsch's Construction-Integration view of the inhibition process, and on Gernsbacher's approach to the suppression process. Then I describe the coherence-cue specificities developed by Gernsbacher (1990) and Zwaan, Langston, and Graesser (1995) and how they are related to the five situational dimensions viewed as central to the maintenance of coherence (Gernsbacher, 1990; Zwaan, Langston, & Graesser, 1995; Zwaan, Magliano, & Graesser, 1995). Finally, the last part of this chapter is devoted to the concept of relevance, presumed to be involved in access to information that has been put into the background. This is done in terms of the Memory-Based Text Processing approach to the comprehension process.

4.1. COHERENCE AS A DYNAMIC COMPONENT OF COMPREHENSION: AN INTEGRATED VIEW (GERNSBACHER, 1990; KINTSCH, 1988, 1998)

The Construction-Integration Model (Kintsch, 1988, 1998) and the Structure Building Framework (Gernsbacher, 1990, 1991, 1996) describe the comprehension process as guided by a dynamic mechanism for establishing and maintaining coherence. Both authors assumed (see also Albrecht & Myers, 1995, 1998; Lorch, 1998; Myers & O'Brien, 1998) that comprehension first requires activating information that is already present in memory and is related to the text information currently being processed. This occurs regardless of information congruence or context. Comprehension then involves the intervention of a second mechanism that selects necessary information and allows readers to make the correct text interpretation. Information selection is associated with the deactivation of information that is irrelevant to the current representation, and the reinforcement of information that is relevant.

Kinstch (1988, 1998) argued that during the construction phase, as readers process the first word of a text, information provided by that word activates several possible meanings (see chapter 2 for empirical evidence and for a detailed description of meaning activation of a homonym). The activation level of these different meanings varies with the lexical, syntactic, and semantic context: Some meanings are highly activated , whereas others receive a lower activation level, and still others get a null activation value. Finally, only one of the word's meanings benefits from an increase in activation and is integrated into the mental structure that is developing; the others are inhibited. This takes place during the integration phase.

In the first phase of Gernsbacher's model, all of a word's meanings are activated, no matter what the context is. This is basically equivalent to the way Kintsch described the initial activation of the meaning of homonyms (see Kintsch & Mross, 1985; Till et al., 1988). In the second phase, the selection phase, some pieces of information must be reinforced, whereas others are suppressed. In order for the contextually appropriate meaning to be selected, the inappropriate ones have to be suppressed from the representation. In contrast to the first phase, these last two mechanisms (reinforcement and suppression) imply the active participation of the reader and are guided by both the context and information relevance. The suppression mechanism facilitates the retrieval of appropriate word meanings by suppressing the less plausible meanings relative to the context (Swinney, 1979). When inconsistent information is suppressed, coherence is established and integration is successful.

Several empirical studies have demonstrated that the repetition of an anaphoric word not only reinforces the activation of its antecedents, but also suppresses the activation of other concepts (Gernsbacher, 1989, 1990, 1991; Stevenson, 1986). For example, Stevenson (1986) showed that when readers read sentences such as *Anne apologizes to Joan at the end of the class because she regrets making trouble*, the processing of the pronoun *she* leads to the activation and maintenance in memory of *Joan* and *Anne*. However, when *Joan* is replaced by *John*, only the protagonist with the appropriate gender *Anne* is activated. These findings confirm the existence of the two main steps in the comprehension process stated earlier. First, when the context does not provide enough elements for readers to select the relevant information or suppress inappropriate information, all of the potential information remains activated (i.e., activation). Second, when the context provides just enough information, the inappropriate meaning is suppressed and only the appropriate one remains activated (i.e., selection).

In both theoretical approaches (Kintsch, 1988, 1998; Gernsbacher, 1989, 1990), the initial activation process is conceived of as automatic, irrepressible, and not influenced by the linguistic, semantic, or situational context. Thus, at this particular point in the process, the representation does not need to be coherent. It is assumed that this activation process allows for the construction of a rich and complex network (propositional, or built from memory nodes) that involves irrelevant or contradictory elements and that necessarily lacks coherence. On the other hand, the selection process (or integration) reinforces relevant information, and inhibits or suppresses irrelevant information in order to establish coherence. However, whether coherence emerges "automatically" or "actively" is a matter of the theoretical view, and the distinction as to how the selection or integration process causes the memory maintenance of only the appropriate meaning creates distance between Gernsbacher's and Kintsch's models. According to Kintsch (1988), the deactivation of irrelevant representational elements emerges from an automatic inhibition process. Conversely, Gernsbacher (1990) claims that irrelevant information is suppressed "actively."

I argue that although these two mechanisms have the same general function in the two theories (i.e., maintaining coherence), they are not identical and should be defined as distinct. In particular, it seems unlikely that the processes carried out for sentence comprehension are identical to those for text understanding. When readers process a sentence, they establish coherence but at a local level only (i.e., they make connections between adjacent units). By contrast, the processes required for text comprehension involve establishing both local and global coherence (this chapter, §4.3.) in order to make connections between adjacent as well as distant units (Albrecht & O'Brien, 1993; Rizzela & O'Brien, 1996). Also, not only do the processes themselves differ between sentence and text understanding, but so do their temporal courses. Unlike text processing, sentence processing presumably does not involve subsequent integration of new elements into information previously processed. In this sense, suppressing information during sentence processing and text processing should not have the same consequences on the construction of the representation. Finally, an interesting question, not explicitly addressed by the authors, arises regarding the extent to which inhibition or suppression of irrelevant information affects the reader's mental representation, namely whether it only decreases or rather eliminates the accessibility and retrieval of this information. For instance, O'Brien et al. (1995) brought forward some new insights on the impact of antecedent reactivation and suppression on the text representation stored in memory. The authors' assumption was that the processing of new text information triggers reactivation of all elements in the episodic representation to which it is related, leading to the intervention of a suppression mechanism during text reading (Albrecht & Myers, 1995; McKoon, Gerrig, & Greene, 1996; O'Brien, Plewes, & Albrecht, 1990). In one study, the authors used passages with two potential antecedents, one displayed at the beginning of the text and one presented later in the text. In each passage, the comprehension of the last sentence required reinstating the first antecedent (i.e., no longer active in working memory). The results of a statement-verification task showed longer reading times for statements about the last antecedent compared to those about the reinstated antecedent (i.e., first antecedent presented). In addition, there was no difference between the response times of the two types of statements when comprehension of the last text sentence did not require reintegrating the first antecedent. This study confirmed the idea that during comprehension, readers are sensitive to all potential antecedents in a text, while suppressing those that are less relevant for the current processing. Also, the suppression mechanism seems to disrupt but not restrict subsequent access to information on which it has operated.

Activating information that is irrelevant to the information currently being processed appears from these results to be eliminated from the active part of the elaborating representation but may still be represented in memory at the end of the comprehension process. This argument is strengthened by the idea that, due to a reader's limited memory capacity, the discursive memory representation is built gradually, cycle by cycle. Several models have accounted for this inherent constraint of the memory system by distinguishing the content of the representation during reading from the content of the final text representation (Ericsson & Kintsch, 1995; Glenberg & Langston, 1992; Sanford & Garrod, 1981; van den Broek et al., 1996; Zwaan & Radvansky, 1998). This distinction is based on the assumption that some elements available during reading may be absent from the final representation, and conversely, certain elements not accessible at a given time during reading may still be present in the final representation. This implies that during the reading process, some pieces of information are removed from episodic memory, whereas others are inhibited and then recovered. It therefore seems worthwhile to assume that inhibition or suppression takes place when activated information is not necessary or relevant to the information currently being processed (see O'Brien et al., 1995), and that a distinct deletion process (that could be called a suppression process) takes place when information is eliminated from the episodic text representation. Thus, the "search" for coherence may lead first to the inhibition of irrelevant or contradictory information, with deletion being postponed until subsequent text elements are processed.

Guéraud, Blanc, and Tapiero (2001)[1] attempted to determine the existence of these two mechanisms, that is, inhibition (or suppression as defined by Gernsbacher) and deletion, in the resolution of inconsistencies in narratives. Each passage either provided an explanation of the inconsistency or strengthened it. In the case where subsequent information provided an explanation aimed at resolving the contradiction, the inhibited information was reactivated and was thus assumed to still be present in memory at the end of the comprehension process. Reinforcement of the contradiction was aimed at triggering the deletion mechanism that would cause the initially inhibited information to be removed. The participants had to perform a word recognition task (online task) right after the display of the inconsistency, and were also tested on an inference-making task after reading each passage. The main results indicated that the contradictory information was reintegrated when it was further explained by subsequent text information, whereas it was eliminated when the contradiction was maintained and strengthened. From these findings, we concluded that the suppressed or inhibited irrelevant information is first put in the background (or maintained temporarily) until subsequent information is provided. Only then can inconsistent information be reintegrated into the representation or definitively removed. This work was a first attempt to study the intrinsic nature of a general process that allows readers to elaborate a coherent mental representation. Further investigations are needed to deepen our knowledge of this question. Currently, I am conducting follow-up studies that should provide new insights for exploring the validity of assuming that two mechanisms are carried out to resolve text inconsistencies and maintain coherence: a first, fast-acting inhibition process as the reader processes irrelevant meanings with respect to other text elements, and a second, strategic, context-dependent elimination process.

This discussion indicates that establishing coherence is regarded as a fundamental dynamic of text comprehension: readers attempt to reinforce relevant information, to inhibit or suppress irrelevant information, and depending on the subsequent text information the irrelevant information may be reintegrated or not into the reader's mental representation. In this respect, Gernsbacher's and Kintsch's models are powerful enough because both emphasize the crucial roles of reinforcement, which enriches the developing representation, and suppression or inhibition, which is devoted to eliminating irrelevant text elements. However, despite their similarities, these two models differ in their assumptions about the way coherence is attained. In Kintsch's Construction-Integration Model, coherence automatically emerges from the text and knowledge networks. For Gernsbacher

---

[1] This study was conducted, under my direction, by Sabine Guéraud and Nathalie Blanc at the University of Lyon 2 (France). Portions of this work were presented at the Meeting of the French Society of Psychology (Paris, October 2001).

(1990, 1996), coherence relies on cues from five dimensions based on the assumption that the reader's mental representation is multidimensional. More specifically, the reader is capable of using textual cues as signals or instructions for interpreting the referential, temporal, spatial, causal, and structural dimensions in terms of his or her specific and general knowledge. These signals allow the reader either to integrate new information into the currently developing substructure (i.e., mapping or integration process) or to build a new substructure (i.e., shifting process).

4.2. Construction, Updating, and Coherence: Situational Continuity as a Cue for Coherence (Gernsbacher, 1990; Zwaan, Langston, & Graesser, 1995; Zwaan, Magliano, & Graesser, 1995)

Because the text world is close to the real world, the mental representation readers construct should reflect the multiple dimensions implied by the situation described in the text. Based on the definition of a situation model, and on the assumption that several dimensions contribute to situation-model elaboration, the coherence of facts and events mainly depends on several factors, including space (Morrow, Bower, & Greenspan, 1989; Morrow, Greenspan, & Bower, 1987; Zwaan & van Oostendorp, 1993), time (Anderson, Garrod, & Sanford, 1983; Zwaan, Madden, & Whitten, 2000), and causation (Fletcher & Bloom, 1988; Magliano, Baggett, Johnson, & Graesser, 1993; Trabasso & van den Broek, 1985), and many authors have investigated the internal structure of situation models by studying this multidimensional aspect (Tapiero & Blanc, 2001; Zwaan, Langston, & Graesser, 1995; Zwaan, Magliano, & Graesser, 1995). Johnson-Laird (1983) was one of the first to theoretically define situation models as multidimensional representations that include individuals, and temporal, spatial, causal, and motivational information. More recently, in the Structure Building Framework, Gernsbacher (1990) accounted for the multiple aspects of situation models by considering these dimensions as sources of coherence that determine the ease with which incoming information will be mapped to the existing mental representation. According to this author, the matching process, that is, the gradual integration of subsequent information into the structures initially built, is performed on the basis of coherence. In this sense, readers interpret coherence cues as signals to map new information into a structure or substructure they are developing, and those signals are mainly based on the notion of situational continuity related to five main dimensions: reference, time, space, causality, and structurality.

Zwaan, Magliano, and Graesser (1995) also underlined the merits of accounting for the multiple dimensions of the mental representation readers build, and in line with Gernsbacher's assumption, they provided evidence of the importance of situational continuity for establishing coherence. According to the authors, time, space, and causality participate in the establishment of situational continuity. Next, some arguments in favor of their account of these three dimensions are presented.

Temporal continuity occurs when a sentence that is being processed describes an event, action, or state that occurs in the same temporal interval as the preceding sentence. In contrast, a sentence that is temporally discontinuous relative to the preceding context occurs when there is a change in the temporal interval. In other words, temporal continuity is disrupted when the text mentions breaks in time (e.g., "one hour later," "the next day"), or when the text describes events that will occur in the near future. This conceptualization relies on several studies in which temporal discontinuities were shown to disrupt comprehension and to slow down reading time (Anderson, Garrod, & Sanford, 1983; Mandler, 1986; Ohtsuka & Brewer, 1992; Zwaan, 1996). In Anderson et al.'s (1983) study, the authors collected estimates of the typical temporal framework for 20 common events. They showed that the typical time frame for "changing a baby" varied between 30 seconds and 15 minutes; the time frame for "having lunch at a restaurant" varied between 30 minutes and 3 hours. After collecting these estimates, subjects had to study stories in which the title referred to these common events, namely "changing a baby" or "having lunch at a restaurant". In the latter case, the first story sentence, *John was sitting at a table in a restaurant*, was followed by a second sentence that contained an adverbial phrase that was either consistent (*Five minutes later, the waiter arrived*) or inconsistent (*Five hours later, the waiter arrived*) with the time frame of the typical event. The results indicated that the sentences that started with a consistent adverbial phrase were read faster than ones with an inconsistent phrase. These findings suggest that readers use their prior knowledge of the typical duration of events to interpret temporal coherence cues, and that they use coherence cues, such as adverbial phrases, as signals to match new information to the structure or substructure they develop.

Spatial continuity occurs when the text describes events, states, and actions that occur in the same spatial framework, and spatial discontinuity is the result of a change in this framework. Spatial discontinuities affect comprehension (Ehrlich & Johnson-Laird, 1982), and information that pertains to the previous locations may be less accessible (Morrow et al., 1987, 1989). Adverbial phrases and the narrator's point of view (i.e., the location where the narrator is assumed to be) are two cues thought to signal spatial coherence. Black, Turner, and Bower (1979) demonstrated that the readers interpreted the narrator's viewpoint as a spatial coherence cue. After reading the sentence *Bill was sitting in the living room reading the newspaper*, which establishes the narrator's location inside the living room, the sentence *Before Bill had finished reading his newspaper, John came into the room* was read faster than *Before Bill had finished reading his newspa-*

per, John went into the room. Haenggi, Gernsbacher, and Bolliger (1994) also demonstrated that readers inferred the location of a protagonist in a story, and that they used this inferred knowledge as a cue for establishing coherence. In particular, readers used their prior world knowledge of spatial relations to interpret spatial coherence cues, and matched that coherent information with the structures and substructures they developed.

Causal continuity occurs when there is a direct link between the sentence currently being processed and the previous sentence, that is, when a possible cause from a preceding context is identified. Without causal continuity, readers attempt to infer a causal link, and this corresponds to an elaboration process that is reflected by a longer processing time (see Bloom, Fletcher, van den Broek, Reitz, & Shapiro, 1990; Fletcher & Bloom, 1988; Magliano et al., 1993; Trabasso & van den Broek, 1985; van den Broek & Lorch, 1993). Keenan, Baillet, and Brown (1984) found some variations resulting from the connection strength between the cause and its consequence, where making the connection required several inferential steps. In their study, participants had to read sentence pairs, and the reading time of the second sentence was measured. The consequences (i.e., the second sentence) could be associated with four types of causes, all of which could lead to the same consequence to a greater or lesser degree (i.e., four degrees of causal connection). The authors compared the reading times of the consequences associated with the four types of causes. For example, when the consequence was *The next day he was covered with bruises*, this sentence was preceded by the following causes:

> Strength 4: *Joey's brother punched him again and again.*
> Strength 3: *Racing down the hill, Joey fell off his bike.*
> Strength 2: *Joey's mother became furiously angry with him.*
> Strength 1: *Joey went to a neighbor's house to play.*

The authors observed that the more the contextual sentences induced the consequence (i.e., strength 4 being the strongest cause), the more the "consequence" was read rapidly. These data suggest that readers interpret causal coherence as a cue for matching new information to the structures and substructures they develop.

Therefore, various sources of coherence appear to be fundamental to explaining the mapping or integration process. Consistent with both Gernsbacher's (1990) and Zwaan et al.'s (1995) theoretical frameworks, establishing coherence is not automatic but strategic, and it is a function of situational continuity. Two situationally continuous events are processed faster than two situationally discontinuous ones. When information is continuous (in terms of situational continuity), integration or updating can occur and the reading comprehension process is not disrupted. When situational continuity is not maintained, however, it causes an increase in processing time and disrupts comprehension (Anderson et al., 1983; Black et al., 1979; Daneman & Carpenter, 1983). In this case, the mapping process cannot be successful and a new mental structure is built under the influence of the shifting process (Gernsbacher, 1990).

The principle of situational continuity is of crucial importance in several respects, then. First, it determines the nature of the updating process, and gives considerable weight to the coherence readers attribute as they process textual information. Second, it provides finer measures of the importance of each dimension in this process and encourages us to investigate the nature of each of these dimensions in depth. Finally, it stresses the necessity of conducting further studies to examine the respective weights of each of these dimensions in the reader's mental representation, as well as their potential relationships.

4.3. COHERENCE AND RELEVANCE: TWO CORE CONCEPTS FOR INTEGRATING BOTTOM-UP AND TOP-DOWN APPROACHES TO THE READING COMPREHENSION PROCESS (MYERS & O'BRIEN, 1998; SANFORD & GARROD , 1981, 1998)

In normal, successful reading, text representations in memory are coherent wholes. Because texts are processed sequentially, text comprehension requires integrating information across sentences to build a coherent representation of the entire text. Prior text representations should be accessible so that the information currently being processed can be tied to the previously read text and thereby create local and global coherence. Models differ in their analysis of this coherence-building process. There are local coherence models, also called minimalist or linear models by van den Broek and Lorch (1993). Kintsch's (1988) and McKoon and Ratcliff's (1992) models are examples of local coherence models. These models focus on readers' attempts to link each discourse unit with the immediately preceding unit. McKoon and Ratcliff (1992) proposed a minimalist hypothesis (see chapter 5 for a detailed description of this hypothesis), according to which readers create connections between current information and information that is stored in short-term memory. Connections between current information and information retrieved from long-term memory are also made, but only when there is a break in local coherence. In several studies, McKoon and Ratcliff illustrated the psychological validity of this minimal processing by showing that inferences that maintained local coherence were generated during comprehension, whereas those required for global coherence were not made unless local coherence failed (McKoon & Ratcliff, 1992).

On the other hand, global coherence models assume that readers establish links both between adjacent units and with other units occurring earlier in the text, even when local connections are successfully made (Collins,

Brown, & Larkin, 1980; Garrod & Sanford, 1988; Glenberg & Langston, 1992; Graesser & Clark, 1985; Graesser, Singer, & Trabasso, 1994; Johnson-Laird, 1983; Kintsch, 1998; Myers & O'Brien, 1998). Readers match current information with information still active in memory, and with relevant information that is no longer active in memory as well. Theories of mental models belong to this category, as does the Constructionist Theory proposed by Graesser, Singer, and Trabasso (1994). The Constructionist Theory (see chapter 5) explicitly adopts two hypotheses that are the building blocks for distinct predictions about the type of inferences made during comprehension. First, the explanatory hypothesis states that readers try to explain why actions and events are mentioned in a text. This may be achieved, for example, by generating plausible causal antecedents of an event mentioned in the text. Second, the coherence hypothesis establishes that readers try to construct a coherent representation at both the local and global levels. It implies that readers make not only causal antecedent inferences but also inferences pertaining to the characters' goals and emotions because they play a role in the overall patterns of story plots and are necessary for establishing global coherence. Thus, these two hypotheses underline the crucial role of causality and emotion (see Part III). This approach emphasizes global coherence, and several findings show that readers are sensitive to global inconsistencies, even when local coherence is maintained.

In this vein, and in contradiction to McKoon and Ratcliff's (1992) findings, O'Brien and Albrecht (1992) showed that readers detected inconsistent information at a global level even when local coherence was maintained. In their studies, the authors manipulated the compatibility between information about a character's location in a specific environment and information mentioned earlier in the text. The inconsistent information could be easily integrated locally but not globally. The results showed that when a sentence was globally incoherent, subjects experienced comprehension difficulties even though it was locally coherent. This means that spatial information that was not compatible with the initial location of the character was detected despite the maintenance of local coherence.

Local and global coherence are created through different mechanisms. Local coherence is especially dependent on textual characteristics (Halliday & Hasan, 1976; Mann & Thompson, 1986) and is closely related to cohesion. Cohesion refers to local connections that are primarily based on the text's surface characteristics rather than on background knowledge (Graesser et al., 1994, p. 378). Kintsch and van Dijk's (1978) original model of text comprehension and the subsequent Construction-Integration Model (Kintsch, 1988) include mechanisms for establishing local coherence. According to these models, texts are processed in cycles, and certain propositions are kept in a memory buffer from one cycle to the next. Connections may be made between propositions in each cycle and propositions in the buffer. The default criterion used to link propositions is argument overlap, or common noun-phrase referents that are shared between propositions. However, other criteria can be used to link propositions, including the case of two propositions sharing the same place or time (Kintsch, 1998). When a connection to propositions in the buffer is impossible, a search in long-term memory (LTM) is initiated in order to find a connection to other propositions.

The more distant connections that have to be made to establish global coherence are less dependent on surface cues in the text. Global coherence requires that incoming pieces of information be related to other information in the text that may not be currently active in short-term memory (STM) due to limitations of STM capacity. This process has been conceptualized in various ways: as a backward parallel spreading of activation (O'Brien & Albrecht, 1992; O'Brien, Plewes, & Albrecht, 1990), a passive resonance process (Albrecht & Myers, 1995, 1998; Klin & Myers, 1993; Myers & O'Brien, 1998; Rizzella & O'Brien, 1996), a passive automatic constraint-satisfaction mechanism (Graesser et al., 1994), or an active meaning-seeking process (Graesser et al., 1994). In particular, the Resonance Model explains the reinstatement of relevant textual and background knowledge by means of a process where traces in STM send signals to all of LTM. Information in LTM that shares features with these traces is reactivated and brought to STM. Several text-related and reader-related variables may affect the passive resonance process that is responsible for the establishment of global coherence, including overlap of target-proposition features and the previous traces to which it may be related (Albrecht & Myers, 1995; Huitema, Dopkins, Klin, & Myers, 1993; Klin & Myers, 1993; Rizzella & O'Brien, 1996), distance in the surface structure between the target trace and previous related traces (Albrecht & Myers, 1995; O'Brien, Plewes, & Albrecht, 1990; Rizzella & O'Brien, 1996), and trace elaboration (O'Brien, Plewes, & Albrecht, 1990). Defined as passive, the resonance process is conceived of as a fast-acting (Klin & Myers, 1993; Myers & O'Brien, 1998; Rizzella & O'Brien, 1996), autonomous process, and because it relies on memory retrieval processes, it is based on the Memory-Based Text Processing approach (McKoon et al., 1996).

The Memory-Based Text Processing Approach can be distinguished from other theoretical views by several crucial hypotheses on the nature of text processing:

> Reading comprehension efforts are subserved by a highly automated memory retrieval process (Myers & O'Brien, 1998; O'Brien & Myers, 1999). The search process is automatic in several senses: it is triggered by individual lexical items, access to associated information is rapid and does not consume

central processing resources, it is unrestricted in that any concept that shares features with information in working memory will be activated, and it is "dumb" in that sufficiently activated information is returned to working memory regardless of its relevance. (Lorch, 1998, p. 215)

In other words, this process is viewed as the first mechanism by which prior information can be reactivated, and models of the second and third generations (see the detailed account in chapter 1) provide mechanisms that are consistent with this process (see Kinstch, 1988; van den Broek et al., 1996, 1999).

The Scenario-Mapping and Focus Theory (Sanford & Garrod, 1981, 1998) is also based on the memory-based text processing view: Information in explicit focus activates the scenario through a passive resonance process (Garrod et al., 1990). However, the authors of this theory assume that the retrieval process is guided and restricted by discursive pointers that prime relevant background information. In this sense, the authors reject the assumption that the process has an unrestricted scope (O'Brien & Albrecht, 1991; O'Brien et al., 1995; O'Brien et al., 1990). In the former view, occurrences that represent entities explicitly mentioned in the text and maintained in explicit focus serve as pointers (see Glenberg & Langston, 1992) and, via a passive resonance process, prime "appropriate" information from the scenario in implicit focus. Therefore, activation of backgrounded information differs in these two views of the resonance process (unrestricted versus restricted).

Cook, Halleran, and O'Brien (1998) contrasted the memory-based approach, which assumes an unrestricted resonance process, to the scenario-based approach, according to which discourse pointers guide the resonance process toward relevant information (i.e., restricted process). Consistent with the memory-based approach (see Myers & O'Brien, 1998), backgrounded information becomes available through a passive resonance process and information relevance has no effect on the retrieval of information. Conversely, in the scenario-based models (Garrod & Sanford, 1988, 1990; Glenberg & Langston, 1992), reactivation of backgrounded information is restricted by discourse pointers to scenario-relevant information.

In four experiments, Cook et al.(1998) tested whether backgrounded information became readily available to the reader regardless of information relevance. They used passages (Cook et al., 1998, Experiment 2A) in which two characters were introduced. One of four possible elaboration conditions followed the introduction part of the text. In the first-character elaboration conditions, the characteristics of the first character were described as being consistent or inconsistent with an action that the same character would carry out in the critical sentence. In the second-character elaboration conditions, the same characteristics as for the primary character were used, but they referred to the second character. The critical sentence always de-

TABLE 4.1

Sample Passage With the Introduction Part, the Four Elaboration Parts,
and the Critical Sentence
(Taken From Cook, Halleran, & O'Brien, 1998, Experiment 2A)

Introduction: Ken and his friend Mike had been looking for summer hobbies for quite some time. They were both college professors and they had the summers off from teaching. This meant that they both had plenty of time to try new things.

First-character consistent elaboration: Ken was a big man and always tried to keep in shape by jogging and lifting weights. His 250-pound body was solid muscle. Ken loved tough physical contact sports which allowed him to match his strength against another person.

First-character inconsistent elaboration: Ken was a small man and didn't worry about staying in shape. His small 120-pound body was all skin and bones. Ken hated contact sports, but enjoyed non-contact sports, such as golf and bowling which he could practice alone.

Second-character consistent elaboration: Mike was a big man and always tried to keep in shape by jogging and lifting weights. His 250-pound body was solid muscle. Mike loved tough physical contact sports which allowed him to match his strength against another person.

Second-character inconsistent elaboration: Mike was a small man and didn't worry about staying in shape. His small 120-pound body was all skin and bones. Mike hated contact sports, but enjoyed non-contact sports, such as golf and bowling which he could practice alone.

Critical sentence: Ken decided to enroll in boxing classes.

scribed an action that was carried out by the first character. Table 4.1 shows a sample passage used by Cook et al. (1998).

According to both the memory-based view and the scenario-based models, when the critical characteristics describe the first character, reading the critical sentence should reactivate those characteristics. When the characteristics are inconsistent with the action carried out in the critical sentence, readers should experience comprehension difficulty. However, according to the model with discourse pointers (see Sanford & Garrod, 1998), when the characteristics describe the second character, actions carried out by the first character should not reactivate those characteristics because they are irrelevant to the first character (i.e., no comprehension difficulty). The results obtained by Cook et al. (1998) indicated that information that was not scenario-relevant was reactivated through an unrestricted passive resonance process where overlapping features guided the reactivation process.

I assume that the nature of inconsistent information has an effect on the retrieval process, as well as on how readers attribute relevance to backgrounded information in order to integrate text information. If relevance is not a necessary factor in the reactivation of backgrounded information, not all pieces of information that are reactivated should be integrated into the representation. Because of this, I conducted two studies to investigate how relevance is attributed when readers retrieve backgrounded information, and I proposed an alternative hypothesis to Cook et al.'s (1998) interpretation of their results.

In the first study,[2] Cook et al.'s (1998, Experiment 2A) procedure was used, but the experimental materials were modified. Contrasting with Cook et al.'s (1998) passages, in which reactivation was tested via character actions that were inconsistent with the description of a previously mentioned character, our experimental passages, taken from Gernsbacher, Goldsmith, and Robertson (1992), concerned characters' basic emotions. We translated them into French and modified them for the purposes of this experiment. Similar to Cook et al.'s study, all passages had two characters, and the introduction part was followed by four possible elaboration conditions. However, the critical information was found in two sentences, so that we could study the temporal course of the reactivation process (compared to only one sentence in the original study). The two critical sentences always dealt with the primary character's emotional state as implied by the story. For two elaborations, the implied emotional state pertained to the first character (i.e., the same character as in the critical sentences) and the critical information was either consistent or inconsistent with the elaboration information. The other two elaborations concerned the emotional state of the second character and were either consistent or inconsistent with the emotional state implied in the critical sentences (i.e., about the first character). Table 4.2 presents an example of a passage where "shyness" was the implied emotional state.

Reading a text requires representing several dimensions in order to build a coherent situation model (Zwaan, Magliano, & Graesser, 1995), and emotions might be part of this representation. Using inconsistencies in this dimension should cause readers to focus on information that is scenario-relevant. Consistent with the memory-based view and with the scenario-based models, when the description gives emotional information about the first character, reading the critical sentences should reactivate this information. When the emotional state implied is inconsistent with the emotional information stated in the critical sentences, readers should have trouble understanding. However, readers should also be sensitive to the relevance of emotional information. According to the scenario-based models, emotional information about a first character should not reactivate emotional properties pertaining to a second character. Consequently, when the elaboration was about the second character, no difference between the consistent and inconsistent conditions was

---

[2] This study was conducted, under my direction, in 2002 by Emilie Aurouer in fulfillment of the requirements for a Master's Degree at the University of Lyon 2 (France).

TABLE 4.2

Example Passage Including the Introduction, the Four Elaboration Parts,
and the Two Critical Sentences: The Implied Emotional State Was Shyness
(Translated From Aurouer, 2002)

Introduction: Eric really wanted to go to the party organized by the students but he didn't know when it was. He thought he could ask Sabine, another student who was in his history class. He would have liked her to agree to join him in going to the party.

First-character consistent elaboration: Eric is not very daring with girls. He always worries because he's afraid of being ridiculous and blushes easily. He's nervous when he has to start up a conversation with them. And he feels uncomfortable when he has to talk to them.

First-character inconsistent elaboration: Eric is very daring with girls. He's never afraid of being ridiculous and doesn't blush easily. He's very confident when has to start up a conversation with them. And he's always comfortable when he has to talk to them.

Second-character consistent elaboration: Sabine is not very daring with boys. She always worries because she's afraid of being ridiculous and blushes easily. She's nervous when she has to start up a conversation with them. And she's uncomfortable when she has to talk to them.

Second-character consistent elaboration: Sabine is very daring with boys. She's never afraid of being ridiculous and doesn't blush easily. She's very confident when she has to start up a conversation with them. And she's always comfortable when she has to talk to them.

Critical sentences: Eric is filled with feelings of shyness. He is very hesitant when he wants to ask a girl out.

expected because information brought by the critical sentences was irrelevant to the previously stated elaboration.

The results confirmed the existence of the resonance process. Readers detected inconsistencies when the emotional information stated in the critical sentences (about the first character) did not correspond to what was previously presented in the elaboration part, and longer reading times on critical sentences were observed for inconsistent conditions than for consistent ones, $F(1,59) = 8.051$, $p < .01$. This result confirms what has already been observed and replicates Cook et al.'s (1998) findings. The resonance process is a fast-acting process that leads readers to reactivate information related to what is currently being processed. In this way, readers are able to maintain both local and global coherence. However, and although both critical sentences in this experiment led to an inconsistency effect, our findings showed that they were not equally sensitive to the inconsistencies: The reading-times difference between the inconsistent and consistent conditions was greater for the first target sentence, $F(1,59) = 18.614$, $p < .01$, than for the second, $F(1,59) = 4.443$, $p < .05$, indicating a decay of the inconsistency effect over time (see Figure 4.1).

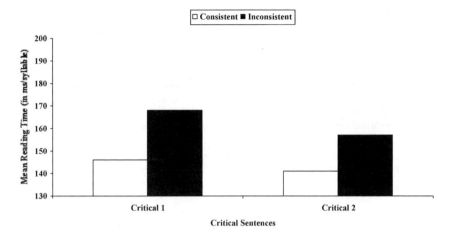

FIGURE 4.1.   Mean reading time as a function of coherence and critical sentence number (from Aurouer, 2002).

Moreover, and as shown in Figure 4.2, whereas a slower reading time was expected for critical sentences only, this pattern also occurred for the last sentence in the passages (i.e., conclusion). This provides some insight into the temporal course and strength of the inconsistency effect: It lasted over time but decreased in intensity.

A second unexpected result was that the emotional state implied for the second character was reactivated, regardless of information relevance. Reading times were longer in the inconsistent condition than in the consistent condition (for the second-character elaboration). Therefore, when

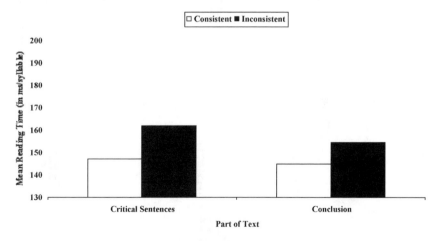

FIGURE 4.2.   Mean reading time as a function of coherence and text structure (critical sentences and conclusion; from Aurouer, 2002).

readers processed information about the first character (i.e., the target sentences), they accessed to the characteristics of the second character, which means that irrelevant information was reactivated. This is consistent with the memory-based approach. However, the strength of the inconsistency effect depended on what characters were mentioned in the elaboration and where the critical information was located (i.e., first and second critical sentences). When the information stated in the critical sentences concerned the elaborated character (first character), the inconsistency effect persisted

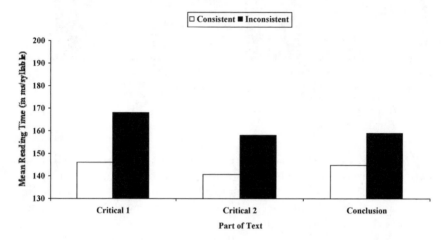

FIGURE 4.3a.   Mean reading time as a function of coherence and text structure (critical sentences and conclusion) for the first character only (from Aurouer, 2002).

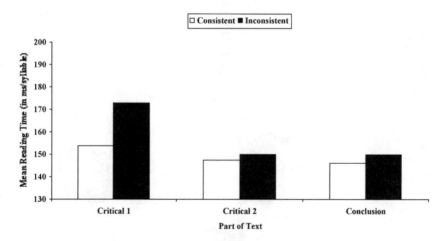

FIGURE 4.3b.   Mean reading time as a function of coherence and text structure (critical sentences and conclusion) for the second character only (from Aurouer, 2002).

in time, with longer reading times for the two critical sentences as well as for the conclusion sentence (see Figure 4.3a). On the other hand, when the information stated in the target sentences was irrelevant to the elaborated character (second character), the inconsistency effect did not persist (see Figure 4.3b). The reading-time difference between the inconsistent and consistent conditions was only significant for the first critical sentence. Therefore, the inconsistency effect seems to have lost its strength and to have been less durable when the target sentences dealt with a character other than the one described in the elaboration condition (compared to when they concerned the same character).

Thus, readers did not reactivate information on each character (first and second) in an equal way. When a character's reactivated emotional profile (second character) was irrelevant to the information currently being processed (first character), the inconsistency effect did not last as long as when the profile of the same character was activated. Therefore, the relevance of reactivated information was taken into account, at least at certain particular points in the reading process, presumably as readers attempt to integrate text information in order to establish coherence.

From these results, one can postulate the existence of two main steps in the comprehension process: a first, fast-acting resonance process that causes reactivation of information previously processed, regardless of information relevance, and a second, more strategic process that may be conceived of as a restricted process that allows readers to maintain relevant information and integrate it into their memory representation. Interpreting these findings in line with Sanford and Garrod's restricted view of the resonance process (Garrod & Sanford, 1998), it is likely that elements kept in focus (i.e., about the first character) served as pointers and primed relevant information in the scenario. Because this matching between explicit and implicit focus takes time, the inconsistency effect began as readers processed the first sentence, but had decreased in strength by the time the readers were processing the second critical sentence and the conclusion.

To extend the results obtained in this first study, a second study[3] was carried out with a similar procedure (see Aurouer, 2002; Cook et al., 1998, Experiment 2A). All passages had the same structure as in the first study and described two characters. The introduction conveyed the same amount of information about each of the two characters and was followed by four possible elaboration conditions. Also, two critical sentences that dealt with the first character's emotional state were presented before the concluding sentence. The content of the four elaborations differed from Cook et al.'s (1998) passages (see Table 4.1) and from the passages used in the previous study (see Table 4.2). The main goal was to determine whether the character token (i.e.,

---

[3] This study was conducted, under my direction, in 2005 by Céline Rossetti, in fulfillment of the requirements for a Master's Degree at the University of Lyon 2 (France).

relevance) and/or the nature of information that overlapped with the critical information (unrestricted resonance) affected the extent of the reactivation process assumed to occur. One type of elaboration (first-and-second-character elaboration conditions) conveyed information about both characters: The first two sentences presented emotional information about the second character that was consistent or inconsistent with the first character's emotional state described in the critical sentences. Here, elaborated emotional information about the second character could match or not match the emotional information described in the critical sentences (about the first character), but there was no match in terms of the relevance of the character token. The last two sentences were about the first character but gave neutral information (i.e., nonemotional). This information matched the critical information in terms of the relevance of the character token, but not in terms of properties attributed to the first character. The two remaining elaboration conditions only concerned the second character (second-character elaborations). The first two sentences gave emotional information about the second character that was consistent or inconsistent with the first character's emotional state described in the critical sentences. This information was identical to the content of the first two sentences of the first-and-second-character elaboration conditions. The last two sentences supplied neutral information. Thus, unlike the second-character elaboration conditions in the previous study (Aurouer, 2002), not all elaborated information overlapped with information in the critical sentences because emotional information was only described in the first two sentences. Table 4.3 shows an example of a passage where "shyness" was the emotional state.

In line with the memory-based view, and no matter what elaboration conditions readers are assigned (first-and-second-character, or only second-character elaborations), critical-sentence processing (about the first character) should reactivate all traces related to the characteristics in question, that is, emotional information. Consequently, when the emotional state implied in the elaboration part is inconsistent with the emotional information stated in the critical sentences, readers should have comprehension problems and longer reading times for both critical sentences. This effect should occur in the first-and-second-character elaboration conditions, as well as in the second-character elaboration conditions. In line with the scenario-based theory's assumption and our previous findings (see Aurouer, 2002), readers should have comprehension problems when the information conveyed in the critical sentences and elaborated information are relevant to each other. So, an inconsistency effect should be observed in the first-and-second character elaboration conditions, with longer reading times in the inconsistent condition than in the consistent condition. This should occur because tokens about the first character's emotional state maintained in focus should serve as pointers and prime reactivation of con-

TABLE 4.3

Example of an Experimental Passage Including the Introduction, the Four
Elaboration Conditions, the Context, the Two Critical Sentences, and the
Conclusion: The Implied Emotional State Was Shyness
(Translated From Rossetti, 2005)

Introduction: Eric and Sabine really want to go to the party organized by their
classmates but they don't know when it is. They both attend the same history
class. They like each other very much and want to go together to the party.

First-and-second-character consistent elaboration: Sabine is not very daring with
boys. She is nervous when she has to start up a conversation with them and is
uncomfortable when she has to talk to them. Eric is studying very hard and
doesn't go to parties very often. However, all the students want to go to this
party because it is the last one in the academic year.

First-and-second-character inconsistent elaboration: Sabine is very daring with boys.
She is very confident when she has to start up a conversation with them and is
comfortable when she has to talk to them. Eric is studying very hard and
doesn't go to parties very often. However, all the students want to go to this
party because it is the last one in the academic year.

Second-character consistent elaboration: Sabine is not very daring with boys. She is
nervous when she has to start up a conversation with them and is
uncomfortable when she has to talk to them. She is studying very hard and
doesn't go to parties very often. However, all the students want to go to this
party because it is the last one in the academic year.

Second-character inconsistent elaboration: Sabine is very daring with boys. She is
very confident when she has to start up a conversation with them and is
comfortable when she has to talk to them. She is studying very hard and
doesn't go to parties very often. However, all the students want to go to this
party because it is the last one in the academic year.

Context: Today, Eric and Sabine have a history class together. It will give them
the opportunity to talk about the party. Unfortunately, the class gets cancelled
at the last minute. They won't be able to see each other. But, by chance, they
meet in the corridor and can talk.

Critical sentences: Eric is filled with feeling of shyness. He is always afraid of
being ridiculous and blushes easily.

Conclusion: Sabine is a perfect person for him.

---

textually relevant information through a passive resonance process.
Although no emotional information about the first character was elaborated, mentioning the first character should prime trace reactivation. In the
second-character elaboration conditions, however, a difference in reading
times between consistent and inconsistent conditions should occur, but only
when readers are processing the first critical sentence; this inconsistency
effect would be due to a first, fast-acting reactivation process. For the
remaining sentences (second critical sentence and conclusion), however,

reading-time differences between consistent and inconsistent conditions should drastically decrease because of the activation of retrieval cues assumed to allow relevance to take effect, and because no information was relevant when occurrences in explicit focus matched information in implicit focus (i.e., character token and character properties).

First, and as predicted, the reading times tended to be longer in the inconsistent conditions than in the consistent conditions, $F(1,59) = 3.592$,

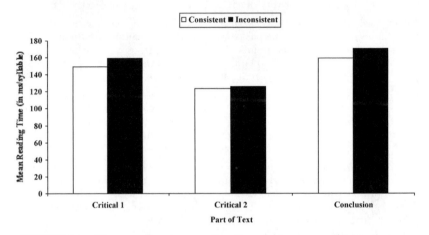

FIGURE 4.4.   Mean reading time as a function of coherence and text structure (two critical sentences and conclusion; from Rossetti, 2005).

$p = .06$. This result confirms the occurrence of the resonance process. As Figure 4.4 shows, the difference in reading times between inconsistent and consistent conditions was significant for the first critical sentence, $F(1,118) = 7.129, p < .001$, and for the conclusion, $F(1,118) = 9.440, p < .001$, but not for the second critical sentence ($F < 1$).

Moreover, although a reliable difference between consistent and inconsistent conditions appeared when the critical information concerned the first and second characters, no reading-time difference between the two conditions was noted when the elaboration only pertained to the second character (see Figure 4.5). This finding demonstrates a differential effect of elaboration on the resonance process, and indicates that at certain points in the reading process, readers relied on relevance.

Finally, Figures 4.6a and 4.6b present the reading times in the consistent and inconsistent conditions for first-and-second-character elaborations, and for second-character elaborations. When both characters were elaborated, the reading-time difference between the consistent and inconsistent elaboration conditions was significant for the first critical sentence as well as for the conclusion. Thus, readers had trouble understanding, and this ef-

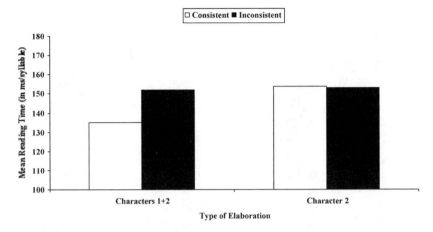

FIGURE 4.5.   Mean reading time as a function of coherence and type of elaboration (from Rossetti, 2005).

fect was maintained through to the conclusion. Conversely, for the second-character elaboration conditions, the lack of a difference in the reading times between consistent and inconsistent elaborations reflects an increase in processing time in the consistent condition. Unexpectedly, readers did not process critical information faster when they were assigned to the consistent condition as compared to the inconsistent condition (see Figure 4.6b).

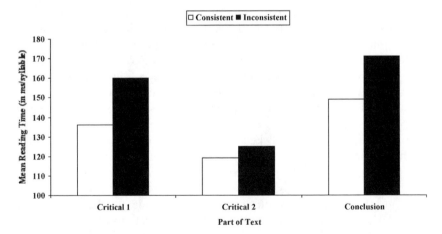

FIGURE 4.6a.   Mean reading time as a function of coherence and text structure (critical sentences and conclusion) for the first and second characters only (from Rossetti, 2005).

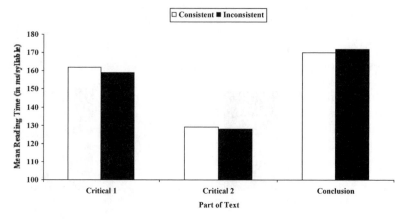

FIGURE 4.6b.   Mean reading time as a function of coherence and text structure (critical sentences and conclusion) for the second character only (from Rossetti, 2005).

The difference in the response patterns for the two types of elaboration is intriguing and unexpected. As predicted by both theories, when the first and second characters were elaborated, readers had trouble understanding the first critical sentence. Although this effect was no longer present on the second critical sentence, it re-occurred when readers processed the conclusion. Once again, these data confirm the existence of a first, fast-acting resonance process (see O'Brien & Myers, 1999) that is not restricted to the character properties described. Processing emotional information about the first character (in the critical sentences) primed emotional information about the second character. It is likely, then, that the implied emotional information about the second character was associated to information stated in the critical sentences about the first character. Nonetheless, although this finding supports the idea of an unrestricted type of resonance process, it is also consistent with the idea that the protagonist the sentence is about is likely to be the principal retrieval cue that primes the scenario (Sanford & Garrod, 1981). Because the readers distinguished information about the character himself or herself (i.e., first versus second character) and about his or her characteristics (i.e., emotional versus neutral information), when they processed critical information about the first character, a token associated with it in explicit focus probably served to reactivate contextually relevant information (from the scenario). The results for the second-character elaboration conditions reinforce this interpretation.

In the second-character elaboration conditions, and in line with both theories, an inconsistency effect was expected based on the assumption that readers access all memory traces that share some features with the critical information. Consistent with Sanford and Garrod's view of the resonance process (1998), however, and also with the data obtained in the first study (Aurouer, 2002), readers were expected to experience comprehension difficulties only on the first critical sentence because occurrences that were maintained in explicit focus primed contextually relevant information via a passive resonance process. This effect was expected to decay rapidly, though, because the critical information was not relevant to the information described in the elaboration parts (different characters and topic shift). Consequently, no reading-time difference between the consistent and inconsistent conditions was predicted for the second critical sentence or the conclusion. Unexpectedly, the data obtained for the second-character elaboration conditions did not completely fit with any of the predictions that follow from the two views of the resonance process because readers had comprehension problems in both the consistent and inconsistent conditions, that is, even when the emotional information implied for the second character was consistent with the information stated for the first character. On one hand, if resonance occurred regardless of information relevance, no comprehension difficulties in the consistent condition should have been observed because emotional traces activated by the critical information about the first character sent signals to all memory traces related to it: Emotional information stated in the critical sentences shared features with the elaborated information about the second character. On the other hand, in line with Sanford and Garrod's theory (1981, 1988), shorter response times in the consistent condition as compared to the inconsistent condition should have been obtained for the first critical sentence but not for the second critical sentence or for the conclusion, where short reading times were predicted in both conditions (i.e., consistent and inconsistent).

The results for the second-character elaboration conditions suggest that readers relied on relevance in some way because they experienced comprehension difficulties in both the consistent and inconsistent conditions. The data indicated that critical emotional information sent signals to all memory traces related to it. However, if this passive resonance was the only factor readers were relying on, they should have had shorter reading times in the consistent condition than in the inconsistent condition because emotional information in the critical sentences sent signals to emotional information in the elaboration. This is not what the findings showed, and the difficulties encountered by the readers in the consistent condition indicate that they had no access to the cue that could help them establish coherence.

The comparison of the data from the two types of elaboration conditions (first-and-second-character and second-character) suggests that readers probably relied on the interplay between two kinds of information when retrieving information from memory: the character token and the type of elaborated information. In the first-and-second-character elaboration conditions, the second character was described as a shy person (first two sentences), but then neutral information was associated to the first character (last two sentences). Therefore, there was a shift in the nature of the information conveyed, but a match in the character token was nevertheless possible for readers. Accordingly, it is likely that discourse pointers to the first character (character token and character properties) were activated and thus primed information associated with that character, leading to the occurrence of the inconsistency effect. In the second-character consistent elaboration condition, however, the same character (the second character) was implicitly described as a shy person (first two sentences) and as a hard worker (last two sentences). As in the first-and-second-character elaboration conditions, there was a topic shift, but to this shift was added the lack of character-token relevance. In this condition, reactivation occurred passively, but there was no possible matching between the critical sentences and the elaboration information pertaining to the character token or to emotional information. Because the elaborations supplied emotional information and then shifted to neutral information, and because in the critical sentence, in addition to the lack of a match with the character token, there was no occurrence that could prime relevant information (i.e., neutral), readers experienced difficulties in both the consistent and inconsistent elaboration conditions. Thus, the shift in topic, combined with the lack of character-token relevance, probably caused the response pattern observed in this condition.

This interpretation is consistent with the results obtained in the earlier studies previously described (see Cook et al., 1998; Aurouer, 2002). Indeed, in the second-character elaboration conditions of both studies, although two different characters were described, an inconsistency effect was observed, at least at first (see Aurouer, 2002). However, in those studies, the information conveyed in the elaboration part of the materials did not involve a shift in topic, and the nature of the information remained the same (i.e., emotional). This probably strengthened the associations between the concepts in the critical sentences and those in the elaborated parts. In the present study, because there were no occurrences that could prime neutral information, difficulties arose in both conditions (consistent and inconsistent).

Overall, these findings confirmed what was already observed in the Cook et al. (1998) study: Comprehension difficulties result in the occurrence of a passive resonance process that is fast-acting. However, passive resonance is not the sole mechanism to cause this reactivation. Another relevance-based mechanism presumably occurs. According to both approaches to the resonance process (see Myers & O'Brien, 1998; Sanford & Garrod, 1998), reactivation of backgrounded information is triggered by an initial unrestricted resonance process. However, this process gradually turns into a restricted process through the use of discourse pointers. These pointers are thought to be flexible enough to trigger the integration of pieces of information from the scenario, and this would help readers build the most "coherent" mental representation. In the two studies reported here (Aurouer, 2002, Rossetti, 2005), I showed, first, that pointers were at play in the second phase of the reactivation process, that is, as readers attempt to integrate elaborated information into their representation (Aurouer, 2002), and second, that the character token as well as the nature of elaborated information (Rossetti, 2005) played a prevalent role in this process.

Thus, these two studies contribute to improving our understanding of the main characteristics of the resonance process and the factors that potentially influence it. They also deepen our knowledge of how tokens in explicit focus serve as pointers that direct the reactivation process toward relevant pieces of information. Finally, they point out the need to make the Memory-Based Approach and the Scenario-Based Theory converge in their principles so that we can account, in a "comprehensive" way, for how readers reactivate backgrounded information and establish coherence.

How do readers access backgrounded information and how do they integrate it into their mental representation? As the findings presented here emphasize, further insight into these questions can only be gained by conducting studies devoted to thoroughly investigating the magnitude of the resonance process as a function of the nature of the information read. The theoretical frameworks (Gernsbacher, 1990; Zwaan, Langston, & Graesser, 1995) and empirical findings on the importance of various situational dimensions as cues for establishing coherence have to be taken into account in an attempt to understand how readers reactivate information that has been put into the background. In this sense, the nature of the information to be reactivated should modulate the extent of the resonance process. In the studies described earlier in this chapter, I focused in particular on emotional information, but other dimensions, alone and in interaction, should be investigated as well.

I also showed that the nature of the information to be reactivated has an impact on the temporal course of the resonance process and on the temporal boundaries of the integration process. In the two studies reported (Aurouer, 2002, Rossetti, 2005), the strength of the inconsistency effect decayed as readers proceeded through the text. Consistent with Kinsch's theoretical framework (Kintsch, 1988, 1998), it is likely that a passive reactivation process acts first during reading. However, this "dumb" process must somehow be guided by relevance, its role being a function of several factors including the reader's knowledge of the situation and the nature of elaborated information, both contributing to the building of an adequate situation model. In other words, I would be tempted to define the resonance process as a general activation mechanism that allows for unrestricted access to any memory trace that shares some features with information in working memory (similar to the activation process in the Construction-Integration Model; see Kintsch, 1988). However, in order for integration to occur, activation has to be constrained by more top-down processes: Pointers or relevance assigned to information could fulfill this function. As I mentioned earlier, activation only partly explains comprehension, so other mechanisms that guide coherence and discourse interpretation must be taken into account in order to fully understand what "comprehension" really means. Therefore, it seems critical that theories of comprehension be able to determine how top-down processes interact with more bottom-up processes. In other words, the issue of how mechanisms that lead to coherence affect the passive reactivation of backgrounded information is a crucial one, and an understanding of these mechanisms will deepen our knowledge of their respective weights and relationships in the reading comprehension process. Accordingly, accounting for the vast and complex interplay between bottom-up and top-down process (see Kinstch, 1998, 2005; van den Broek, Rapp, & Kendeou, 2005) should be the best way to approach the nature of the reader's mental representation and should allow us to define comprehension as accurately as possible.

4.4. CONCLUSION: WHAT KINDS OF RELATIONSHIPS EXIST BETWEEN THESE COGNITIVE PROCESSES AND THE POSTULATED "INTERNAL OBJECTS" OF SITUATION MODELS?

In this section (chapters 3 & 4), my goal was to present how coherence is understood in theories of comprehension. The various approaches to coherence that I discussed show that building a coherent mental representation relies on mechanisms that are powerful enough to disregard the type of unit that readers are activating and using when facing a situation of text comprehension. In other words, what seems to matter is more the nature and flexibility of the configuration of units than their format per se. Explaining and deeply investigating the main processes involved in establishing coherence, such as activation, mapping, inhibition, resonance, and integration, cannot be confined to the use of any one kind of unit, regardless of its intrinsic nature (symbolic or analogical). Rather, beyond unit specificity, what I have described emphasizes the large explanatory power of the processes related to how coherence is established, maintained, and achieved. In Kintsch's Construction-Integration Model (Kintsch, 1988; 1998), coherence emerges from the interplay between construction and integration processes, and the raw material for this representation relies on propositional format. In Gernsbacher's (1990) framework, structures and substructures are built from memory cells, and coherence is achieved via linguistic cues that map the current text information to previously processed information.

In Sanford and Garrod's model (1981, 1998), integration is the result of a mapping, by way of discourse pointers, between tokens in explicit focus and script-based knowledge in implicit focus. In this view, propositions are only regarded as a product of an interpretation. Finally, Zwaan and Radvansky's (1998) model is based on three main theoretical frameworks that do not necessarily use the same structural units but nonetheless allow for the description of the main processes involved in the comprehension and updating processes.

As I described the main processes assumed to underlie readers' mental representations, our focus of attention gradually shifted from the types of units activated to the type of cognitive operations readers carry out, in such a way that a more prevalent role was accorded to the functional aspect of situation models than to their structural aspect. In this sense, the mechanisms described have proven to be just general enough to subsume several representational formats.

Therefore, and as already discussed in the first chapter, a complete theory of comprehension should account for the various types of units activated by readers because a model's explanatory power depends on the possibility of generalizing the underlying mechanisms to the various postulated units. However, and although investigating the type of units readers activate when trying to understand a text is necessary, it is more crucial to determine how those units are interrelated and what kind of relations are brought to the fore while others are put into the background so that a coherent representation can emerge. This representation is constrained by bottom-up factors, but also by more top-down factors. A critical task for future research will be to determine the respective weights and two-way relations between these processes in the construction of a coherent representation.

Part III

Contribution of Readers' Knowledge to the Establishment of Global Coherence

A reader's mental representation is not a set of unconnected elements, but rather a coherent whole that requires integrating the content of the sentence currently being processed into the mental representation previously constructed. This "updating" process allows readers to access their long-term memory and use both their world knowledge and relevant discourse information. However, coherence does not emerge from the text. It is the result of a mental construction: Readers go beyond explicit information when building their mental representations. Consequently, an adequate psychological theory of text comprehension should account for how the reader generates these various pieces of information (called *inferences*) that result from the interaction between text input and memory traces, and should also emphasize how readers access global or remote information. Although all theories of reading comprehension assume that readers are engaging in some kind of inferential processing (e.g., Graesser, Singer, & Trabasso, 1994; McKoon & Ratcliff, 1992; van Dijk & Kintsch, 1983), no general consensus has been reached yet regarding the mechanisms that lead to the activation of inferential processes or concerning the extent to which readers make inferences. Some theories focus on the passive activation of inferential information (e.g., Kintsch, 1988; McKoon & Ratcliff, 1992; Myers & O'Brien, 1998; O'Brien & Myers, 1999); others bring inferencing to the fore as an active part of the comprehension process (e.g., Graesser et al., 1994; Zwaan & Radvansky, 1998). In addition, and regardless of the processes underlying inference generation (whether passive or

115

more strategic), models of comprehension disagree on the nature of the updating process, and consequently on the way readers establish coherence. As already stated in chapter 4, some models called "linear" or "minimalist" (Kintsch, 1988; Fletcher & Bloom, 1988; McKoon & Ratcliff, 1992) assume that, because of the constraints of the memory system, readers processing textual information relate the current discourse unit to the immediately preceding unit, and establish distant connections only when adjacent connections fail. Consistent with this minimalist theoretical approach (McKoon & Ratcliff, 1992), representation building is primarily defined as local, consisting of connections between adjacent text units and in the activation of readily available information. In this view, global inferences are thus drawn only when local coherence cannot be achieved automatically.

The Linear-Causal Chain Model developed to describe the causal structure of stories relies on this assumption: Causal connections are only created between adjacent text units (see Black & Bower, 1980; Fletcher & Bloom, 1988; van Dijk & Kintsch, 1983; Trabasso & Sperry, 1985; Trabasso, Secco, & van den Broek, 1984). In this type of model, a story's causal structure can be described by a set of connected actions, events, or states that relate the beginning of the text to its end. Statements that are in the causal chain maintain the causal flow of the text and play a crucial role in achieving story coherence in the memory representation. The events not belonging to the causal chain, that is, dead-end statements, remain peripheral because they are not relevant to the outcome of the text and thus do not contribute to textual coherence (Black & Bower, 1980; Omanson, 1982; Schank, 1975; Schank & Abelson, 1977; Trabasso et al., 1984). For instance, Trabasso et al.(1984) showed that events that belonged to the causal chain were better recalled, were more often included in summaries, and were judged as being more important than dead-end events. Therefore, in causal-linear models, if a connection between two text units is identified, the processing is successful and the reader can go on to the next text unit. Connections are not established between nonadjacent units as long as adjacent text units can be constructed (Fletcher & Bloom, 1988; Kintsch, 1988; Schank & Abelson, 1977). However, because the representation of an event leads to at most one antecedent and one consequence, several other kinds of causal relations cannot be integrated.

In contrast to this "local" assumption, global or maximalist models assume that coherence, and consequently the inferential process, does not rely solely on local connections or on readily available information but also on global connections: Readers establish both local and global connections, whether or not the local connections are successful (Garrod & Sanford, 1988; Glenberg & Langston, 1992; Graesser & Clark, 1985; Graesser et al., 1994). Depending on the underlying theoretical framework, however, coherence may be triggered either by a passive resonance process (Albrecht &

Myers, 1995, 1998; Klin & Myers, 1993; Rizzella & O'Brien, 1996; Myers & O'Brien, 1998) or by more strategic processing (Graesser et al., 1994) guided by reading goals, task requirements, the reader's prior knowledge, and the situation model elaborated.

In this section, I point out the relevance of the coherence assumption assumed by global models (Garrod & Sanford, 1988; Glenberg & Langson, 1992; Graesser & Clark, 1985; Graesser et al., 1994) and exemplified by the Causal Network Theory (Bloom et al., 1990; Fletcher, van den Broek, & Arthur, 1996; Trabasso & Sperry, 1985; Trabasso & van den Broek, 1985; van den Broek, 1990a,b; van den Broek & Lorch, 1993). I then provide empirical evidence of the assumption that the situation model (i.e., referential model) built by readers strongly influences the updating process and thus, comprehension. I assume that higher level units, such as situation models, function as relevant retrieval cues, emphasizing the role of the reader's prior knowledge and mental representations in the retrieval and integration processes. I contrast this position with the one held by researchers who assume that access to backgrounded information is underlain by a more passive reactivation process (i.e., the resonance process) triggered by the overlapping of low-level features.

Chapter 5

Establishing Global Coherence: An Account of Readers' Naive Theories of Causality

5.1. ESTABLISHING LOCAL AND GLOBAL COHERENCE: THE MAIN HYPOTHESES

Although there is a large consensus on the idea that readers connect each current processing unit to the immediately preceding ones (i.e., local coherence), theories of comprehension have evoked certain conditions under which distant units in the surface text structure are related and incorporated into the reader's mental representation. For example, such connections are more likely to be made when participants are engaged in special comprehension strategies (McKoon & Ratcliff, 1992). The experimental situation, including the texts and the nature of the task to perform, may encourage readers to access distant information and build a global representation. A break in local coherence may also increase the likelihood that readers will seek to establish global coherence. These are the main factors in the minimalist view (Dell, McKoon, & Ratcliff, 1983; Haviland & Clark, 1974; Kintsch & Keenan, 1973; McKoon & Ratcliff, 1992). McKoon and Ratcliff (1992) consider the processing carried out by readers to be "minimal" in the sense that they will draw only those inferences necessary for establishing local coherence (i.e., automatic inferences), or based on readily available information. Global coherence would therefore depend on nonautomatic, strategic processing and would be established only when local coherence fails. Contrasting with the Minimalist Theory of the inferential process, the Constructionist Theory embraces a principle of "search after meaning" that may or may not be successful regarding reading conditions (see Graesser et al., 1994). In this vein, inferences that are drawn during reading (i.e., online) are knowledge-based, because they are crucial to situation-model construction. The principle of "search after meaning" has three critical assumptions that make clear distinctions between the two theories of inference generation (i.e., minimalist and constructionist) and that constrain the types of inferences readers will generate. First, it is assumed that when readers comprehend a text, they are motivated by one or more goals, and therefore construct inferences that address those goals; this is the goal assumption. Second, in contrast to the Minimalist Theory, which assumes that global (or strategic) inferences are constructed only when local coherence cannot be established during clause interpretation, and that these inferences are not encoded as consistently during comprehension, readers attempt to construct a meaningful representation that is coherent at both a local and a global level (i.e., the coherence assumption). As already discussed in chapter 4, the distinction between local and global coherence is an important one. Local coherence refers to structures and processes that organize elements, constituents, and referents of adjacent clauses or short sequences of clauses; global coherence is established when local pieces of information are organized and interrelated into higher order elements. This higher level of coherence requires accounting for relationships between nonadjacent units, and consequently, is not as dependent on surface text cues as adjacent relations are. Also, unlike local inferences, global inferences are more time-consuming (see also McKoon & Ratcliff, 1992) because a reinstatement search has to take place. Thus, in line with this "global" approach to inference generation, text understanding requires readers to construct the most global representation of meaning, based on text information in interaction with background knowledge (for a typology of global inferences, see Graesser et al., 1994).

Consistent with the coherence assumption, Suh and Trabasso (1993) provided empirical support for a causal text structure in the form of a network by demonstrating that causal goal-oriented inferences are generated during reading. The authors constructed stories that included a protagonist's goal related to subgoals within a given episode (see Trabasso & van den Broek, 1985). The participants had to read a story and generate inferences aloud after reading each sentence. They also had to perform a lexical decision task online during reading, with target words that referred to the story's goals and subgoals. The authors constructed two types of stories. In the first type, the initial goal (main goal) was attained at the end of the story only (failed-goal story). In the second type, the initial goal was attained at the beginning of the story (control story). The different measures converged: Readers retained information about the initial goal as long as it had not been reached. This result is consistent with the Constructionist Theory:

The main goal justifies all story actions until it has been reached. Until attained, it still belongs to the causal field that triggers causal connections and the causal inferences required for comprehension. In parallel, when the main goal is reached, forward or predictive inferences can also be generated. This finding emphasizes the idea that the narrative causal structure is complex, and one text unit can have several other possible connections to other units. These connections include the ones defined by the Linear Chain Model (i.e., adjacent) as well as others that relate distant units in the surface text structure (Graesser & Clark, 1985; Trabasso & van den Broek, 1985).

Finally, in line with the "explanation" assumption, readers attempt to explain why actions, events, and states are mentioned in a text and why the author mentioned them. These explanations involve naive theories of causality to explain actions, events, and states (see chapter 2) and play a central role in the understanding of narratives and the establishment of coherence. According to this assumption, a coherence break occurs when an incoming clause cannot be readily explained by prior-text or background-knowledge structures. In the Minimalist Theory, this "explanation" assumption has no relevance because only "minimal inferences" are drawn during reading.

In this global approach of coherence, then, readers are assumed to match current information to information still active in memory and to relevant information that is no longer active. As such, they are sensitive to global inconsistencies even when local coherence is maintained. Several empirical findings support this assumption and thereby weaken McKoon and Ratcliff's (1992) minimal hypothesis.

The three critical assumptions of the Constructionist Theory just described provide strong support for the central role played by causal relations in the construction of a coherent mental representation of narrative texts (Black & Bower, 1980; Omanson, 1982; Trabasso et al., 1984; van den Broek & Lorch, 1993). For instance, the explanation assumption argues that successful text comprehension requires the reader to detect the relationships between the different parts of the text, and between the text and the reader's world knowledge. Two events causally related in the world should be causally related in the representation, so a text is perceived and represented in memory as a coherent structure. The construction of this coherence is thought to result from the inferential processes that take place during text reading (Fletcher & Bloom, 1988; McKoon & Ratcliff, 1992; Trabasso & van den Broek, 1985; van den Broek, 1990a,b; van den Broek, Risden, & Husebye-Hartmann, 1995).

Story representations match the reader's naive theories about a possible world, and two types of reader knowledge have been described and investigated: linguistic knowledge (van Dijk, 1972) and knowledge of the domain represented in the text. These two types of knowledge have the same schematic structure. Linguistic knowledge not only affords a conceptual frame-work that allows readers to go beyond syntax, defining supraphrastic units such as episodes, stories, and their combinatory rules, but also supplies information about the semantic aspects of the text, including the micro- and macrostructures (see chapter 1). Nezworsky, Stein, and Trabasso (1982) studied the recall of story components defined in the story grammar (see Stein & Glenn, 1979) by controlling their semantic content. They showed that goal-oriented information was always well recalled, regardless of its location in the story, indicating that coherence established by the goal seems to dominate that established by the story schema. Other studies based on a different theoretical framework (Black & Bern, 1981; Bower, Black & Turner, 1979; Keenan, Baillet, & Brown, 1984; Miller & Kintsch, 1981) showed that cognitive invariants must be studied not only in the text, but also in the world knowledge evoked by the text.

In story comprehension, domain knowledge can be described in terms of (a) causal schemas, which include the concept of causality and the naive theories about the physical and social worlds possessed by nonexpert readers; (b) scripts, which are stereotyped representations of actions or familiar event sequences; and (c) plans that use intentional relations to organize sequences of actions as a hierarchical structure of goals. For instance, the predictable parts of a text are shown to be read faster than unpredictable parts (Miller & Kintsch, 1981), due to the reader's use of causal knowledge including scripts and plans.

It has been widely acknowledged that readers use their naive theories about causality to understand a text, that is, to construct a coherent representation of what is described therein. The effects of causal knowledge have been investigated across the different phases of text processing. The role of causal knowledge has been found to vary independently of the reader's linguistic representations during the detection of relations, the incorporation of text information into the reader's prior knowledge and/or world knowledge, and information retrieval from memory representations. Data on reading times has shown, first, that causally related events are read faster than other types of related events (temporal, and/or argument overlap; see Haberlandt & Bingham, 1978), and second, that reading time increases with the number of inferential steps required to causally connect two sentences (Bower et al., 1979; Keenan, Baillet, & Brown, 1984). Other experiments using free and cued recall tasks (Black & Bern, 1981) have shown that two sentences related causally are recalled better than ones related temporally or referentially (i.e., argument overlap). Moreover, two causally related sentences tend to be recalled as a whole. Black and Bern (1981) also showed that readers encode the causal relations in their text memory representation: A higher proportion of recall was obtained when a cued event was causally related to the event to be recalled. In addition, Omanson (1982) and Black and Bower (1980) provided evidence of readers' use of their causal knowledge to assign importance to semantic information and to introduce coherence into their representation. In particular, they showed that an event that belonged to the causal path relating the beginning of a text to its end was rated as more important than any other textual event or state. Finally, a goal-oriented action was found to be recalled better than a subgoal-oriented action.

This set of results emphasizes the idea that meaning reaches its full coherence via interpropositional relations. Causal relations from the physical and social worlds, including goals, plans, and human protagonists' intentions, are the most studied because a text's semantic interpretation appears to be determined by the explanatory activity: Readers construct a representation to explain a possible world, establishing relations of causality between the facts of that world. Because causal knowledge allows readers to establish these relations, it plays a crucial role in text processing.

5.2. THE CAUSAL NETWORK MODEL AS REPRESENTATIVE OF READERS' NAIVE THEORIES OF CAUSALITY

The Linear Causal-Chain Model and the Causal Network Model are the two models proposed to describe causal reasoning (see Black & Bower, 1980; Bloom et al., 1990; Fletcher & Bloom, 1988; Trabasso & Sperry, 1985; Trabasso et al., 1984; van den Broek & Lorch, 1993; van den Broek et al., 1990; van Dijk & Kintsch, 1983), but several authors have demonstrated the greater psychological relevance of the network representation (McKoon & Ratcliff, 1986; Trabasso & van den Broek, 1985; van den Broek & Lorch, 1993). Trabasso and van den Broek (1985) assume that as the first sentences of a story are being read, readers construct a possible world using the protagonist's characteristics and the story location and time, all elements that are organized to form the story setting. This possible world sets the circumstances by which subsequent events will be interpreted. It will be modified as, and whenever, the causal changes appear. To establish the causal field and isolate the cause from the effect, readers use both their naive theories of causality in the world and their abstract causality schemas. If these are lacking, they use the closeness of the events in time and space as a basis for establishing a relation of causality. The memory representation that results from this is organized as a network: Event representations form the nodes and the causal relations, the links. These authors assume a network-like representation of a causal structure rather than a linear order, because "Causes are often disjunctions or conjunctions of sufficient conditions rather than simple causes" (Trabasso et al., 1984, p. 84). Accordingly, the causal chain goes through the network, connecting the most important story events (i.e., events located on the critical path that defines the transition between the initial and final states). This chain starts with the statements in the introduction that establish the circumstances by which the subsequent events will be interpreted. It ends with the consequences that are implied by the achievement of the superordinate goal, the latter usually being inferred during story processing. The authors not only assume that the recall probability of an event is a function of whether or not that event is in the causal chain (Black & Bower, 1980; Omanson, 1982), but that it also depends on the number of causal relations it has to other events (Graesser & Clark, 1985; O'Brien & Myers, 1987; Trabasso & van den Broek, 1985). Therefore, although the causal-chain and network models include causal connections between adjacent units, the Causal Network Theory involves causal connections between two nonadjacent units, and therefore accounts for the multiple consequences an event might have along with other events.

van den Broek and Lorch (1993) attempted to find out if the mental representation of a text was better described as a network of multiple relations than as a linear chain. Their main goal was to determine whether individual relations were incorporated into the memory representation of a text in a direct way (McKoon & Ratcliff, 1986). In their studies, subjects read a series of experimental stories and were then tested on their memory of story events. A recognition priming procedure aimed at implicitly testing the readers' memory representations was used. The subjects' task was to read a prime statement (general or related) and then to determine whether a target statement (true or false) appeared in a story previously read. The true target statements paraphrased either an action or an outcome of the story. The prime statements were related either to the general topics of the story from which the targets were selected (general prime), or to the topics of the target's causal antecedent (related prime). Related primes included adjacent actions and adjacent and nonadjacent goal statements. Finally, goal statements were separated from the true target by an intervening event for one of the true targets and by eleven intervening events for the remaining true targets.

Priming effects were measured by calculating response-latency differences on positive trials between general primes and the two types of related primes. The authors' main assumption was that the targets would be recognized faster when the textual representation included a causal relation between the prime and the target than when the prime and target were unrelated. In addition, the distinction between the linear-chain and the causal network models was investigated by determining if causally related events, although nonadjacent in the text, were represented as related. In line with the network model, such relations will be included in the representation if they are required for an appropriate explanation of the target event. By contrast, and in line with the linear chain model, these relations should not be incorporated into the representation because the target is only related to the previous text via an adjacent relation.

The results indicated that goals primed the actions and the issues to which they were causally related but nonadjacent in the surface text structure. This finding is consistent with the causal network model but not with the linear model. Therefore, causally related events are directly connected in mental text representations even when they are far apart in the surface text structure.

van den Broek and Lorch (1993) carried out another study to find supporting evidence for a Causal Network Model and a Mediational Linear Chain Model, based on the assumption that goals prime nonadjacent targets via mediation by intervening events. They tested the priming of a final action by a nonadjacent goal and by action primes. In both conditions (i.e., goal and action primes), prime and target events were separated by the same eight actions in the surface text structure. Two text versions were created, a long text version in which the action primes corresponded to the first story action, and a short text version in which the first action was removed from the text. This caused the targets to be related to the goal primes by the same number of events as when they were related to the action primes. Table 5.1 presents an example of a story used in this study (long-text version).

According to the Linear Chain Model, because the two primes (i.e., action and goal) were connected to the targets by an identical chain of causally related events, they should result in identical priming effects. In line with the Network Model, however, whereas the goal prime was directly related to the target, the action prime was indirectly related to it via the eight intervening actions. So, this model would predict reliable priming by the goal, but little or no priming by the action. Also, a control comparison was made to see if the goal and action primes had similar effects when associated to a target action that was directly related and adjacent in the surface text structure.

The main results indicated that goal statements primed adjacent and nonadjacent targets in a similar way. However, a differential effect occurred for the action primes. Action statements paired with adjacent targets led to faster reaction times than action statements paired with nonadjacent targets. In addition, an intriguing result was the lack of a reliable reaction-time difference between action and goal primes paired with adjacent targets. Because the mental representation of stories was assumed to resemble a network more than a linear-causal chain, the activation of a statement connected to several other statements presumably activated all connected events, and an inhibition effect occurred for goal primes paired with adjacent events as compared to action primes that had only one connection in the text structure (i.e., the consequence). Quintana (1994)[1] carried out a study to contrast the assumption of a direct connection (i.e., linear model)

---

[1] Marie-Pilar Quintana conducted this study in 1994, under my direction, in fulfillment of the requirements for a Master's Degree at the University of Lyon 2 (France).

TABLE 5.1

Example of a Long Version Story
(Taken From van den Broek & Lorch, Experiment 3, 1993)

Setting (S). There once was a boy named Bob.

Initiating event (IE). One day, Bob saw his friend's new 10-speed bike.

Goal (G). Bob wanted to get a 10-speed bike.

Action (A1). He looked through the yellow pages.

Action (A2). He called several stores.

Action (A3). He asked them about the prices for bikes.

Action (A4). He found out what store had the lowest prices on bikes.

Action (A5). He went to the bike store.

Action (A6). He asked the salesperson about several models.

Action (A7). The salesperson recommended a touring bike.

Action (A8). Bob looked at the selection of touring bikes.

Action (A9). He located some that were his size.

Action (A10). He found a bike that was metallic blue.

Outcome (O). Bob bought the beautiful bike.

---

to that of a chain of connected events as mediations (i.e., network model), and to directly test the inhibition effect. A recognition priming procedure was used, and the experimental material, although in French, followed the same rules as in van den Broek and Lorch's (1983) study. It was assumed that causally related events would be directly connected to the mental representation of stories even when they were distant in the surface text structure (see Trabasso & van den Broek, 1985; van den Broek & Lorch, 1993). Because the reader's representation resembles a network, a priming effect was expected to occur with goal primes but not with action primes. Goal primes were directly connected to nonadjacent targets, whereas action primes were connected to targets via story actions. In addition, because action primes only had one connection to other events compared to goal primes which had several, an inhibition effect was predicted based on the assumption that readers attempt to deactivate all inappropriate statements activated during the reading of the prime.

A set of 24 stories was constructed, in two versions of 12 stories each: a long version and a short version. Each long-version story consisted of fourteen sentences with the following structure: a setting, an initiating event, a goal, 10 actions, and an outcome sentence, that is, the attained protagonist's goal (see Table 5.2 for an example of a story). The short-version stories only differed from the long-version ones by the number of intermediate actions, which was reduced to nine in the short versions by removing the first story action (i.e., the fourth sentence in the long version story). Both story versions (long and short) could be described as a linear-causal chain or as a causal network, and there were no coherence breaks between adjacent units. For each story, two pairs of target statements were generated. A pair of true targets (adjacent and nonadjacent) that corresponded to paraphrases of the second and tenth actions (for long versions) and of the first and ninth actions (for short versions), and a pair of false targets (adjacent and nonadjacent). These statements were plausible events but were unrelated to the text sentences. For each target, three types of primes were proposed: a general prime used for both versions,

TABLE 5.2

Sample of the Experimental Material: A Long-Story Version
and Its Related Primes and Targets (From Quintana, 1994)

Setting. Xavier liked to camp in the heart of the calm forest.

Initiating event. During a bad stormy night, his tent was torn.

Goal. He decided to look for a shelter to spend a dry night.

Action 1. So, he went to find a possible house.

Action 2. He didn't see anything or anyone in that part of the forest.

Action 3. He came back somewhere near the location of his campsite.

Action 4. He decided to build a shelter of his own.

Action 5. He searched in his bag for his perfect-camper handbook.

Action 6. He read only the chapter he was interested in.

Action 7. He gathered four strong pieces of wood.

Action 8. He sharpened the pieces of wood so as to make stakes.

Action 9. He drove the stakes into the ground to form a square.

Action 10. He attached the rest of his tent cloth to them.

Outcome. This gave him a shelter for the rest of the night.

Recognition Priming Task: General, Action, and Goal Primes

General primes: Remember the story about Xavier. (Paraphrase of the setting, sentence 1).

Action primes (for the long-text version): So, he planned to find a house to stay in (paraphrase of action 1, sentence 4).

Goal primes (for the short-text version): He wanted to find a dry place to sleep (paraphrase of the goal, sentence 3).

Adjacent True and False Targets:

Sentence 5. Action 2: He didn't see anything or anyone in that part of the forest.

True: Nobody or nothing was alive in the forest.

False: He didn't see anything or anyone in that part of the reserve.

Non-Adjacent True and False Targets:

Sentence 13. Action 10: He attached the rest of his tent cloth to them.

True: He put pieces of his tent cloth to them.

False: He hung the rest of his sleeping bag on it.

---

that is, a paraphrase of the first story sentence, and two related primes, an action prime and a goal prime. The action and goal primes were paraphrases of the fourth sentence (i.e., the first action for long versions) and of the third sentence, (i.e., the goal for short versions). Action primes were paired with targets for long-version stories, whereas goal primes were paired with targets for short-version stories, which created an equal distance between action primes and nonadjacent targets for the long versions, and between goal primes and nonadjacent targets for the short versions.

General primes were paired with true and false adjacent and nonadjacent targets. Action primes were associated to true and false adjacent targets, and goal primes were associated to true and false nonadjacent targets. Table 5.2 presents a sample of the experimental material used (including a long-story version and its corresponding prime statements and target statements).

Subjects were tested individually in a soundproof room and were randomly assigned to one of two reading conditions: read six long-version stories followed by six short-version stories, or six short-versions followed by six long-versions. The order of the stories for each version was counterbalanced across subjects. After reading the first six stories, the participants had to perform a priming recognition task (see van den Broek & Lorch, 1993). They were presented with pairs of sentences displayed on the screen, one sentence after the other. For each pair, they had to read the first sentence (the prime statement), which automatically disappeared after being displayed for 3,700 milliseconds, followed by the second sentence (the target statement). The subjects had to respond as fast and as accurately as possible by answering YES or NO as to whether the second sentence referred to a sentence read previously in one of the six stories. For the long-version stories, general and action primes were paired with adjacent and nonadjacent targets. For the short-version stories, general and goal primes were paired with adjacent and nonadjacent targets.

Several predictions were made based on van den Broek and Lorch's (Experiment 3, 1993) results. First, a reliable priming effect for targets preceded by related primes (action and/or goal) was expected, but no effect for targets preceded by general primes. Second, assuming that the story's mental representation included direct connections between nonadjacent units in the text surface structure, no difference in reaction times between adjacent and nonadjacent units preceded by goal primes was expected, whereas a reaction-time difference between adjacent and nonadjacent units preceded by action primes was predicted. Finally, faster reaction times for adjacent targets preceded by action primes than for ones preceded by goal primes were expected. Because in these stories, the goals were directly connected to several actions whereas the action prime event was only connected to its consequence, the action prime should only activate its consequence, and faster reaction times for action primes than for goal primes were expected. By contrast, processing a goal prime was assumed to activate all connections related to that goal, and subjects should tend to deactivate inappropriate pieces of information in order to answer. Because this process required additional processing time, longer reaction times for goal primes than for action primes were predicted.

The main results showed a prime effect, $F(2,40) = 30.05$, $p < .001$. As predicted, reaction times to targets preceded by general primes ($M = 5170$ ms.) were significantly longer, $F(1,40) = 59.96$, $p < .01$, than those preceded by related primes ($M = 3748$ ms and $M = 3823$ ms, for action and goal primes, respectively). Causal relations were thus encoded in the readers' mental representations of the stories. A main target effect also occurred, $F(1,20) = 11.63$, $p < .01$: Reaction times to adjacent targets ($M = 4001$ ms) were faster than reaction times to nonadjacent targets ($M = 4493$ ms). Therefore, the relations between primes and nonadjacent targets seem to be less direct than the relations between primes and adjacent targets. This effect was assumed to be due to mediations in the linear causal chain for nonadjacent pairs. The data also indicated a significant primes-by-targets interaction, $F(2,40) = 4.75$, $p < .02$. As shown in Figure 5.1, reaction times differed significantly between adjacent and nonadjacent targets for action versus goal primes: $F(1,40) = 8.32$, $p < .01$. The reaction time difference between adjacent and nonadjacent targets was greater for action primes ($d = 1171$ ms) than for the other two types of primes ($d = 248$ ms and $d = 56$ ms, for general and goal primes, respectively).

Thus, it seems that goal statements primed adjacent and nonadjacent targets in the same way. This effect was predicted by the Causal Network Model, which claims that direct causal connections between two units are possible in mental representations, even when they are far apart in the surface structure of the story. Action statements primed adjacent and nonadjacent targets, but faster reaction times were observed for adjacent than for nonadjacent ones. It is likely that no direct link between action statements and nonadjacent targets exists, and the difference in the reaction times of adjacent and nonadjacent targets is presumably due to the time taken by subjects to explore the mediations in the causal chain. The time required to recognize an event could thus be a function of its distance from a prime. The data also revealed a reaction-time difference for adjacent targets between action and goal primes. As expected, reaction times for action primes paired with adjacent targets ($M = 3163.45$ ms) were faster than those for goal primes ($M = 3795.33$ ms), indicating that recognition was slowed down by the amount of information activated during prime presentation and was faster when the participants did not have to select any information and only had to base their judgment on one statement. The subjects presumably activated all information related to goal primes during

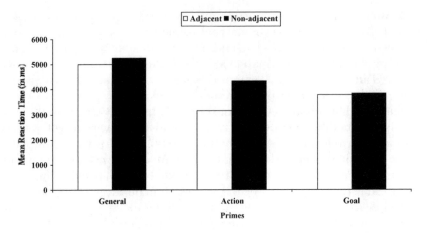

FIGURE 5.1.   Mean reaction time as a function of the three types of primes and
the two types of targets (from Quintana, 1994).

prime presentation, and in order to recognize target statements, they had
to deactivate inappropriate information. Whereas goal primes had several
connections to story events, an action prime had only one connection: its
consequence (corresponding to adjacent targets). This finding extended
what was previously obtained in van den Broek and Lorch's (1993) study.

Thus, it appears that processing a story event facilitates the recognition
of its causally related events, and causal relations seem to be integrated into
the reader's mental representation. This was shown to be true for closely related events in the story's surface structure but also for distant, causally related events. The data collected in this study also provide evidence of the
relevance of network models over linear models for representing causal
knowledge that readers might have. The main prime effect (general vs. related) suggests that related primes facilitate information retrieval from
memory. Reaction times were faster for targets paired with related primes
because the relationship between the related primes and the targets was
stronger. The reliable prime-by-target interaction was also consistent with
network models. Indeed, goals were perceived as directly connected to the
different subsequent events, resulting in the lack of a difference in the priming effect between adjacent and nonadjacent targets. The present experimental material consisted of the same number of pairs of statements for
adjacent and nonadjacent targets paired with goal (short versions) and action (long versions) primes. No difference in reaction times between adjacent and nonadjacent targets paired with goal primes occurred, whereas a
difference in reaction times for targets paired with action primes was observed. These findings show that direct causal connections are possible between nonadjacent units in a text's surface structure, but mediations are

necessary to access information that is not next to the prime and not directly connected to it in the causal text structure. The farther away from the primary cause (in a causal chain) a consequence is, the longer it takes to access that consequence. This is consistent with the idea that a causal chain is included in causal-network representations (Trabasso & van den Broek, 1985; Trabasso & Sperry, 1985; van den Broek, 1990a,b; van den Broek, Trabasso, & Thurlow, 1990, van den Broek & Lorch, 1993). Finally, the lack of a significant difference between adjacent and nonadjacent targets paired with general primes confirmed the prediction that all story events make sense relative to the topic described in the "setting" category (Kintsch & van Dijk, 1978; Trabasso & van den Broek, 1985; van Dijk & Kintsch, 1983). The first sentence that introduces the reader into the story world, exposing the protagonist, the location, and the time, "enables" the processing of the text (see Trabasso & van den Broek, 1985; Trabasso et al., 1989; Shapiro, van den Broek, & Fletcher, 1995).

In sum, a text's memory representation is better characterized as a causal network than as a linear chain (see van den Broek & Lorch, 1993). Events in a narrative are often the result of a combination of causal antecedents rather than of only one cause, and they frequently have multiple consequences. Readers' representations include those multiple connections, adjacent as well as nonadjacent in the surface structure of the text (Trabasso et al., 1984; Trabasso et al., 1989; van den Broek & Gustafson, 1999). The Causal Network Theory has the advantage of enabling those multiple connections.

Another advantage of the Causal Network Theory over the Linear Chain Model is that the former provides a set of formal criteria for identifying the causal relations in a text and for combining events and their interrelationships into a network-like textual representation (Mackie, 1980; van den Broek, 1990a,b; Trabasso et al., 1984; Trabasso et al., 1989). Two properties are required, temporal priority (a cause never occurs after its consequence), and operativity (a cause must be active when its consequence appears), and two properties determine causal strength, necessity, and sufficiency. Necessity reflects the fact that if a cause does not happen, its consequence will not take place given the text circumstances (*If the china vase did not fall, would it have broken into thousands of pieces?*). This property is used to identify a relation between a given event and the preceding events, and has been tested using the counterfactual test: Event A causes event B if it is true that if A does not occur in the text circumstances, then B will not occur. Sufficiency reflects the fact that if a cause appears, the consequence will probably appear, given the text circumstances (*The fall of the china vase caused it to break*). A cause is sufficient for the occurrence of the consequence if it is true that if A appears in the general text circumstances, and if the world proceeds from there, B will appear. This property concerns an identified relation between an event and succeeding events. Four types of causal relations have been identified in the literature (Trabasso & Sperry, 1985; Trabasso & van den Broek, 1985; Trabasso et al., 1989; van den Broek, 1994): Physical causality (Phy), which connects events describing changes in physical states of objects and persons (*The china vase fell off the coffee table. It broke into a thousand pieces*); motivation (M), which describes the relationship between a goal and its consequences (*The little boy wanted to see his grandmother. He bought a train ticket to visit her*); psychological causation (Psy), which refers to causal relations that are internal states such as emotions, plans, and thoughts (*Paul liked to do outdoor activities. He decided to play football with some friends*); and finally, enablement (E), which describes the link between an event and a precondition that is necessary but weak in its sufficiency for the consequence (*John liked red bicycles. He went to the store to buy one*). These four relations play different roles in the construction of text coherence because they differ in their connection strength, that is, whether or not they satisfy the causal criteria of necessity and sufficiency.

Trabasso and van den Broek (1985) formalized causal text information in terms of a network of interrelated links (i.e., Causal Network Models) and developed a general Recursive Transition Network Model (RTN Model; van den Broek, 1990b), which incorporates a recursive transition network for story representation (Trabasso & van den Broek, 1985) and a taxonomy for labeling causal relations (Warren, Nicolas, & Trabasso, 1979). This model also uses the properties of temporal priority, operativity, necessity, and sufficiency in the circumstances, in order to identify relationships between event pairs in a text. Figure 5.2 presents a diagram of the RTN model (see Trabasso et al., 1989).

In this model, the conceptual category of a proposition (i.e., letter nodes), as well as possible relations between two propositions, are determined. Regarding letter nodes, the setting (S) introduces the protagonists in space and time, and provides the general conditions that enable the occurrence of states and actions in the episodes. It can also "enable" other settings, or be temporally coexistent or successive with them. Goals (G) are states, activities, or objects (desired or not). If a goal is desired, it is assumed that the protagonist wants to attain or to keep a certain state, activity, or object. If it is not desired, the protagonist is assumed to leave or avoid a certain state, activity, or object. Goals motivate attempts and other subordinate goals. Attempts (A) are actions carried out by the protagonist in order to reach a goal. Attempts (physically) enable other attempts; they enable or physically cause outcomes. The outcome (O) has a special status because it determines the principal causal chain of states and actions in narratives. It is used to refer to those events that represent consequences and also changes in the states. Outcomes cause reactions, physically enable actions and physically cause or enable other outcomes. Reactions (R) are typically internal states, changes of state, or internal reactions such as emotions or cognitions.

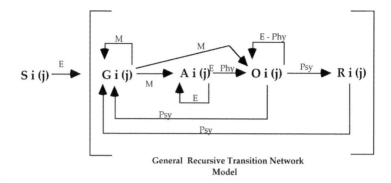

General Recursive Transition Network
Model

FIGURE 5.2. Diagram of the Recursive Transition Network model (from Trabasso et al., 1989). [Legend: I and j indicate the degree I of the category (degree of the episode in which it appears) for a proposition of level j in the temporal proposition sequences (level of the proposition in the narrative)].

A reaction is psychologically caused by outcomes or by other internal states or reactions. When outcomes follow attempts, they indicate goal success or failure. If the goal is reached, the episode ends. If the goal is not reached, it can be reinstated, abandoned, and/or replaced by another goal. In this sense, outcomes indicate the success or the failure of the goal, and can psychologically cause goals. Goals and outcomes are viewed as the most important categories because they anchor the episode and are the causes and consequences of the story content. Relations between pairs of conceptual categories are also represented in this model, by the four causal relations previously defined, namely, *physical causality, motivation, psychological causation*, and *enablement*, respectively labeled Phy, M, Psy, and E.

The psychological relevance of different properties of causal relations was first tested by Trabasso et al. (1989) and then extended by Quintana[2] (1996; Tapiero, van den Broek, & Quintana, 2002). In Trabasso et al.'s study, participants read several stories constructed as stipulated in the RTN model (see Trabasso & van den Broek, 1985; Trabasso et al., 1989), and then rated pairs of story events according to either a criterion of necessity or a criterion of causality. Pairs of events were selected from each of the four types of causal relations. The main results showed that the various types of causal relations differed in connection strength. Physical causality tended to be highly connected, followed by motivation and psychological causation, and then enablement, the last relation being considered necessary but not causal by the participants. Necessity seems to be a broader criterion

---

[2] Marie-Pilar Quintana conducted this study in 1996, under my direction, in fulfillment of the requirements for the first year of her PhD at the University of Lyon 2 (France).

than causality per se: Causal relations have to satisfy both necessity and sufficiency. To extend Trabasso et al.'s (1989) findings and to further examine the effect of distance on the reader's mental representation, Quintana (1996; Tapiero et al., 2002) looked into whether the distance between two statements in a text's surface structure can affect the perception of possible causal relations, depending on their importance to goal success or failure (van den Broek & Lorch, 1993). Readers evaluated the strength of the relationship between pairs of sentences taken from narratives generated in accordance to the Recursive Transition Network Model (see Trabasso & van den Broek, 1985). The pairs extracted were either adjacent or nonadjacent in the surface text structure, and varied in necessity and sufficiency as well as in the type of causal relation. Ratings were made either without reading the narratives, after a single reading of the narratives, or after two readings. The results indicated an effect of distance on the way readers perceived the four types of causal relations (Phy, Psy, M, and E). As predicted, the pattern of rated strengths for adjacent pairs followed the causal strength order found by Trabasso et al. (1989), and thus replicated and reinforced what was previously obtained (i.e., the causal strengths of the various types of relations in the text's surface structure). Physical causality was judged to be the strongest relation, followed by motivation, psychological causation, and finally enablement. For nonadjacent pairs, however, the pattern of strengths for the types of relations was different. As distance increased, some relations lost strength whereas others gained importance and were foregrounded in the reader's representation. Here, psychological causation and motivation were judged to be strongly connected, followed by enablement, and finally, physical causality. Thus, relations that involved a goal or internal state (as a cause in the case of motivation, as a consequence in the case of psychological causation) were considered strongly connected even when the elements of the relation were separated in the text structure. This suggests that readers tried to connect all of the sentences to the goal, paying special attention to information that could indicate goal success or failure. This is consistent with the network theory and with the importance attributed by readers to the thematic and goal structure of narratives (see van den Broek, Bauer, & Bourg, 1997). In contrast, physical causal relations less related to the text theme were strongly affected by distance. Whereas these relations had the strongest causal connections when adjacent to their consequences (because the cause was still operative), they became very weak when their operativity declined with distance. This reflects the major role of operativity as a property of causal relations: If a cause is still active when the consequence occurs, the perceived strength of the relation is great. For the nonadjacent physical causal relations, the fact that distance separated the cause from its consequence reduced operativity, and this lowered the perceived strength of the relation.

This study also provided evidence in support of the network theory because a clear distinction was made between the necessity and sufficiency criteria (Mackie, 1980; Trabasso et al., 1989). Perceived necessity tended to be more sensitive to story context than did perceived sufficiency. Whereas there was almost no difference between the two criteria in either reading condition, sufficiency led to higher ratings than did necessity in the no-reading condition. Therefore, the fact of whether event A is necessary for event B depends on context, but the fact of whether A is sufficient for B depends on the causal strength of the relationship between A and B. Thus, reading appeared to facilitate the identification of the necessary circumstances, but necessity was shown to be a broader criterion than sufficiency because it includes other criteria than causality, such as temporality as determined by text circumstances (see Trabasso et al., 1989).

Finally, the comparison of single and double reading provided insight into how readers represent a text and how their representation can change through several readings. First, reading the text helped participants perceive the causal strength of the four types of relations, but only when the pairs were adjacent in the text's surface structure. For nonadjacent pairs, however, reading had no effect on the perceived strength of physical causality and enablement, whereas for goals and internal states, rating strengths were higher in the reading conditions than in the no-reading condition. The second reading underlined the importance of goals and internal states in a story's mental representation, evidenced by higher ratings in the double reading condition for motivation and psychological causation. However, the second reading increased the perceived connection strengths for adjacent pairs only. It was predicted that with a second reading, distant relations would come to be seen as more important. Apparently, on the second reading, readers had already established the circumstances with respect to which distant relations could be detected. This is consistent with the fact that when readers processed the text the first time, setting statements led to longer reading times than other statements did, but in the second reading, this was no longer the case. One possible interpretation is that increased recognition of adjacent relations may put distant relations into the background or even decrease the perceived importance of a particular distant relation. However and once again, the importance of goals and internal states in the network-like memory representation was confirmed, and although readers processed the different stories' categories (including goals) at the same rate, the importance of goal's causal structure increased with the second reading.

Thus, these findings confirm and extend our knowledge of the mental representation of a text in network format. Distance, relation type, and the necessity/sufficiency criteria affected the perceived relation strengths, and those strengths were readjusted when a second reading took place. The relationships between goals were particularly important for the reader, and they became more so after a rereading. Thus, a text representation is more complicated than a simple network would suggest: The connections in a network differ in strengths (see Mackie, 1980; van den Broek, 1990a,b), and the "landscape" of perceived connection strengths changes as readers reread the text. These findings reinforce the idea that the construction of a coherent memory representation is a dynamic activity. Moreover, the importance attributed to information by the reader fluctuates between the first and second readings. This is consistent with the landscape view of reading, which focuses on comprehension processes, memory representation, and most importantly, on the relationship between the two (see van den Broek, Young, Tzeng, & Lunderholm, 1999).

The Causal Network Model relies on the assumption that comprehension is a problem-solving activity in which readers have to detect causal relations (i.e., adjacent and nonadjacent) between actions and events from the beginning to the end of a text. In this view, the "search for coherence" is a strategic process primarily guided by the reader's prior knowledge and expectations. Nonetheless, although this theoretical orientation has received a great deal of support in the literature, not all researchers embrace this position. Some define comprehension (i.e., the establishment of coherence) as a more passive, automatic, and irrepressible process. In line with the coherence assumption, however, the proponents of the latter approach see the construction of the reader's mental representation as being guided by both local and global coherence, even when local coherence is successful. Let us now turn to some empirical arguments that defend this view of comprehension.

Chapter 6

The Reader's Mental Representation: Search for Coherence or Passive Resonance?

Unlike a knowledge-based view of coherence, and in particular the explanatory theory assumed by global models, several authors have argued that readers access backgrounded information through a passive resonance process. Because it is assumed that a fast and automatic checking of the fit of new input to existing representations occurs, both in relation to background knowledge and to the representation of prior text, local and global connections are possible even when local connections are successful (Albrecht & O'Brien, 1993; Huitema et al., 1993; O'Brien & Albrecht, 1992). In this sense, it counters one of the main assumptions brought to the fore by the Minimalist Theory (McKoon & Ratcliff, 1992). Huitema et al. (1993) looked at whether readers access global information even when local information is successful for establishing coherence. In Huitema et al.'s (1993) study, subjects had to read stories that were similar in content to those in McKoon and Ratcliff's (1992) experiments. First, a protagonist's goal was mentioned: (*Dick ... wanted to go to a place where he could swim and sunbathe.*) Then some intermediate sentences were inserted: (*... he went to his local travel agent.*) Finally the story ended with a description of an action that was compatible (*... and asked for a plane ticket to Florida*) or incompatible (*... and asked for a plane ticket to Alaska*) with the initially stated goal. The authors observed longer reading times when the sentence described an incompatible action than a compatible action. This increase in reading time was at-

137

tributed to a fast-acting process (i.e., resonance) that allows readers to reinstate initial goal-related information. These data also support the Constructionist Theory, as well as other theories of comprehension that claim that readers maintain not only local but also global coherence (Graesser et al., 1994; Kintsch, 1998; van Dijk & Kintsch, 1983).

Global coherence thus implies that incoming pieces of information are related to other information in the text that may not be currently active in short-term memory. The resonance process also relies on this coherence assumption (Albrecht & Myers, 1995, 1998; Klin & Myers, 1993; Myers & O'Brien, 1998; Rizzella & O'Brien, 1996). As previously stated (see chapter 4), several textual and reader-related variables may affect this resonance process, which is responsible for the establishment of global coherence: overlap of the features of the target proposition and the previous traces to which it may be related (Albrecht & Myers, 1995; Huitema et al., 1993; Klin & Myers, 1993; Rizzella & O'Brien, 1996), distance in the surface structure between the target and previous related traces (Albrecht & Myers, 1995; O'Brien et al., 1990; Rizzella & O'Brien, 1996), and trace elaborateness (O'Brien et al., 1990).

Albrecht and Myers (1995) examined whether the resonance process contributed to a change in the availability of previously relevant information. In particular, they tried to find out whether a reference to a previously known episode could reactivate information that was relevant to the goal of the previously known episode (Experiments 2 and 3). In their experiments, each passage described a character motivated by a specific goal. For example, one of the passages dealt with Mary, who had to make an airline reservation before midnight. Two goal conditions were constructed, an unsatisfied-goal condition and a satisfied-goal condition. In the unsatisfied condition, Mary was interrupted before she could book a flight because she had to finish a project. In the satisfied condition, however, she was able to make the booking and then work on the project. After some filler sentences, the reactivation of previously relevant information was manipulated. In one condition, a statement after the filler sentences provided a contextual overlap with the goal of the episode: A direct reference was made to some of the aspects of the context in which the goal was originally introduced (e.g., a leather chair). This corresponded to the context-reinstatement condition. In another condition (the nonreinstatement condition), the statement did not provide any contextual overlap and did not make any references to the previous episode. This statement was immediately followed by two target sentences that described the character implied in actions that were inconsistent with the previously unsatisfied goal (going to bed without booking the flight, putting on pajamas). If participants access goal information and detect the inconsistency, reading times should be longer for target sentences in the unsatisfied-goal conditions than in the satisfied-goal conditions.

The results indicated that target sentences were read longer in the unsatisfied-goal condition, but only when the reinstatement sentence contained concepts that were also present in the context of the initial goal. This demonstrates that the contextual cue in the reinstatement sentence served to reactivate information in the goal episode. Albrecht and Myers (1995) explained this outcome by the fact that concepts and propositions derived from the context-reinstatement sentence, including the contextual sentence, were combined with the contents in working memory and a signal was sent to LTM. The elements of discourse representation that shared some features with the signals resonated in response and, in turn, caused the related propositions, including goal propositions, to be activated. Hence, these elements provided the participants with access to the goal information that allowed them to detect inconsistencies. By contrast, when the contextual cue was absent from the reinstatement sentence, there was no overlap with the goal episode and thus, no way in which the episode could be accessed.

In another study, Albrecht and Myers (1998) looked at whether the resonance process was influenced by the amount of elaboration of the contextual cue in memory and by the specificity of the context-reinstatement sentence. In three experiments, subjects had to read a series of stories, each one composed of five sections. Each passage included either an elaborated contextual cue (i.e., a noun plus adjective: "leather chair") or an unelaborated contextual cue (i.e., the noun alone). The contextual cues were always presented in the goal section and in the reinstatement sentence. Based on this design, three context conditions were constructed: an adjective–adjective condition that included an elaborated cue in the goal section as well as in the reinstatement sentence, and an adjective–noun condition that included an elaborated cue in the goal section but an unelaborated cue in the reinstatement sentence. Finally, a noun–noun condition was generated in which an unelaborated cue was used both in the goal section and in the reinstatement sentence. If the subjects access a proposition related to an unsatisfied goal when reading a target sentence, they should notice an inconsistency, and this should lead to an increase in reading time for the target sentence in the unsatisfied-goal conditions. The reading-time difference between the unsatisfied- and the satisfied-goal conditions was called the *inconsistency effect*. According to the authors, when the contextual goal was elaborated by including an adjective, a stronger memory trace ought to be encoded. The results indicated an inconsistency effect in the adjective–adjective condition. The reading times for the two target sentences were longer in the unsatisfied-goal condition than in the satisfied-goal condition. It follows that the reinstatement of a modifier reactivated information about a preceding episode in the text. The results of the noun–noun condition indicated the inconsistency effect for the second target sentence only. Thus, when a noun was used as a retrieval cue, it led to a decrease in the activation level or to a slower activation-building pace. Finally, in the adjective–noun condition, the inconsistency effect was three times greater for the first than for the second target sentence. This was interpreted as showing that the removal of the adjective from the context-reinstatement sentence reduced overlap between traces, thereby weakening resonance.

6.1. ESTABLISHING GLOBAL COHERENCE: SITUATION MODELS AS RETRIEVAL STRUCTURES

This discussion highlights the idea that coherence in text representations depends on the retrieval structures available in long-term memory. Textbases and situation models are those retrieval structures in discourse processing (Ericsson & Kintsch, 1995). But the textbase and situation-model levels have different relative degrees of importance in readers' text representations. Emphasis on one of the levels may depend on several factors and have several implications. Characteristics of the reader, including the amount of relevant world knowledge, may have an impact on the creation of a situation model. Likewise, there are texts characteristics that may facilitate or disrupt situation-model building (Johnson-Laird, 1983). Johnson-Laird (1983) argued that "models, like images, are highly specific" (p. 157), and "a propositional representation processes in a similar way determinate and indeterminate spatial relations, whereas situation models handle better determinate than indeterminate relations" (p. 158). Accordingly, the level of specificity and determinacy, or the extent to which a description in a text rules out states of affairs in the world, or alternatively is consistent with several of them, should influence the creation of situation models.

The relative importance of the textbase versus the situation model has implications on the ease with which coherence is established in a text representation, but situation models have been conceived of as more efficient retrieval structures than textbases in creating coherence in text representations. van Dijk and Kintsch (1983) already pointed out the importance of situation models in creating coherence: "A sequence of sentences can be said to be coherent if the sentences denote facts in some possible world that are related" (p. 150), and "A prerequisite for coherent text representation is the ability to construct a coherent situation model. Without that, memory for text is stored in disjoint bits and pieces ..." (p. 361). Finally, Johnson-Laird (1983) made a similar point: "A necessary and sufficient condition for a discourse to be coherent, as opposed to a random sequence of sentences, is that it is possible to construct a single mental model from it" (p. 370). Establishing coherence, that is, linking the representation of the currently read sentence to the memory of the read text, relies on two types of connections: textbase connections (i.e., local) and situation-model connections (i.e., global). Textbase connections are explicit connections between propositions (e.g., argument overlap), and also include the coherence relations classified by van Dijk and Kintsch (1983) and Kintsch (1998) under the headings "direct coherence" (Kintsch, 1998, p. 39) and "subordination" (Kintsch, 1998, p. 39). Direct coherence relations are explicitly marked by connectives; subordination corresponds to a meaningful unit that is a condition of another unit, indicated by a subordinate clause. These types of relations were considered by Kintsch and van Dijk (1978) in their initial model of text comprehension, and contribute to coherent discourse by creating connections between propositions in a textbase without a situation model having necessarily been built. For example, a reader may easily relate propositions resulting from two sentences through argument overlap, without having built a corresponding referential representation or situation model. On the other hand, two objects that are related in a real-world situation may be unrelated in the surface or textbase structure of the text describing that situation. The following text developed by Bransford and Johnson (1972) is a well-known example of this situation: "If the balloons popped, the sound would not be carried since everything would be too far away from the *correct floor*. A *closed window* would also prevent the sound from spreading …" *Correct floor* and *closed window* are presumably hardly related by readers who create a representation emphasizing the textbase, as most readers of this text would do, but these propositions are assumed to be related to the appropriate situation model. The model might involve a man serenading a woman from a tall building, where a loudspeaker is held at the appropriate height by means of some balloons, and where the *closed window* is located on in the *correct floor*. Another example of propositions that may be unconnected to the textbase but closely related to the situation model is that of coreferential noun phrases. "*The man standing by the window*" (see Johnson-Laird, 1983, p. 381), and another noun phrase that occurs in the same paragraph, "*The Portuguese with the Port wine*," may correspond to the same token in a situation model (i.e., they may have the same referent). But these two statements are not very related when one considers their meaning representation in the textbase. Spatial relations are also excellent examples of the difference between links in situation models and in textbases. Two objects may be close together or far apart in a reader's representation of a text, depending on the spatial situation model built. Such a configuration is clearly illustrated in Glenberg, Meyer, and Lindem's (1987) experiment. The authors provided readers with versions of a text including two different sentences: *After doing a few warm-up exercises, John put on his sweatshirt and began jogging*, or *After doing a few warm-up exercises, John took off his sweatshirt and began jogging*. After reading these sentences, both groups of subjects read *John jogged halfway around the lake* and were then asked if "sweatshirt" was a word that appeared in the story. The subjects who read that John put on his sweatshirt said "yes" faster than those who read that John took off his sweatshirt. The sweatshirt thus seemed to be differently linked to the representation of the sentence describing John halfway around the lake, even though the textbase representation of this last sentence should be the same in both cases. Therefore, there were different links between the information units corresponding to *John* (*halfway-around-the-lake*) and *sweatshirt* in the situation model and in the textbase. Thus, there are two alternative connection possibilities for propositions. A proposition may be connected to others at the textbase level, or two propositions may not have an explicit connection through textbase links but may be related to situation-model objects and these referents should be connected through situation model links. This occurs when two propositions share the same time or location, as *correct* (*floor*) and *closed* (*window*) in the prior example. This corresponds to *indirect coherence* in Kintsch's (1998) classification. Indirect coherence would also include other relations that are not always explicitly indicated in texts, such as antecedent-consequent, enablement, and implication relations (see Graesser & Clark, 1985). In short, coherence depends on relations between elements in the retrieval structures used by readers, and these relations in situation models may be different from those existing in textbases.

Situation model links should be better than textbase links at establishing coherence in text representations because situation models have some advantageous characteristics. First, although situation models have been occasionally represented as propositions (see chapter 2), as textbases have been (Graesser & Clark, 1985; Kintsch, 1998; Tapiero, 2000; Tapiero & Otero, 1999), they are conceived of as analogical representations, that is, as structural analogues of the world. The analogical nature of situation models implies that there is a parallelism between represented and representing relations. Consequently, relations in the real world should be more faithfully represented in the relations existing in situation models than in the relations existing in textbases. Second, spatial situation models are similar to images because they have an integrated character, that is, many elements of the represented situation are simultaneously available (Johnson-Laird, 1983). This means that there are more conceptual "hooks" to connect the representation of a sentence being read to previous text information when a situation model rather than a textbase is used as a retrieval structure.

Because research on global coherence has mainly focused on narrative comprehension (Albrecht & Myers, 1995, 1998; Klin & Myers, 1993; Myers & O'Brien, 1998; Rizzella & O'Brien, 1996; Suh & Trabasso, 1993; van den Broek & Lorch, 1993; Trabasso et al., 1989), Otero and I (Tapiero & Otero, 2002) attempted to determine the effect of situation models on the construction of global coherence in science-text representations. We did this by investigating detection of implication relations in these representations. Implication relations may exist between two objects or tokens in a situation model that correspond to two events or two states described in a text. Examples of implication relations are the ones created through syllogistic reasoning. The generalization *Dancers are sexy*, together with the fact that *X is a dancer*, imply that *X is sexy* (Graesser & Clark, 1985, p. 64). Similar relations can often be found in science-text representations. The generalization *Viscous drag is proportional to speed* and the fact that *The speed of particle P moving within a viscous fluid is increasing* imply that *Viscous drag on particle P is increasing*. In fact, according to the Nomological-Deductive Model, scientific explanation consists in showing that the explanandum is implicated by general laws, together with statements about particular facts. For example, the particular orbit traced by Uranus is explained by showing that it may be deduced from Newton's Law of Gravitation and facts such as the existence of the sun and other planets orbiting in the relative vicinity of Uranus. Readers who create a globally coherent representation may recognize an implication relation between two propositions that are far apart in the textbase structure. This can be achieved without explicit signaling of the implication relation. In fact, these signals are more often than not omitted in science texts. For example, one of the texts used in our study (see Table 6.1) contained the following information: *In the city of Hammerfest, located in Northern Norway, there are months when the sun never rises ... More electricity is needed to light up the streets*. Although no textbase connection exists between the meanings of these two sentences, a reader may relate one to the other through an implication relation: *Sun never rises* → (*No natural light*) → *More electricity is needed to light up the streets*.

Tapiero and Otero (2002) tested the claim that creating a situation-model representation of a text was a powerful way of establishing global coherence. This is because tokens corresponding to information in a text can be easily related within the situation model. In the cited example, a reader may easily relate the absence of sun in the sky to the need for more electricity to light up the streets when a situation model corresponding to a town at night with street lights on was constructed. The integrated nature that situation models share with images may provide simultaneous availability of one element of the situation (i.e., no sun in the sky) and of another element (i.e., increase in electricity consumption for street lights). In addition, a reader who builds a situation model should recognize this relation regardless of distances in the surface representation or textbase.

We conducted a study that compared predictions of a model based on the assumption that situation models play a critical role in constructing coherence in science texts (i.e., a referential model of global coherence) to those of a model based on textbase resonance (i.e., through trace overlap). Special texts were designed to have an inconsistent implication relation between target information and earlier related sentences (memory traces). For example, in the text discussed earlier (see Table 6.1), we replaced *There*

TABLE 6.1

Example of Versions of Experimental and Knowledge Texts
(From Tapiero & Otero, 2002)

Contradictory, Far, Indeterminate Version

Text 1: Variations in Energy Consumption.

1. The duration of days and nights is quite different at higher latitudes near the North Pole than at lower latitudes. 2. *In some places, there are months when the sun never rises.* 3. During these months, working activity is reduced, as are educational activities. 4. There is less consumption of energy for transportation during these months. 5. Several energy requirements also change during this period. 6. The consumption of energy during these months is different from the rest of the year. 7. *Less energy is needed to light up the streets.* 8. Heating relies on fossil fuels and depends less on electricity.

Non-contradictory, Near, Determinate Version

Text 2: Variations in Electricity Consumption

1. The duration of days and nights is quite different at higher latitudes near the North Pole, than at lower latitudes. 2. *In Hammerfest, located in the north of Norway, there are months when the sun never rises.* 3. The consumption of electricity during these months is different from the rest of the year. 4. *More electricity is needed to light up the streets.* 5. During these months, working hours are reduced as well as school hours. 6. There is less consumption of fuel for cars and public transportation during these months. 7. Several electricity requirements change also during this period. 8. Heating relies on fossil fuels and depends less on electricity.

Specific Knowledge Text 1 (prior to the reading of the experimental text): Environmental Conditions Are a Function of Latitude

There are geographical changes that depend on latitude. Regions at higher latitudes have a colder climate than regions nearer the equator. The reason is the different amount of radiation received from the sun. The position of the sun's orbit relative to the earth also explains the important differences in day length at northern latitudes. The sun never sets in places near the North Pole during the summer months of the northern hemisphere. The opposite is true during the winter, and there is a long period of night. This causes quite different patterns of behavior for people living there.

General Knowledge Text 2 (prior to the reading of the experimental text): Influence of Geographical Variables

Geographical variables have many effects on the social and economic characteristics of countries and cities. Climate, for example, depends on variables like latitude, proximity to the sea, or orographical characteristics. It has a large impact on the economy. Climate is an important factor in determining what type of agriculture that can be sustained in a country. Climate also affects energy consumption. Other characteristics of a country, like orography, strongly affect transportation. This influences trade, communications within the country, and relations with neighboring countries.

144

are months when the sun never rises ... More electricity is needed to light up the streets by *There are months when the sun never rises ... Less electricity is needed to light up the streets.* As these two sentences were separated by one or more intervening sentences (depending on the experimental condition), the detection of the inconsistency was expected to provide a measure of global coherence in the readers' representations.

In order to compare predictions of the resonance model with those based on the referential model, four variables were manipulated in the texts: (a) consistency of the implication relation, (b) distance in the surface structure between target information and previously related traces, (c) readers' knowledge of the topic discussed in the text, and (d) level of determinacy of textual information. It was predicted that Variable 2 would affect the resonance process, whereas Variables 3 and 4 would affect the capacity to build a situation model. The consistency of the implication relation was manipulated as previously explained. The distance between the target and previous related information was manipulated by introducing a different number of sentences between the two elements of the implication relation (see Table 6.1). In addition, subjects were given paragraphs with either specific knowledge about the implication relation or general knowledge, before actually reading the experimental texts. The difference in knowledge specificity should independently help the reader create an appropriate situation model. For example, the experimental text on variations in electricity/energy consumption (Texts 1 and 2, respectively in Table 6.1) was preceded by a knowledge text dealing with either the influence of latitude on environmental conditions (i.e., specific knowledge Text 1) or the influence of geographical variables on the social and economic characteristics of countries (i.e., general knowledge Text 2). The construction of a situation model by subjects who lacked the appropriate knowledge was expected to be facilitated in the first case more than the second. Finally, the experimental texts were made more or less determinate in order to differentially affect the creation of a situation model. As an example of a variation in the level of determinacy, the original first sentence—*In the city of Hammerfest, located in Northern Norway, there are months when the sun never rises*—was changed into a less determinate phrase: *In some places, there are months when the sun never rises.*

The four experimental science texts were eight sentences long. Each text included an implication relation, as discussed earlier, and was written in eight versions, depending on the manipulations of the consistency, distance, and determinacy variables. There were "inconsistent" versions (one of the elements of the implication relation was inconsistent with the other) versus "consistent" versions (the elements of the implication were consistent with each other). There were "near" versions (the sentences related by implication were in the second and fourth places) versus "far" versions (these sentences were in the second and seventh places). And there were "determinate" versions (specific terms were used in the text) versus "indeterminate" versions (general terms were used). In addition, each of the experimental texts was preceded by a knowledge text, seven sentences long, that provided readers with either specific or general prior knowledge about the domain of the experimental text (i.e., the reader's knowledge was the fourth variable). The presentation order of the experimental texts was counterbalanced between subjects, and three filler texts came between the experimental texts.

The texts were presented sentence by sentence, and reading times were recorded. An increase in target-sentence reading time (the second element in the implicational structure) was taken as evidence of detection of the inconsistency in the implication relation, and consequently, of the creation of global coherence in the text representation.

The results indicated no significant effects for distance or reader's knowledge. Determinacy almost reached the significance level, $F(1, 24) = 3.57$, $p < .07$: Readers tended to take more time to read target sentences when information was determinate ($M = 7.4$ s) than when it was indeterminate ($M = 6.6$ s). In addition, there was a main effect of consistency, $F(1, 24) = 24.11$, $p < .0001$). As expected, the subjects in the inconsistent condition had longer reading times ($M = 8.0$ s) than those in the control condition ($M = 5.9$ s). With respect to second order interactions, the resonance model would predict longer reading times in the near condition as compared to the far condition when the text was inconsistent because more readers should detect the inconsistency in the near condition where memory traces would resonate more easily. However, our analysis failed to show the significant distance-by-consistency interaction predicted by the resonance model. Finally, a determinacy-by-consistency interaction occurred in the direction predicted by the referential model, $F(1, 24) = 8.41$, $p < .01$. Subjects processed the target sentence longer in the inconsistent condition when information was determinate than when it was indeterminate, and no difference was found in the consistent condition (see Figure 6.1). However, and contrary to the prediction of the referential model, we did not find a reader's knowledge-by-consistency interaction.

In line with our argument concerning the role of situation models in establishing coherence, determinacy appeared to help readers detect inconsistencies in the implication relations, thereby showing that the creation of a situation model had an influence on global coherence. In the inconsistent version, reading times were significantly longer for subjects who read determinate information. In the consistent version, however, subjects took the same amount of time to process target sentences in the determinate and indeterminate conditions. Contrary to our prediction, though, no interaction was found between the reader's knowledge and consistency. Reading target

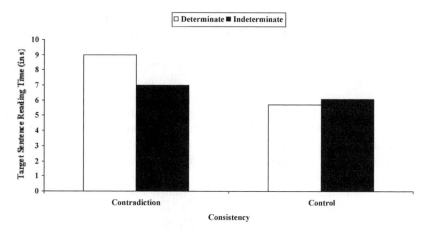

FIGURE 6.1. Target sentence reading time as a function of determinacy and consistency (from Tapiero & Otero, 2002).

sentences after having been provided with specific knowledge about the implication relation did not help the readers identify the inconsistency. A possible explanation for this may be that the specific knowledge paragraphs were ineffective in helping readers create a situation model. The knowledge that readers could obtain from these short paragraphs may have been insufficient to create a situation-model representation of the target texts. Also, we did not find any distance effect on the establishment of global coherence. This result contradicts predictions obtained from the resonance model but is consistent with our claim that situation-model links play an important role in creating coherence in science texts, independently of resonance processes at the textbase level. Overall, these findings show that global coherence in science texts can be established through situation-model links, and they confirm the idea that situation models are more efficient retrieval structures than textbases for creating global coherence. The construction of a situation model enabled readers to set up links among many pieces of information that were not explicitly stated in the text, regardless of textbase connections. These related elements of information in turn helped enrich the situation model. Thus, it is crucial to account for the knowledge readers called on when building their mental representations.

The next and final section of this book is fully devoted to exploring this point: the effect of knowledge on readers' mental representations. I highlight the contribution of several types of knowledge that readers are calling on when processing textual information, underlain by both local and global coherence establishment. In particular, I demonstrate the prevalence of global coherence over local coherence in the reader's elaboration of mental representation. To do so, I focus mainly on two crucial dimensions that readers are assumed to represent as they process text information: causality and emotion. First, I provide a description of the different types of causal inferences, whether necessary or not, for the comprehension process to occur. I then focus on one particular type of inferences: predictive or forward inferences. Contrary to the widely accepted assumption that predictive inferences are merely generated when the immediately preceding context strongly constrains them, I embrace the strong assumption that contextual and situational knowledge may largely affect the type of predictive inferences generated, sometimes even overriding constraints imposed by the local context. In the last part of the next section, I focus on emotion and how it can affect text comprehension. I provide an overview of the theoretical frameworks, as well as empirical findings about readers' representations of emotion. If emotional information is easily accessed by readers, it should serve as an appropriate retrieval structure to help readers correctly match the information currently being processed to previously processed units (from the preceding text or from prior knowledge). Finally, I conclude by discussing some new directions of research that might better our understanding of this dimension, alone and in relation to others.

Last, because theories of comprehension have recently incorporated memory processes in a more straightforward way (see Ericsson & Kintsch, 1995), and because principles of memory theories have been called on to investigate discourse comprehension, particularly the updating process (Myers & O'Brien, 1998; Sanford & Garrod, 1981; 1998), the opposition between automatic and strategic processes has led us to clearly separate the main principles assigned by theories that assume the contribution of one or the other process (i.e., automatic or strategic). I do not ignore this debate, but I go beyond it. In line with several authors (Kintsch, 2005; van den Broek et al., 2005), my conviction is that it is necessary to develop a single integrated theory that makes both passive and strategic processes a necessary part of its structure. For instance, some textual situations may require shallow processing that minimizes the cognitive resources allocated by readers to the inferential process. Conversely, other more demanding situations may require readers to generate goal-oriented inferences. For those who are interested in what "comprehension" means, determining the relative contributions of both of these processes in a fine-grained way, and delimiting their boundaries, are crucial issues.

Contribution of the Reader's Knowledge and the Multidimensional Aspect of Situation Models: Importance of Causality and Emotion

In the previous section, I brought out the importance for readers to establish global coherence in order to integrate previous information stored in long-term memory into the text elements currently being processed. I stated that readers mental representations go beyond text representations because other types of information (i.e., concepts and relations) not necessarily explicitly mentioned in the text have to be represented as well (see chapter 6). In particular, readers need to call on actions, events, situations, and general knowledge that are drawn from their prior knowledge. Therefore, it is crucial to consider the direct inferential processes readers engage in when they process any type of text, as different as those types may be regarding the nature of the knowledge they bring to bear (e.g., narratives vs. science texts). In the previous chapter, I also relied on two main views of the retrieval process, one that sees it a passive reactivation process, and the other, as a less automatic, strategic process. The basic assumption of the former view is that the focused event sends signals to all information in long-term memory, thereby generating passive resonance. These theories revolve around the passive activation of inferential information (Kintsch, 1988; McKoon & Ratcliff, 1992; Myers, & O'Brien, 1998). In the "causality-based" view, however (i.e., the latter view), readers are assumed to pro-

149

cess the text more deeply and to actively "search after meaning" (Bartlett, 1932, cited in Graesser et al., 1994). Hence, comprehension is regarded as a problem-solving activity aimed at discovering causal relations between text units (adjacent or not). In this view, readers have to specify the reasons, motivations, and causal antecedents of events and actions (Craik, 1943; Schank, 1986), with these explanations being a function of their semantic or schematic knowledge, or their reasoning strategies. Understanding a text, then, would mean justifying it on the basis of one's knowledge, often approached in terms of causal relations, each corresponding to one inference. Inference making is thus viewed as an active part of the comprehension process (see Graesser, Singer, & Trabasso, 1994; Zwaan & Radvansky, 1998).

Chapter 7

Causal Inferences in the Reading Comprehension Process

Consistent with the theoretical approach that relies on a causality-based search for coherence, the Causal Network Theory provides strong predictions as to what types of inferences readers generate online, and what mechanisms underlie inference generation (see chapter 5). In particular, van den Broek (1990a) developed a model of inferences called the Causal Inference Maker (CIM), which proposes a classification of the inferences readers are assumed to make, regardless of whether those inferences are necessary for comprehension. In this chapter, I describe this model, and then focus on one particular type of inference, predictive or forward inferences, assumed to be drawn only under very specific conditions. My attempt here is to highlight the fact that, although it has been widely acknowledged that predictive inference generation is constrained by a strong, immediately preceding context, other more distant information may have an effect on the inferences made. Some recent findings (Cook, Limber, & O'Brien, 2001; Peracchi & O'Brien, 2004) have shown that the process of generating predictive inferences combines two types of context information as readers process a focus statement: the immediately preceding context, and more distant knowledge (episodic or semantic). It has also been demonstrated (Guéraud, Tapiero, & O'Brien, submitted) that readers' episodic and semantic knowledge may override the immediately preceding context during predictive inferencing. I describe some of the studies that have underlined these aspects of the inferential process, and I also show that the nature of contextual information located far from the immediately preceding context influences this process (Galletti & Tapiero, 2004).

7.1. THE CAUSAL INFERENCE MAKER MODEL
(CIM MODEL, VAN DEN BROEK, 1990A)

Inferences are all pieces of information that lead the reader to connect two events during text comprehension, or all information added by readers to information explicitly stated in a text (Campion & Rossi, 1999). Two broad categories of inferences that can be drawn during reading have been defined in the literature: necessary inferences and elaborative inferences. Necessary inferences are ones that are required for full comprehension. Their main function is to ensure the coherence of the mental representation at both the local level (i.e., between adjacent units) and the global level (between nonadjacent units). Local inferences are made online, and doing so increases comprehension time (Bloom et al., 1990; Myers, Shinjo, & Duffy, 1987). These inferences include anaphoric or referential inferences (O'Brien, Duffy, & Myers, 1986), bridging inferences (Haviland & Clark, 1974; Keenan, Potts, Golding, & Jennings, 1990; McKoon & Ratcliff, 1990), and causal antecedent inferences (van den Broek, 1990a, 1990b). Global inferences are made when readers attempt to organize text information into higher order chunks. These inferences include thematic inferences, although no evidence of the online nature of these inferences has yet been found (Graesser et al., 1994). Elaborative inferences belong to the second category. Because their generation allows readers to go beyond what has been explicitly stated in the text, they are considered unnecessary for comprehension. They are assumed to be generated online only when a strong constraining context precedes the focal event. Category instantiation and predictive or forward inferences belong to this category.

It has been widely acknowledged that causal inferences are the basis of successful comprehension (see Part III), and the properties of causal information conveyed in texts may determine not only whether an inference will be generated but also the type of inference it will be. The Causal Inference Maker Model (CIM) developed by van den Broek (1990a; van den Broek, Fletcher & Risden, 1993) addresses precisely those questions. It was aimed in particular at determining the processes underlying the elaboration of a network representation and, consequently, the causal inference process. This model provides a classification of causal inferences grounded on two main assumptions that determine the content and type of inferences that get made and the constraints that operate on the inferential process (see van den Broek, 1990a,b). First, this model adopts causality criteria as principles that guide the inferential process. Second, it accounts for limitations in short-term memory capacity or attentional resources. Figure 7.1 presents a diagram of the different types of inferences drawn during reading.

The CIM model (van den Broek, 1990a,b) calls on the postulate of immediacy in the inference-generation process because one of its basic assump-

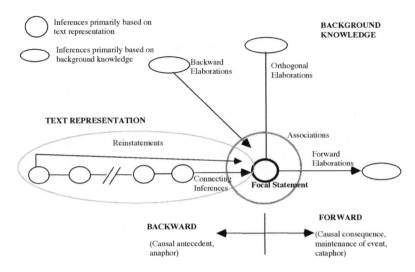

FIGURE 7.1. Different types of inferences in reading (from van den Broek, Fletcher, & Risden, 1993).

tions is that causal inferences are drawn as readers process a focal event. The concept of focal event is crucial because it provides readers with information about a set of possible other events that might be described in the text. Thus, as an event becomes a focal event, it triggers the activation of associations, as well as general semantic knowledge stored in memory required for the inferential process to occur. When those activations, combined with residual activation from previous reading cycles, go beyond a certain threshold, an inference is drawn. However, because the focal event continues to generate inferences even once other statements are being read, inferences are assumed to occur in a backward or forward direction, hence two main types of inferences: backward and forward inferences.

Backward inferences are considered as necessary for comprehension. They connect a focal event to prior events in order to establish and maintain causal coherence in the representation of a narrative text. The CIM description of backward inferences assumes a "minimalist" reader who makes only those inferences that are required to maintain local coherence (see chapter 5). In this model, two main constraints operate on the inferential process. First, causal coherence is maintained if antecedents of a focal event meet the four criteria that determine whether a relationship between two events is causal: temporal priority, operativity, necessity, and sufficiency. If one of these criteria is not met, additional inferences that provide the missing information are required. Second, due to the reader's short-term memory capacity or attentional limitations, relevant causal information may not be readily available. The availability of information determines what kind of inference is required to attain coherence, and three types of backward inferences are postulated. In the first type, readers attempt to find adequate causal justifications as they encounter an event. Therefore, the first event to be considered is the immediately preceding or causally most recent one because it is likely to be still activated. If the preceding event meets all criteria, the inferential process stops and a connecting inference is generated. If, however, the criteria are not met, a coherence break occurs and readers have to resolve the break by means of reinstating and/or elaborating inferences, the second and third types of backward inferences. If the text itself provides information that meets the causal criteria, and if such information is not too far from the focal event (i.e., in episodic memory), a reinstated inference is drawn. If the information is too far away from the focal event to be easily reinstated, then readers may infer events that are not explicitly stated in the text but are plausible explanations of the focal information (i.e., elaborating inferences). Therefore, these elaborative inferences rely on and are constrained by readers' knowledge about events and about causality in general, and their generation enables readers to reach a high level of comprehension.

Forward inferences anticipate information that will be subsequently described in the text (the consequences of events), and they are not necessarily required for comprehension. The CIM model (van den Broek, 1990a,b) defines two types of forward inferences: predictive inferences and anticipations. Predictive inferences refer to expectations about future events that help readers establish a causal relation between a focal event and the subsequent event they are expecting. They are seen as probable hypotheses about the causal consequences of the focal event and are drawn from the initial text representation and focal information. When a prediction is confirmed by the processing of a new event, it is instantiated and used as an integrative function between two text sentences. The occurrence of predictive inferences is difficult to evidence because these inferences are only constrained by their antecedents. However, it has been shown that sufficiency is a crucial criterion for their occurrence: Inferences with highly sufficient causal antecedents in the text are more easily generated than those for which the text does not provide a sufficient causal explanation. The second type of forward inference concerns expectations about the role that a prior event, person, or object, still active in the current cycle, will play in subsequent text information. These inferences rely on the reader's anticipations about statements that are necessary for the future importance of prior events. Consequently, readers are assumed to anticipate the causal role of a just-read event and to keep it active in order to explain future information. It will still be active as its consequence occurs, provided two conditions are fulfilled: the event has not yet been explained, or it has no consequence.

Thus, the CIM model (van den Broek, 1990a,b) assumes that readers have the ability to anticipate the necessary event when it is in the attentional focus of future events.

Finally, two other types of inferences mentioned in the CIM model, but not specific to causality, have also been described: orthogonal inferences (i.e., spatial and visual inferences) and associative inferences (Kinstch, 1988), but it is beyond the scope of this chapter to describe them here.

Thus, the generation of causal inferences and the type of causal inference generated comply with several constraints. Moreover, although there is a large consensus on the idea that necessary inferences are activated and generated as readers proceed through the text, the conditions under which elaborative, that is, predictive inferences become activated are subject to substantial debate regarding what factors trigger them and when (encoding or retrieval). As stated earlier, forward inferences are ones that are about "what is going to happen next" and are defined as unnecessary for comprehension. They are not very prevalent and are generated online only when highly constrained by the story context (i.e., a highly sufficient context). They are also generated when they are readily available, based on the reader's general knowledge and when few alternative consequences are available (e.g., Calvo & Castillo, 1996; Cook et al., 2001; Fincher-Kiefer, 1995, 1996; Graesser et al., 1994, Keefe & McDaniel, 1993; Klin, Guzman, & Levine, 1999; Klin, Murray, Levine, & Guzman, 1999; McKoon & Ratcliff, 1986; Murray, Klin, & Myers, 1993; Peracchi & O'Brien, 2004). Their activation is short-lived, and depending on the method used, they may or may not be instantiated in the long-term memory representation of the text. Finally, some authors have argued that forward inferences are not generated in an all-or-none fashion (see Calvo & Castillo, 1996); others have stipulated that they may be encoded in an all-or-none way by some readers, whereas others would need more contextual cues to generate the predictions and then draw the inferences (Zwaan & Graesser, 1993a,b). Next, I review some of the empirical data that has brought those constraints to the fore.

7.2. THE MAIN CONDITIONS FOR THE GENERATION OF FORWARD INFERENCES: IMPORTANCE OF CONTEXTUAL CONSTRAINTS AND TIME COURSE FOR THIS GENERATION

Under what conditions are forward inferences generated? Several authors have shown that when a constraining context immediately precedes the point at which activation is measured, predictive inferences are available in active memory (e.g., Keefe & McDaniel, 1993; McKoon & Ratcliff, 1986; Murray et al., 1993). The assumption that constraints play a crucial role in the generation of predictive inferences has been tested directly. One important source of constraints is the most recently processed event. If this event provides substantial support for a specific inference, a predictive inference will be drawn. The strength of the causal relation between the focal event and the possible inference is one crucial aspect of this support (see van den Broek, 1990a,b). In illustration, let us consider the study by McKoon and Ratcliff (1986). These authors presented subjects with the following sentences (A and B):

A. "While shooting a film, the actress accidentally fell out the *first floor* window."

B. "While shooting a film, the actress accidentally fell out the *fourteenth floor* window."

Readers more easily activated "the actress died" in sentence B than in sentence A because B provided readers with more causal sufficiency to generate a predictive inference and constrained the generation of that specific inference in a stronger fashion. In sentence A, sufficiency was moderate, and readers activated and generated a wider range of possible inferences that were less specific than for sentence B. Therefore, the degree of sufficiency of the focal event constrained the strength of activation and the specificity of the inference that was drawn. However, the activation level of the inferred concept was low, due to the relative weakness of the context that led to the activation of that inference.

Klin, Guzman, and Levine (1999) not only confirmed the influence of a strong contraining context on the generation of forward inferences, but also looked at whether they were integrated into the memory representation or were only activated in a "minimal" way. In their first experiment, participants had to read short passages in which some events were highly predictable consequences of actions described in the stories (see Murray et al., 1993). Two elaboration versions of each passage were constructed: an inference version and a control version that did not lead readers to generate an inference. Both versions were followed by a probe word that corresponded to the to-be-inferred event in the inference version. After the readers processed the following two statements—*He tried to cool down, but felt his resentment building. No longer able to control his anger, he threw a delicate porcelain vase against the wall.*—they had to respond to a specific probe word, "break." The authors' prediction was that if readers infer that the vase is going to break, they will be faster at naming the probe word "break" in the inference elaboration condition than in the control condition where no action from the main protagonist induced the to-be-inferred information: *He reacted by acting cool toward her. He then apologized for getting angry and offered to clean up her delicate porcelain vase to make up for it* (from Klin, Guzmàn, & Levine, 1999, Experiment 1, p. 595). As expected by the authors, the results showed shorter naming latencies after the reading of the inference version than after the control version, which provides support for the argument that forward inferences were activated, at least temporarily, when the current information highly constrained the information to be inferred. In their second experiment, the authors tested whether predictive inferences were maintained in memory over time. In particular, they used naming time and reading time to see whether predictive inferences were momentarily activated and then lost from the memory representation after a certain time, or if they were encoded and integrated into the reader's memory representation. For this purpose, the authors added neutral information at the end of each passage used in Experiment 1. The added pieces of information were unrelated to the inference to be generated and was aimed at putting the inference into the background. A target sentence inconsistent with the to-be-generated inference, but not with information explicitly stated in the text, followed this neutral information. In line with the authors' assumption, the readers should notice the inconsistency only if they had generated the inference (i.e., about the broken vase), and in that case, reading time should be longer. The results showed that readers generated predictive inferences, and in this sense they confirmed the authors' assumption. They also indicated that forward inferences were encoded in a more permanent way than evidenced in several other studies (Fincher-Kiefer, 1996; Keefe & McDaniel, 1993; McKoon, & Ratcliff, 1986). In two follow-up studies, Klin, Guzmàn, and Levine (1999) investigated the boundaries of the previously observed effect. In particular, the authors wanted to determine whether text variables significantly affected the generation of predictive inferences. The same passages as those used in Experiment 1 were modified by adding some pieces of information to the introduction (in both the inference and control versions). This new information was aimed at activating an additional consequence of the final event (i.e., his wife wanted to leave him if he continued to be violent). According to the authors, such additional information in the introduction should lessen the activation of the target sentence in the inference version, because activation should be divided between the event to be inferred (i.e., the vase breaks) and this additional consequence (i.e., his wife leaves). In the control version, however, the additional information did not lead to any critical consequence. According to the authors, when readers were processing the final line of the passage, the probability that the inference "the vase breaks" is available should decrease.

Their results showed no difference in naming time between the inference and control versions, and thus confirmed that predictive inferences were only drawn when few consequences were available (Fincher-Kiefer, 1996). However, the opposite results were obtained with regular reading-time measures, showing that an additional consequence did not eliminate the activation of predictive inferences (see Weingartner, Guzman, Levine, & Klin, 2003). These findings indicate that several factors may influence the conditions under which predictive inferences are drawn. Klin, Guzmàn, and Levine (1999) showed that predictive inferences were drawn when there was more than one consequence of the predictive context, and thus appeared to be more prevalent than what has been assumed in several other studies. However, when conditions were not optimal, they were only minimally encoded (see also, Weingartner et al., 2003).

An implicit consideration in the work on predictive inferences is that the supportive context must always contain strong semantic associates of the inference, must immediately precede the point at which activation of the predictive inference is measured, or must maintain the predictive inference in active memory (e.g., Murray et al., 1993; Keefe & McDaniel, 1993; Schmalhofer, McDaniel, & Keefe, 2002). In a series of experiments, Cook, Limber, and O'Brien (2001) demonstrated that the constraining context did not have to appear immediately prior to the point at which activation was measured, but could be presented in a much earlier portion of the situation or "discourse" model. The authors argued that even when the immediately preceding context was neutral with respect to a predictive inference, information contained in the situation model could result in the activation of the inference. Their assumption relied on the idea that reactivation of earlier portions of a discourse representation, and thus the generation of necessary and elaborative inferences, was available through a passive resonance process. In addition, the authors wanted to determine whether a strong context necessary for the activation of a predictive inference could be created without the use of direct semantic associates of concepts representing that inference. The authors presented subjects with passages in which a context either strongly primed the inference assumed to be generated (high-context version) or in which the to-be-generated inference had only a low likelihood of occurring (low-context version). The last sentence of each passage (i.e., inference-evoking sentence) was assumed to lead to the predicted inference only in conjunction with information from the high-context version. For example, the authors used passages in which a protagonist "Jimmy" was playing with his friends. The participants read one of the two context versions (high- or low-context). In the high-context version, the participants read, *Jimmy was delighted and ran across the street to play with them. They taught him a fun game that involved throwing rocks at a target to get points.* For the low-context version, only one word distinguished this version from the high-context version because "rocks" was changed to "Nerf balls." Both context versions were followed by several sentences that maintained the contextual information as part of the active portion of the situation model (e.g., "Jimmy and his friends were having a great time."). The last sentence of each version of the passage said that Jimmy missed the target and accidentally hit the door of a new car. After the last sentence of each passage, the probe word "dent" was presented to the subjects for 500 ms (Experiment 1) or for 250 ms (Experiment 2). This probe was assumed to be strongly primed in the high-context version but not in the low-context version, and shorter naming times were thus expected in the high-context condition. The authors assumed, however, that the mere priming of the inference-evoking sentence, or the situation alone described in the high-context version, could not lead to the generation of the predictive inference. Rather, the activation of the to-be-generated inference should result from both the contextual features contained in the situation model and the inference-evoking sentence. The results of these first two experiments were in line with the authors' predictions: Naming times for the inferred concept "dent" were faster following the inference-evoking sentence in the high-context version than following the inference-evoking sentence in the low-context version. The authors concluded that because the inference-evoking sentence in isolation was not sufficient to produce activation of the predictive inference, the inference had to be the result of a convergence of activation emanating from both the inference-evoking sentence and information contained in the earlier portion of the situation model. Thus, these findings showed that contextually constraining information contained in an early portion of the situation model modulated predictive inference activation.

Peracchi and O'Brien (2004) further investigated the idea that information contained in situation models can modulate inference activation even when the immediately preceding context strongly supports a particular predictive inference. The authors looked into whether a predictive inference is generated when the immediately preceding context strongly supports a particular predictive inference but information in the situation model is inconsistent with that inference. The participants had to study several passages, each appearing in four different versions: consistent-trait elaborated version, inconsistent-trait elaborated version, neutral version, and finally, a baseline condition. Table 7.1 presents one of the passages used in this study.

As shown in Table 7.1, the inference-evoking statement was preceded by three possible character trait elaborations that described the characteristics of the protagonist. In the consistent-trait condition, the protagonist "Carol" was described as someone who was short-tempered and tended to act without thinking. In the inconsistent-trait condition, Carol was described as someone who never used physical violence and the character trait elaboration was inconsistent with the predictive inference. The neutral-trait elaboration described Carol as someone very devoted to her children, so it was unrelated to the predictive inference. The fourth version of each passage included a baseline condition in which the neutral elaboration was followed by a non-inference-evoking sentence (see Table 7.1). The participants' task was to answer as quickly as possible to the probe word "dump"

TABLE 7.1

Example of a Passage (From Peracchi & O'Brien, 2004, Experiment 1)

Introduction. Carol was a single mother with two young children. She had to work two jobs to make ends meet. She worked full-time as a teacher and part-time as a waitress. She hated not having much free time.

Consistent-Trait Elaborated (Experiments 1 & 2). Carol was known for her short temper and her tendency to act without thinking. She never thought about the consequences of her actions, so she often suffered negative repercussions. She refused to let people walk all over her. In fact, she had just gotten a ticket for road rage. She decided she would never put up with anyone that was not nice to her. One particular night, Carol had an extremely rude customer. He complained about his spaghetti, and he yelled at Carol as if it were her fault.

Inconsistent-Trait Elaborated (Experiments 1 & 2). Carol was known for her ability to peacefully settle any confrontation. She would never even think of solving her problems with physical violence. She taught her students and her own children how to solve problems through conversation. She believed this was an effective way to stop the increasing violence in the schools. Carol also helped other parents learn to deal with their anger. One particular night, Carol had an extremely rude customer. He complained about his spaghetti, and he yelled at Carol as if it were her fault.

Neutral-Trait Elaborated (Experiment 1). Carol loved her kids and would do whatever it took to keep them. She was thankful that she was granted sole custody after the divorce. She didn't know what she would have done if she had lost her children. She tried to make the time that they had together meaningful. They ate dinner together every night and she always planned a fun event for the weekend. One particular night, Carol had an extremely rude customer. He complained about his spaghetti, and he yelled at Carol as if it were her fault.

Inference-Evoking Sentence (Experiments 1 & 2). Carol lifted the spaghetti above his head.

Baseline Condition (Experiment 1). She lifted the spaghetti and walked away.

Probe. dump.

---

after the presentation of the inference-evoking sentence, *Carol lifted the spaghetti above his head.* The authors predicted shorter naming times for the consistent- and neutral-trait elaboration condition, because the subjects were assumed to generate the predictive inference in both conditions. They also predicted the longest naming times in the baseline condition, because no inference was assumed to be drawn due to the lack of evoking information. Finally, and in line with the authors' prediction, if drawing a predictive inference was the result of the inference-evoking sentence plus the situational context, naming times for the inconsistent-trait elaborated condition would be close to the baseline condition because the activation of the predictive inference was assumed to be disrupted by the inconsistent elaborated information.

The results indicated shorter naming times for the predictive inference (dump) in the consistent- and neutral-elaboration conditions than in the inconsistent-elaboration condition. More importantly, naming times in the inconsistent-elaboration condition were not faster than in the baseline condition in which the predictive inference would not have been activated. Thus, even though the immediately preceding context was sufficient to activate the predictive inference—as evidenced by the fast naming times in the neutral-elaboration condition—when information contained in the situation model was inconsistent with that inference, no activation occurred. Thus, these findings show that the characteristics of the protagonist determined whether or not a predictive inference became activated. When those characteristics were consistent with a strong immediate context, a predictive inference was drawn. When, however, the characteristics were inconsistent with the immediate context, no inference was activated. Thus, the situational representation appears to have a strong impact on the generation of predictive inferences (see also Schmalhofer et al., 2002).

Recently, Guéraud, O'Brien, and I (Guéraud, Tapiero, & O'Brien, submitted) further explored the question of whether both the immediately preceding context and information contained in an earlier portion of the discourse model have an effect on the activation of predictive inferences. The experimental materials used were adapted from Peracchi and O'Brien (2004). Each passage introduced a protagonist followed by two character-trait elaboration versions, each leading, in conjunction with the same inference-evoking context (i.e., inference-setting information and inference-evoking sentence), to the activation of a specific inference relevant to the elaboration version. This context presented in isolation was sufficient to generate the specific inference (see Peracchi & O'Brien, 2004). The character-trait elaborations differed in such a way that when presented in combination with the same inference-evoking context, they would lead to the activation of a different predictive inference. For instance, in the first character-trait elaboration version, the protagonist "Carol" worked part-time as a waitress and was described as a short-tempered person. In the second character-trait elaboration, the same protagonist was described as uncomfortable when having to lift something due to a recent shoulder injury. This study was designed to test whether the same inference-evoking context, when combined with different character-trait information, triggered the activation of two different predictive inferences. For example, after both character-trait descriptions, the same inference-setting information was presented (e.g., *One particular night, Carol had an extremely rude customer. He complained about his spaghetti, and yelled at Carol as if it were her fault.*). This was followed by either an inference-evoking sentence (e.g., *Carol lifted the plate of spaghetti above his head.*) or a baseline sentence (e.g., *Carol took the plate of spaghetti and walked away.*). Following each version of the passage, participants were asked to name out loud the specific predictive inference that was consistent with the character-trait elaboration (e.g., "dump" following the first character-trait elaboration, or "pain" following the second character-trait elaboration). If character-trait information combined with the inference-evoking context determined inference activation, then in the first character-trait elaboration condition, "dump" should be named more quickly following the inference-evoking sentence than following the baseline sentence. In the second character-trait elaboration condition, "pain" should be named more quickly following the same inference-evoking sentence than following the same baseline sentence.

As predicted, and consistent with prior findings (e.g., Murray et al., 1993; Peracchi & O'Brien, 2004), the main results showed that information contained in an earlier portion of the situation model, combined with the immediately preceding context, determined inference activation. In the first character-trait condition, Carol was described as a short-tempered person. In this context, the inference-evoking sentence (*Carol lifted the plate of spaghetti above his head*) resulted in the activation of the predictive inference "dump." In the second character-trait condition, Carol was described as someone who was uncomfortable when she had to lift things because she recently had shoulder surgery. When the same inference-evoking sentence was presented following this context, it resulted in the activation of the predictive inference "pain." Thus, the combined results for the first and second character-trait conditions showed that the predictive inference that was activated in response to the inference-evoking sentence was determined by information that had appeared in an earlier portion of the situation model.

Thus, these findings confirmed and extended what had been already obtained (Cook et al., 2001; Keefe & McDaniel, 1993; Peracchi & O'Brien, 2004). Different inferences may be activated, depending on the information contained in the situational context, even when the immediate context in isolation is sufficient to produce activation of a specific inference. The same immediate context can lead to the activation of two very different inferences when combined with information from an earlier portion of the situation or discourse model. This grants the situational context, and consequently the reader's situation model, a preponderant role.

7.3. WHEN AN EMOTIONAL CONTEXT CONSTRAINS THE GENERATION OF PREDICTIVE CAUSAL INFERENCES

Galletti[1] (Galletti, 2004; Galletti & Tapiero, 2004) explored the impact of emotional and causal context information on the strength of predictive causal inference generation. Earlier, I discussed the crucial role of causality

---

[1] Sonia Galletti conducted this study in 2004, under my direction, in fulfillment of the requirements for the first year of her PhD at the University of Lyon 2 (France).

in the construction of a coherent mental representation, and thus in inference-making, and in doing so, I demonstrated the importance of causal sufficiency in the generation of predictive inferences. In parallel, other studies have shown that emotion, and more specifically, a protagonist's emotional states, are part of the reader's mental representation: Readers are able to infer the protagonist's emotional state, so emotion should be viewed as a core dimension in situation models (see chapter 8). Finally, I reported some findings (Cook, Limber, & O'Brien, 2001; Peracchi & O'Brien, 2004; Guéraud, Tapiero, & O'Brien, submitted) showing that predictive inferences are activated on the basis of contextual features contained in the situation or discourse model. The generation of predictive inferences appears to be the result of the representation of the immediately preceding context combined with more distant information, or it may only be dependent on the representation of the discourse situation. In this vein, and in an attempt to better define the factors that affect the inferential process, Galletti (Galletti, 2004; Galletti & Tapiero, 2004) designed an experiment to determine whether the nature of the situational context (i.e., causal and emotional) can influence the generation of predictive inferences. In particular, the respective contributions of emotional and causal contextual information to the activation and integration of predictive inferences were investigated.

The experimental material consisted of eight same-structure stories that were major revisions of Gernsbacher, Goldsmith, & Robertson's (1992) passages. Each story described two characters and was composed of six sections: an introduction, a contextual elaboration part, a section devoted to putting contextual information into the background, a focal statement, two critical sentences, and a conclusion. For each passage, two contextual-elaboration versions were constructed, one dealing with causal information and the other with emotional information. Also, the focal statement could be either high or low in sufficiency, which determined the probability that the predictive inferences would be generated. Finally, the first critical sentence described the main protagonist engaged in a causal action that was consistent with the information conveyed in the focal statement, and with the contextual causal elaboration; the second critical sentence presented the protagonist's emotional state and was reinforced by the content of the emotional-context elaboration.

Each subject was assigned to only one contextual-elaboration version (causal or emotional), but had to read passages that presented a focal statement that was either high or low in sufficiency. Predictive-inference activation was measured in two ways, depending on the subjects' group assignment: Half of the subjects had to answer two inferential questions presented at the end of the reading, that is, causal and emotional offline tests; the other half was probed with a causal inferential question during the reading (online causal test) and with causal and emotional inferential questions at the end of the reading (similar to the first group). Integration was tested by measuring the reading times on the two critical sentences that preceded the conclusion statement in each passage. Response times for the online causal test and for the offline causal and emotional tests were also collected. Prior to running the study, a preliminary test was conducted to check the validity of the materials and the sufficiency of the focal event statements. An example of a passage is presented in Table 7.2.

This study was designed to test whether the generation of predictive inferences resulted in a convergence between contextual information and the representation of the focal event. It was assumed that the likelihood that a predictive inference would be generated depends on the nature of the information presented in the prior context (causal vs. emotional) in relation

TABLE 7.2

Example of a Passage Used in Galletti and Tapiero (2004)

Introduction. The man was lying face down, probably unconscious, on the busy sidewalk. Other men and women bustled by on their way to work. Mark, who was late again, almost tripped over the man and yelled that someone should do something. Peter, a co-worker who was with him, agreed.

Emotional Information Elaborated: Mark jabbed the man with his foot and then continued on his way. Still furious, he muttered, "Why doesn't someone move that guy so people can get through? It's not my job. I'm in a hurry."

Causal Information Elaborated: Mark and Peter went to work together every morning. They liked to walk to their office rather than taking the bus because it was always too crowded. They had both worked at the same company for several years.

Backgrounding Information: A few minutes later, they heard the siren of an ambulance. The man would certainly soon receive all the necessary care. Mark and Peter hurried along more than they usually did. They had to be at work on time. This was a special day for them because their boss planned to present a project on door-to-door selling.

Causal Focal Statement (High Sufficiency): If he didn't arrive too late, Mark *definitely wanted to stop by* the newspaper stand to get some magazines.

Causal Focal Statement (Low Sufficiency): If he didn't arrive too late, Mark *thought that he might stop by* the newspaper stand to get some magazines.

Online Causal Test: Mark will buy some magazines at the newspaper stand.

Critical Sentences: Mark hurried up and arrived early at his office *(causal)*. To say the least, he is not a warm person *(emotional)*.

Conclusion: After meeting with the boss, Mark went back to his office.

Offline Causal Test: Mark bought some magazines.

Offline Emotional Test: Mark is a callous man.

Comprehension Question: Mark drives his car to go to work.

---

to the sufficiency strength of the focal event. With a causal elaboration, a high-sufficiency preceding context should increase the probability of the predictive inference being generated, compared to a low-sufficiency context. Emotional elaboration, however, should weaken the generation of predictive causal inferences in the high-sufficiency prior context only, but also trigger the generation of emotional inferences.

The reading-time data showed that emotional critical sentences were processed faster than causal critical sentences (p <.01), indicating that emotional information was easily retrieved from memory. Also, there was a reliable effect of the causal strength on the reading times of the two critical sentences (i.e., causal and emotional; p <.02). As Figure 7.2 indicates, whereas with a high-sufficiency context, a large reading-time difference was found between the causal and emotional critical sentences ($d = 5.25$; i.e., shorter reading times for the emotional sentence than for the causal sentence), a slighter difference was noted between causal and emotional sentences when they were preceded by a low-sufficiency context ($d = 1.89$; see Figure 7.2). Thus, a high-sufficiency context appeared to constrain the generation of predictive inferences but for causal inferences only, leading to their integration in memory. The generation of a wider range of inferences (e.g., emotional and causal) was facilitated solely by low-sufficiency context.

Concerning the response times to causal inferential questions (online and offline), the causal-context elaboration had a facilitating effect compared to the emotional-context elaboration (p <.05). This is fully consistent with the idea that a causal situation better constrains the activation of predictive inferences than an emotional one. In addition, the combined analysis of the response times for online and offline causal tests indicated an interaction between the degree of sufficiency and the type of contextual information, $F =(1, 78) = 10.04, p = .002$. As shown in Figure 7.3, a high level of sufficiency appears to have disrupted the activation of inferences, but only when the content of the elaboration was emotional (longer response times when the preceding context was high in sufficiency compared to low). For a causal elaboration, however, response times for causal inferential tests (online and offline) were shorter when the preceding context was high in sufficiency. This result is consistent with our predictions and confirms the claim that inferences are not activated in an all-or-none fashion (see the Causal Inference Maker Model, van den Broek, 1990a). Compared to a highly constraining context, with a low-sufficiency context, the inference activation appeared to be only minimally encoded in the readers' memory representations, and this allowed readers to activate more candidates for the inferential process.

Finally, the response times to the two types of offline tests (causal and emotional) indicated an effect of the nature of the contextual elaboration, but only when the focal event was high in sufficiency (p <.06): The subjects tended to have shorter response times to both types of offline tests when the

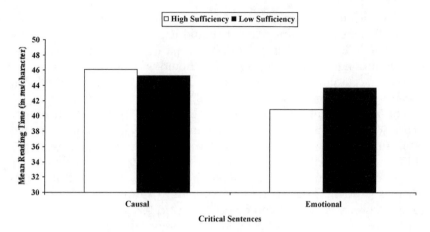

FIGURE 7.2.   Mean reading times by type of critical sentence (causal or emotional) and level of sufficiency (high or low; from Galletti & Tapiero, 2004).

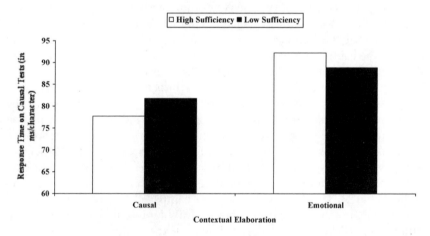

FIGURE 7.3.   Response time on causal tests, by type of contextual elaboration (causal or emotional) and the degree of sufficiency (high or low; from Galletti & Tapiero, 2004).

contextual elaboration was causal compared to when it was emotional. Thus, although emotional information was processed faster than causal information, as evidenced by the reading times on the two types of critical sentences, an emotional context disrupted the generation of causal and emotional inferences. Stated differently, a strongly constraining causal context helped readers activate both types of information, causal and emotional.

The results of this study confirmed the importance of sufficiency strength in the generation of predictive inferences, and are consistent with the Causal Inference Maker Model (see van den Broek, 1990). With a high-sufficiency focal event, predictive causal inferences were generated, whereas with a low-sufficiency focal event, their activation was more diffuse. This study also provided some insight into the impact of contextual information on inference generation and showed that predictive inferences are not necessarily activated in an all-or-none fashion (see van den Broek, 1990a,b). Rather, their activation fluctuated here as a function of information that was far from the causal focal event. When an emotional context preceded the presentation of a focal event high in sufficiency, the process of inference generation was disrupted. When a causal elaboration context preceded the presentation of the focal event, however, the strength of the sufficiency criterion influenced the inference generation process, and a high-sufficiency context constrained inference generation.

Further investigations still need to be conducted to deepen our understanding of how the causal strength of a focal event is affected by an emotional context in predictive inference generation. The next chapter takes a closer look at the importance of emotion in the reader's mental representation.

More broadly, predictions from recent models of comprehension (i.e., the Construction-Integration Model: Kintsch, 1988; the Landscape Model: van den Broek et al., 1996; van den Broek, Young, Tzeng, & Lunderholm, 1999) should help us better define and determine the role of emotion and other types of information in the reading comprehension process, particularly inferencing. Because the underlying principles of these models rely on the convergence of bottom-up processes and top-down processes, this would allow us to determine the relative contributions of each of these processes in modeling the process in question here. However, in order to do so, one crucial requirement is that we determine a way to differentiate between the nature of the input units (e.g., concepts, propositions, events, etc.) and the dimension to which they belong to (e.g., emotional, causal, etc.).

Chapter 8

Emotion and Text Comprehension

Emotions have been commonly defined in terms of the social–cultural context in which they occur (Fischer, 1991; Fridja, 1986): An emotional experience in a certain situation is a result of the way an individual assigns meaning to that situation. Most researchers have regarded this "appraisal process" as a form of cognition (Fischer, 1991; Fridja, 1986; Lazarus, 1982; Mandler, 1975; Ortony, Clore, & Collins, 1988; Scherer, 1982) and have argued that if the cognitive processing of a situation precedes and determines the emotional experience (see Fridja, 1986), the emotional experience itself may in turn influence cognitive processing. Therefore, emotions can trigger cognitive structures, sensitize people to certain types of information, and help them to determine what knowledge is relevant to the situation and what knowledge has to be activated (see Fridja, 1989; Tan, 1994). Emotions punctuate almost all of the significant events in our lives and should thus be considered as cues for determining the coherence of the situation. Because coherence is crucial when readers are processing language, text comprehension is one of the most critical domains in which researchers should take emotions into account. However, although some models of comprehension have attempted to propose a formal description of its structural and/or functional aspects (Gernsbacher, 1990; Kintsch, 1988; van Dijk & Kintsch, 1983; Zwaan & Magliano, & Graesser, 1995; Zwaan & Radvansky, 1998) in conventional stories (Tan, 1994) or in literary texts (Kneepkens & Zwaan, 1994), most authors have not provided us with a clear description of how and when emotions take effect in the reading comprehension process. One of the main reasons is probably that, despite their apparent familiarity, emotions are an extremely subtle and complex topic.

Recent studies on the relationship between emotions and text comprehension can be classified into two main research areas (see Blanc, Ducreux, & Tapiero, in preparation): The reader's emotions are about the fictional world described in the story, and the story induces a particular mood in the reader. In the first area, it has been acknowledged that the strength of the relationship between emotions experienced by readers and those experienced by the main protagonist of a story is a function of the extent to which the reader empathizes with one or more of the protagonists, and numerous studies have underlined that readers commonly represent the protagonists' emotions. The second research area assumes that the mood (or emotion) induced in the reader affects text processing. Next, I describe some of the studies that have focused on those two areas of research.

8.1. REPRESENTATION OF CHARACTERS' EMOTIONAL STATES IN NARRATIVES: ACTIVATION OF EMOTIONAL INFERENCES

Understanding the emotions felt by a story protagonist should enable us to represent and anticipate his or her actions and thoughts (Miall, 1989). In other words, inferring the character's emotions is assumed to facilitate text processing because emotions have the ability to serve as a coherent cue in text understanding. The investigation of inferences about a character's emotions has emerged within the last 13 years or so as an important research area in the field of text comprehension (e.g., Gernsbacher, Goldsmith, & Robertson, 1992; de Vega, Diaz, & Leon, 1997). A very common idea is that as readers process a text, they form a mental representation of it that includes explicit text elements and information pertaining to the people, settings, actions, and events either described explicitly or implied by the text (Oakhill & Garnham, 1996; Graesser, Millis, & Zwaan, 1997; Graesser, Singer, & Trabasso, 1994; van den Broek & Gustafson, 1999). To form such a mental representation, readers are assumed to combine different sources of information (Graesser et al., 1994; van den Broek & Gustafson, 1999) and because they go beyond linguistic processes while comprehending a text (Martins & Le Bouedec, 1998), they construct a relatively complex representation of it. However, the apparent complexity of readers' mental representations raises several questions, mostly concerning the kind of implied information or the types of inferences readers activate during reading. As discussed earlier, two main theories have been advanced to account for this particular issue, the Minimalist Theory and the Constructionist Theory. According to the minimalist approach to the reading comprehension process, in which readers do not adopt a specific goal-directed strategy, the number of inferences generated during reading is limited (McKoon & Ratcliff, 1992). This approach stipulates that only those inferences needed for local coherence, or those based on information that is readily available, are generated during reading (McKoon & Ratcliff, 1992). However, such an approach is somewhat ambiguous regarding emotional inferences because if one considers such inferences to be crucial to global coherence, the minimalist approach would argue that they are not inferred during reading. By contrast, the core principle underlying the constructionist approach (i.e., the search after-meaning principle) assumes that people naturally attempt to construct meaning from texts, social interactions, and perceptual input (Bartlett, 1932, cited in Graesser et al., 1994). Accordingly, readers attempt to build a mental representation of the text that allows them to maintain local and global coherence. In this line of thinking, the constructionist approach sees emotion inferences as general features which, by maintaining global coherence, guide readers' understanding of the text.

Many researchers have studied the representation of characters' emotional states in narratives, assuming that emotional inferences are based on information that is easily retrievable from long-term memory and thus that emotion inferences are generated during reading. Beyond this assumption, the specific versus general character of these inferences has been questioned.

8.1.1. Readers Represent the Protagonist's Emotional State in a Specific Way

In a series of experiments, Gernsbacher, Goldsmith, and Robertson (1992) tried to find out whether readers activate knowledge about emotions during story comprehension. They assumed that a reader uses explicit textual information to activate his or her knowledge about human emotions, and thus is able to build a coherent representation of the characters' emotional states. In two studies, the authors provided readers with 24 stories describing information about the characters' goals and actions without explicitly mentioning their emotions. Half of the stories described emotions with a positive valence (e.g., joyful), whereas the other half evoked a negative emotional state (e.g., sad). Although the passages as a whole implied an emotional state, the last sentence of each one (i.e., the target sentence) was intended to cause readers to make an inference about the character's implied emotional state. The participants' task was to read each story at a natural reading rate. Reading times on the target sentence were recorded (Gernsbacher et al., 1992, Experiments 1 & 2). In a third experiment, participants read the same stories as in the first two experiments but had to read aloud test words displayed immediately after the disappearance of the final word of the last sentence (Gernsbacher et al., 1992, Experiment 3). The last sentence in each passage (i.e., the target sentence, Experiments 1 & 2) or the test words used for the word-reading task (Experiment

3) referred to an emotion that did or did not match the text information (e.g., "guilt" as a matching emotion word, "pride" as a mismatching emotion word). The experimental materials from Experiment 2 differed from the ones used in Experiment 1 by the nature of the mismatched information: Mismatching emotion words had the same valence as in the matching condition, but were different from the opposite emotion (e.g., "sad" as a mismatching emotion word, "guilt" as a matching emotion word). Table 8.1 presents an example of the story entitled "Suzanne" including (Experiments 1 & 2) or not including (Experiment 3) the target sentence containing the emotional word with the different emotion-word matching conditions.

TABLE 8.1

A Sample Story "Suzanne" Including or Not Including the Target Sentence Containing the Emotional Word with the Different Emotion-Word Matching Conditions

---

"Suzanne had just returned from her regular visit to the nursing home. Today, there had been several problems and one elderly patient had died. Another had fallen on the stairs and broken her hip. [...] The sheer magnitude of the problems simply overcame Suzanne. A tear ran slowly down her cheek."

Target sentence (only for Experiments 1 & 2)

"Her visit to the nursing home filled her with feelings of *sadness / joy / guilt.*"

Note. Revised from Gernsbacher, Goldsmith, & Robertson, 1992, Experiments 1, 2, & 3/ http://psych.wisc.edu/lang/materials/emm.html

Gernsbacher et al. (1992, Experiments 1 & 2) found shorter reading times for target sentences that contained matching emotional terms than for those containing mismatching emotional terms. In addition, the authors showed that readers activated knowledge about human emotions during the reading process (Experiment 3). From these results, they concluded that readers activated and mentally represented very specific emotions. Such specificity has not only been found in research on emotion inferences (e.g., de Vega, Diaz, & Leon, 1997; de Vega, Leon, & Diaz, 1996; Gernsbacher, Goldsmith, & Robertson, 1992; Gernsbacher, Hallada, & Robertson, 1998; Gernsbacher & Robertson, 1992; but has also been extended to research on characters' trait inferences (Rapp, Gerrig, & Prentice, 2001), which indicate that readers form a rather specific trait-based model of narrative protagonists, without particular effort.

8.1.2. Representing the Protagonist's Emotional State: A General Feeling

Although it has been considered that readers generate specific emotional inferences during reading (Gernsbacher, Goldsmith, & Robertson, 1992), some critical points about the specificity of the emotions represented by readers have been raised. In several studies, Gygax and colleagues (Gygax, Garnham, & Oakhill, 2004; Gygax, Oakhill, & Garnham, 2003) showed that the protagonist's emotion representation was not as specific as predicted and previously demonstrated. In their first study, participants were asked to read short stories (the same passages as in Gernbacher, Goldsmith, & Robertson, 1992) and then to carry out a sentence-completion task. For each story, the participants had to complete the sentence: "The main character felt ..." and were asked to give a minimum of one answer and a maximum of 10 answers, but there were no specific instructions regarding what emotional terms to write down. The subjects' protocols showed that readers evoked a number of different but mutually compatible emotions in response to a given story, emphasizing the unspecific character of the emotional inference generated. In their second study, Gygax et al. (2003) looked at whether the readers' evaluations of a range of emotion terms for each story led to more specific preferences than when they had to produce terms. The participants read the same stories as those used in the previous experiment, and then had to rate the likelihood of the main character feeling several emotional responses on a 7-point scale (1 = not very likely to 7 = very likely). As the authors predicted, the subjects rated highly a wide range of emotional terms for the same story, indicating that they inferred a general feeling rather than a specific emotion from the text information. In particular, the subjects referred more to the general ideas and the stories' protagonists than to the specific emotional term that was expected. Thus, readers seem to infer a general feeling that is compatible with several emotional terms. Gygax et al. (2003) extended these findings by using a self-paced reading paradigm, assuming that such a paradigm (also used by Gernsbacher, Goldsmith, & Robertson, 1992) could provide a measure of on-line inference processes. The authors distinguished four types of emotion terms: matching (used by Gernsbacher, Goldsmith, & Robertson, 1992), matching synonym, matching similar, and mismatching, and obtained the expected difference between the four conditions. However, when the mismatching condition was omitted, no significant difference was observed between the matching, matching synonym, and matching similar conditions. This finding suggested that readers did infer some emotional information while reading, but not enough to pinpoint a specific emotion. Emotion inferences are thus not as specific as it has been assumed in previous research (Gernsbacher, Goldsmith, & Robertson, 1992): readers infer general emotional information composed of different emotional components that may be shared by several emotional terms.

To further explore why emotional inferences are not specific, Gygax, Garnham, and Oakhill (2004) conducted two additional experiments. They postulated that in the texts used in the previous experiments, the information provided to the readers might not have been sufficient for identifying the components of specific emotions. Moreover, they underlined that a lack of contextual information may result in the generation of unspecific emotional inferences because this kind of information is crucial to the reader's identification with the story characters. In other words, contextual information was assumed to determine the intensity of readers' identifications with the story characters and thus the specificity of the emotional inferences readers generate. In the first study, Gygax, Garnham, and Oakhill (2004) manipulated the length of the stories: one group read a short version of the stories in (those used in Gygax, Oakhill, & Garnham, 2003) and the other group read the same stories in a longer version. At the end of each passage, all participants performed a sentence-completion task: "The main character felt ...". They had to choose one answer from a list of five possible answers that corresponded to the four conditions tested in the previous experiments, plus an extra possibility allowing them to write an alternative answer. As expected, the participants more often chose the matching emotions for the long story versions than for the short versions. It is therefore possible to influence the specificity of emotional inferences by adding extra information about the main character's emotional state. For this process to occur, the stories had to be longer than the stories used in Gygax et al. (2003). Thus, with hypothetically more-engaging stories, readers better understood and more accurately experienced the character's emotional responses. Furthermore, additional information might lead to stronger activation of the character's emotional state, causing readers to generate more specific emotional information. In their second study, the authors postulated that while reading, readers infer specific emotions if provided with sufficient information. The participants had to read the stories, and the reading times on the target sentences were recorded. If readers inferred specific emotions, a difference would be observed between three of the conditions: matching, matching synonym, and matching similar. The results indicated a significant difference between the four conditions, but when the mismatching condition was omitted, no significant difference between the matching, matching synonym, and matching similar conditions occurred. Thus, although readers did infer emotions while reading, they did not infer specific emotions, even when the stories were longer and more relevant to the character's emotional state.

In short, Gygax et al. (2003, 2004) demonstrated that readers do not infer specific emotions while reading, but a more general feeling composed of various emotional components shared by other emotional terms. These components were shared by emotions that were similar, and their combination did not lead to the inference of specific emotions, at least not during reading (see Gygax, Tapiero, & Carruzzo, in press).

8.2. ACTIVATION OF EMOTIONAL KNOWLEDGE:
AN AUTOMATIC PROCESS

As already stated, both the minimalist and the constructionist theories make specific predictions regarding the types of inferences readers make as well as the nature of the inferential process (i.e., automatic or strategic). This question was also addressed by Gernsbacher, Hallada, and Robertson (1998), but for emotion inferences. In a series of experiments, these authors examined the accessibility of emotional knowledge, and whether inferring characters' emotional states consumed cognitive resources. The authors assumed that if readers' ability to activate knowledge about emotions was not compromised when they performed a divided-attention task, the information should be relatively accessible. In their first study, participants read the same stories as those previously used (Gernsbacher, Goldsmith, & Robertson, 1992), but while reading some of the stories, they had to perform a tone-identification task. If inferring fictional characters' emotional states is a relatively effortful component of reading, a diminished difference between the participants' reading times on target sentences containing matching versus mismatching emotion words should be observed when participants simultaneously perform a tone-identification task. The results indicated that the target sentence reading times were considerably shorter when they contained matching as opposed to mismatching emotion words. This advantage was maintained even though the participants had to perform the tone-identification task. Thus, the readers' ability to activate knowledge about emotions was not lessened when they simultaneously performed another task. To confirm this result, the authors conducted a second study in which they used a more demanding divided-attention task, the one previously used by Baddeley and Hitch (1974; see also Baddeley, 1986). For half of the experimental passages, and at four different points in each text, the participants had to remember a string of four consonants as they read the next sentence. Then they had to take a quick recognition test: A string of four consonants was presented and the task was to check whether the test string matched the string they had attempted to remember while reading the sentence. In line with previous findings (see Gernsbacher, Hallada, et al., 1998, Experiment 1), the participants' ability to activate emotional knowledge, assessed by their reading time on the target sentences, was not disrupted by the execution of a divided-attention task. The reading time increased on target sentences that mismatched the protagonist's emotion, regardless of whether the participant had performed the memory-load task. In a third study, Gernsbacher, Hallada, et al. (1998) inserted a cumulative memory-load task. At four random points in the narrative, participants were shown one consonant and had to remember all four consonants as they read the rest of the text. Then recognition of the complete consonant string was tested. Again, the shortest reading times were observed for the matching target sentences, and this pattern of results occurred both when the participants were performing the cumulative memory-load task and when they were not performing that task. Finally, in a fourth study, the authors attempted to directly assess the accessibility of readers' knowledge of fictional characters' emotional states. For half of the experimental stories, they added an initial sentence that explicitly stated the emotional state that had only been implicitly conveyed in the previous experiments (Gernsbacher, Hallada, et al., 1998, Experiments 1, 2 & 3). If activating knowledge about emotional states is a relatively automatic component of reading, a difference of the same magnitude between the participants' reading times on target sentences containing matching versus mismatching emotion words should be observed when participants read the explicit versus implicit forms of the stories. As predicted, the difference in the participants' target sentences reading times for matching versus mismatching emotion words was as great after reading the stories in their implicit form as after reading them in their explicit form. Overall, these data confirm that readers activate knowledge about human emotions during narrative comprehension, and demonstrate that this is a relatively automatic component of the reading process.

8.3. INFLUENCE OF READERS' EMOTIONS ON TEXT UNDERSTANDING: INDUCTION OF EMOTIONAL STATES

Inducing a specific state of mood (or emotion) in individuals provides another way of investigating the effect of emotions on text comprehension. Several induction procedures have been described in the literature, and most results converge in suggesting that when the emotional state or mood induced and the type of materials processed are emotionally congruent, processing is facilitated. One type of induction procedure involves the use of emotion-inducing materials. In this case, the participants are usually presented with a film, a story, or a short description of a situation, and are instructed to imagine the situation and "live" it to get into the suggested emotional state or mood (i.e., try to feel the mood/emotion described in the statement). In Perrig and Perrig (1988), for example, participants were instructed to try to feel either happy or sad and to memorize a list of positive and negative words. Then they had to recall the word list. The results showed that performance was higher for words that were consistent with the participant's emotional state. The authors interpreted these data as being the result of more effective processing of information that was emotionally congruent. Rinck, Glowalla, and Schneider (1992) conducted two experiments to investigate the effect of an induced mood on the incidental learning of emotionally toned words. The participants were put in a happy or sad emotional mood by means of autosuggestion, and had to rate the emotional valence of a list of words. Later, when in a neutral emotional mood, they were asked to recall the words. For words with a high emotional valence, mood-congruent learning was observed: Strongly unpleasant words were recalled better by participants in a sad mood, and strongly pleasant words were recalled better by participants in a happy mood. Thus, an effect of mood-congruency on learning of words with a strong emotional tonality was observed, and emotional intensity appeared to be a component of overall comprehension.

Bower, Gilligan, and Monteiro (1981) looked into whether an emotional state or mood had an effect on learning and memorizing textual information. In one of their experiments, they used hypnotic suggestion (i.e., second type of induction procedure) to induce a happy or sad mood in participants. Then the participants had to read a short story about two college men who met and played a friendly afternoon game of tennis. The story portrayed the emotional reactions of both characters. One was sad because his girlfriend had just broken up with him, and he was also worried about upcoming exams. The other one was very happy: He and his girlfriend were getting along well, and he was thinking of a fabulous dinner date with her on that evening. The same amount of information for both characters was presented. After reading the story, the participants had to fill out a questionnaire that assessed two important points: The character they had identified with, and the character they thought was emphasized the most. Next, they had to recall the details of the story as thoroughly as possible. The results indicated that the participants had identified with the character who was experiencing a mood similar to the one they felt while reading the story. Moreover, that character appeared to influence their perception of the story as well as their recall. The participants not only believed that the story was mainly about the character they had identified with, but also that more details were given about that character. This probably explains why the participants recalled more facts involving the character they had identified with. Thus, the subjects were more likely to remember information corresponding to their own emotional state or mood. The authors concluded that a reader's mood causes selective learning of material that is congruent with that mood. This is consistent with one of the main principles of the model developed by Bower (1981), where mood is assumed to activate mood-congruent concepts in memory, which in turn guide the encoding process (see Bower, 1981; Bower & Cohen, 1982; Bower & Mayer, 1985).

Finally, in the third type of mood-induction procedure, participants are not explicitly asked to get into the suggested emotional state or mood, but have to study highly connoted stimuli (positive or negative linguistic or nonlinguistic information). For example, Peeck (1994) suggested that connoted pictures could induce a perspective on the situation described by the text. This author used texts in which two opposite aspects of the same topic were developed (e.g., positive and negative consequences of the industrial revolution, poor and rich living conditions in 1900). Each text was illustrated with a series of pictures emphasizing only one of the two aspects. At the end of the reading, the author tested the participants' memory of the text. The results indicated that when one of the two aspects of the topic was emphasized and enhanced by pictures, it tended to dominate the participants' memory and assessment of the text. Thus, under the influence of pictures, systematic differences occurred in the participants' memory for and evaluation of the text, even though every participant read the same text.

In line with Peeck's results (1994), Ducreux[1] (2001; Ducreux & Tapiero, 2001) showed that memory for text is a function of the congruency between the reader's emotional state and the affective tone of the text read. The author's assumption was that when a mood is induced in a subject, he or she will notice and more easily retrieve congruent emotional materials from memory (see Bower, 1981; Perrig & Perrig, 1988). In one study, the participants had to read a "natural text" about the shipwreck of the tanker Erika, and then perform a recall task on their memory of the text. The text was composed of 10 negative and 10 positive sentences about general elements of the disaster and about the fate of birds. Before reading, the participants were shown 15 positive or negative pictures (i.e., emotional induction). These pictures had been tested for their valence in a study prior to the experiment proper. The results confirmed Ducreux's assumption and demonstrated the influence of emotional information on natural catastrophe text comprehension. In particular, the prior presentation of positive pictures slowed down negative-sentences reading compared to that of positive sentences. The same congruent pattern was observed with positive sentences, the longest processing times being observed when they were preceded by negative pictures. However, and contrary to the results obtained by Peeck (1994), this congruency effect only occurred at encoding time, not during retrieval.

Ducreux (2001) also examined whether and how readers' emotional states affect their ability to engaged in more elaborate encoding of text information (microstructural and macrostructural information was described in the text). An improvement in reading performance was predicted when the emotional induction and the affective valence of macrostructural information were congruent. A preliminary task to rate the valence of each text sentence indicated that the macrostructure was negatively connoted. Prior to the reading, the participants were presented with 15 negative or neutral pictures. Then they had to perform a recognition task on the micro- and

---

[1] Angélique Ducreux conducted this study in 2001, under my direction, in fulfillment of the requirements for a Master's Degree at the University of Lyon 2 (France).

macrostructural information provided in the text (positively and negatively connoted; see Fletcher & Chrysler, 1990; Kinstch, Welsh, Schmalhofer, & Zimny, 1990). Regarding processing time, the negative pictures influenced readers' performance and led to the differential allocation of processing resources during encoding. Whereas no difference was observed between positive and negative sentences when neutral pictures preceded the text, the presentation of negative pictures slowed down the processing of negative sentences compared to positive ones. More importantly, the participants' recognition performance showed that the retrieval of micro- and macrostructural information was a function of emotional intensity. Positive emotional sentences were recognized better when associated with microstructural information, whereas negative emotional sentences were recognized better when associated with macrostructural information. This intriguing result, although consistent with the overall negative topic of the text, supports the idea that highly intense information was embedded in the level of importance of that information. These results are consistent with other studies (see Bower, Gilligan, & Monteiro, 1981; Perrig & Perrig, 1988) demonstrating a consistent relationship between emotional states and memory performance.

Finally, Blanc and Tapiero (2002) examined the role of emotions in the construction of readers' situation models. Participants had to read a news text composed of negative and positive information (a revised version of the material used in Ducreux & Tapiero's studies, 2001). The reading was preceded by the viewing of a set of highly positive or negative pictures related to the news event. Then, the participants were asked to perform an inference judgment task in which they had to judge both positive and negative information about the described event. As has already been pointed out by previous works on memory (Bower et al., 1981; Peeck, 1994), the results showed that the emotions induced by illustrations promoted the representation of consistently connoted textual information. Specifically, participants presented with positive illustrations mainly selected and integrated positive textual information, whereas those shown negative illustrations favored the selection and integration of negative textual information. Moreover, by comparing the processing and retrieval of positive versus negative information, the authors noted that negative information led to a decrease in reading speed and inference response times. Thus, Blanc and Tapiero (2002) also found evidence of the emotional impact of text constituents, suggesting that the valence of information must be considered in text comprehension. Overall, these findings strengthen the idea that the reader's emotions form an integral part of the comprehension process (see Bower et al., 1981; Ducreux & Tapiero, 2001; Peeck, 1994).

What I have presented here provides some insight into the way readers' emotions have been approached. I have also pointed out the importance of emotion in the processing and comprehension of texts. However, these studies are only a first step toward bettering our understanding of the various effects of emotion on text comprehension, and several issues still need to be addressed. Regarding the protagonist's emotion, and although it has been demonstrated that readers generate specific emotional inferences during reading Gernsbacher, Goldsmith, and Robertson (1992), Gygax et al. (2003, 2004) showed that readers' representations of the protagonist's emotion should be defined more as a general feeling than as a specific one. The question of the semantic components of emotions should therefore be considered. Gygax, Tapiero, and Carruzzo (in press) recently offered new insight into the exact nature of the mental representations of emotions built by readers during reading. In a series of experiments, they demonstrated that readers' mental representations of a text do not include specific emotions, or specific emotional concepts. Rather, they most likely encompass elements related to the protagonist's physical reactions to the situation. These last findings support the idea that participants' mental representations are more likely to include behavioral aspects of the situation than emotion concepts per se. These data offer new perspectives for future research into the semantic constituents of emotions, and will add crucial findings about how emotions influence readers' mental representations of narratives.

Another aspect that should be further investigated is the nature of the texts that influence the way readers represent the protagonist's emotions and the type of emotional inferences made (see van Dijk & Kinstch, 1983). It is very likely that emotions generated from stories are different from those generated from other types of texts, including literary or news texts. Emotions in narratives should be viewed as logical consequences of the events reported, and are undoubtedly mainly based on general emotional knowledge. In the case of literary texts, however, emotional inferences are probably rooted in situational emotion knowledge (i.e., episodic memory). Finally, for news texts, both episodic and semantic structures are likely to be involved.

The type of induction procedure used is itself subject to question, mainly because "real" efficiency and stability over time has never been evaluated for the reading comprehension process. It is easy to imagine a specific emotional state being induced in a particular reader by way of connoted illustrations, at some point in the process. But how can we be sure that the effect of the induction will be maintained (or be stable) throughout the entire processing of the text? It would be more reasonable to see the reader's emotional state as evolving in accordance with the information provided by the text. Assuming that this is the case, the effect of inducing in a reader a specific emotional state or mood should have an impact everywhere in the text to account for this change, with the expectation that it will probably be strengthened.

Finally, the strength of the induction on the "general" or "usual" emotional state of the reader is another important question. The induction procedure is probably not powerful enough to put the reader in a "positive" or "negative" emotional state like the ones a reader could experience in real-life situations. Collecting data from related areas such as cognitive neuroscience or cognitive modeling should help us answer this question and should provide us with greater expertise on how to induce an "effective" emotional state in readers, and how to maintain its effect throughout the experimental session.

8.4. READERS' EMOTIONS AND TEXT UNDERSTANDING: WHEN EMOTIONS PERTAIN TO THE TEXT'S SEMANTIC CHARACTERISTICS

Although the literature on protagonists' and readers' emotions is well documented (Gernsbacher, Goldsmith, & Robertson, 1992; Gygax et al., 2003, 2004), little is known about how individual text components like emotion words, valence, or emotional-information intensity, and their relation to the levels of importance of text information (i.e., micro- and macrostructure), affect reading performance. The relationship between emotional intensity and levels of information importance on retrieval was first investigated by Martins (1982). In particular, this author showed that highly intense emotional text information was better recalled than weakly intense information. Also, Legros (1989) demonstrated that highly connoted information promoted text recall, with a better text recall when secondary information was highly connoted compared to weakly connoted. Thus, although primary information always appeared to be well recalled, the retrieval of secondary information was found to be a function of its emotional intensity. However, Denhière and Legros (1983) obtained contradictory results by showing that the recall of a reported event was poorer when the text contained highly connoted words rather than neutral ones. These contradictory findings highlighted the idea that emotional intensity affects memory performance in different ways, depending on experimental design. Thus, the data collected on the relationship between text components and emotions needs to be interpreted with caution when considering this problem.

Finally, assuming that the reader's representation of a text is multidimensional, one question of interest is whether emotional information influences representations of other dimensions. Although the study I described at the end of the previous chapter was only a beginning in this line of research (see Galletti & Tapiero, 2004), it nevertheless showed that an emotional-situation context has an effect on sufficiency, and consequently on the activation of causal information. It appears relevant, then, to consider the different dimensions of mental representations and to determine whether some dimensions are more crucial than others. If so, what are the main factors that influence this presumed dominance? The next and last chapter of this section is devoted to this question.

Chapter 9

Are Some Dimensions More Crucial Than Others?

9.1. THE EVENT-INDEXING MODEL AND ITS PRINCIPLES (ZWAAN, LANGSTON, & GRAESSER, 1995; ZWAAN, MAGLIANO, & GRAESSER, 1995)

There is no doubt that the representation built by the reader is multidimensional (see chapter 4, §4.2). From a theoretical point of view, Gernsbacher (1990) stipulated that a correct mapping between information currently being processed and information processed previously relies on the coherence of information along five dimensions: referential, temporal, spatial, causal, and structural. Zwaan, Magliano, and Graesser (1995) also underlined, through their Event-Indexing Model (see Zwaan, Langston, & Graesser, 1995), that events conveyed in narratives are connected in memory along the dimensions of time, space, protagonist, causality, and intentionality (Zwaan, Langston, & Graesser, 1995; Zwaan, Magliano, & Graesser, 1995; Zwaan & Radvansky, 1998; Zwaan, Radvansky, Hilliard, & Curiel, 1998). Those two theoretical frameworks are based on the postulate of situational continuity, according to which the processing time of two events is facilitated if those events are situationally continuous along one of the aforementioned dimensions. The comprehension process should therefore be promoted when an incoming event continues on from another event on each of those five dimensions. Another underlying assumption is that the likelihood that events are connected in long-term memory is a function of their relatedness on each of these dimensions, with the strength of the relation between two events being a function of the number of situational cues they share.

Relying on these assumptions, Zwaan, Magliano, and Graesser (1995) studied the reader's capacity to simultaneously monitor spatiality, causality, and temporality assumed to be involved in story representation. Participants had to read two texts in which continuity on the causality, spatiality, and temporality dimensions was manipulated. They were assigned to one of two reading instructions (i.e., normal and memorization) and reading conditions (i.e., one or two readings). The results indicated that reading time significantly increased when the readers encountered temporally and causally discontinuous information, but not spatially discontinuous information. This finding indicates that the different situational dimensions do not benefit from the same monitoring, and the spatial dimension seems to be more difficult to represent than the other two. Zwaan, Magliano, and Graesser (1995) also showed that the monitoring of these dimensions is a function of the reading instructions given. Whereas the dimensions were monitored simultaneously under normal reading instructions, a memorization instruction impaired their processing because the readers' attention focused more on the semantic text components and less on the evoked situation. This points out the importance of reading instructions, which serve as a guide for the reader's goals and strategies. In addition, these findings indicated a differential effect of reading instructions on the monitoring of the multiple dimensions implied by the situation. Reading a text twice enabled the participants to focus on situational dimensions that were not attended to during the first reading. Thus, while the authors provided empirical evidence of the reader's construction of a multidimensional situation model, they also emphasized how sensitive the monitoring of these dimensions is to various experimental conditions.

The studies conducted by Zwaan, Radvansky, Hilliard, and Curiel (1998), brought further findings regarding the monitoring of these dimensions and their potential relationships (Zwaan, Langston, & Graesser, 1995). In their first experiment, these authors looked at whether readers monitor the spatiality, causality, temporality, intentionality, and protagonist dimensions. Consistent with what was already observed (Zwaan, Magliano, & Graesser, 1995), an increase in reading time occurred on causal and temporal discontinuities, but not on spatial discontinuities. Moreover, intentionality and protagonist discontinuities also underwent an increase in reading time. In their second experiment, the authors wondered whether spatiality, which is usually not well represented by readers, is monitored better when participants have to memorize a map of the environment described in the story before reading the text (see Morrow, Greenspan, & Bower, 1987). This task was assumed to help the reader represent spatiality. First, the results confirmed the effects previously observed for the other dimensions. Second, the findings clearly indicated that the experimental design was beneficial to the monitoring of spatiality, as discontinuities in this dimension lead to an increase in reading time. However, Zwaan et al. (1998) noted that spatiality was no longer monitored when the participants did not have to memorize the map of the environment before reading the text, whereas the results obtained for the other dimensions remained stable. This highlights the influence of readers' prior knowledge, goals, and strategies on the representation of text dimensions, and supports the idea that task requirements guide dimension monitoring. A particular task may therefore induce the processing of a dimension that is not spontaneously monitored.

In their attempt to determine whether several situational dimensions participate in the construction of the reader's mental representations, and based on the previous findings, Magliano, Zwaan, and Graesser (1999) proposed and tested four main principles derived from the Event-Indexing Model initially developed, mostly dealing with situational continuity. The first principle refers to a variation in reading times as a function of existing situational links between the information to be processed and the preceding context. According to the authors, the more situational links the information to process shares with the preceding context, the shorter the processing times. Magliano, Trabasso, and Langston (1995) tested this principle in two experiments. In the first, they found a correlation between ratings assigned to the relationship between story sentences and the preceding context, and the reading times of the corresponding sentences. In particular, the rating task scores increased with the number of cues shared by the sentence and the preceding context. The authors confirmed these results in a second study and showed that the rating task scores converged with the reading times obtained: Reading times decreased as the causality and intentionality ratings increased.

Magliano, Zwaan, and Graesser (1999) added two other principles concerning the construction of a multidimensional representation in relation to the inference generation process (i.e., second and third principles). The authors first assumed that readers generate connecting inferences when the information to process is continuous with the preceding situational context, whereas they generate knowledge-based inferences when the common situational links are not sufficient. This assumption could explain variations in the processing times of text information because the generation of connecting inferences is likely to be less resource-demanding than the generation of new inferences based on the reader's prior knowledge. In the latter situation, the readers would have to update their representation in order to resolve the coherence break, this operation requiring more processing time (see also Gernsbacher, 1990). Magliano, Trabasso, and Graesser (cited in Magliano, Zwaan, & Graesser, 1999) looked at whether the type of inferences generated by readers was a function of the situational continuity among the story sentences. The experimental material was composed of stories for which the authors had initially measured the number of discontinuities in each sentence, which varied between 0 to 4. The participants were instructed to read the stories, sentence by sentence, and to report their thoughts aloud, as they understood each processed sentence. The subjects' protocols confirmed that situational continuity determined the type of inferences generated. Discontinuities were resolved by inferences generated on the basis of the readers' prior knowledge (i.e., associative, explanatory, and predictive), whereas causal continuity led to the production of connecting inferences, and hence yielded shorter processing times. Finally, the association between two events was shown to be a function of the number of shared situational cues (see Zwaan, Langston, & Graesser, 1995).

9.2. FURTHER CONSIDERATIONS ABOUT SITUATIONAL DIMENSIONS: TOWARD A POSSIBLE EXTENSION OF THE EVENT-INDEXING MODEL (ZWAAN, LANGSTON, & GRAESSER, 1995; ZWAAN, MAGLIANO, & GRAESSER, 1995; ZWAAN ET AL., 1998)

The theoretical principles just presented, combined with the empirical findings reported earlier, converge in showing that readers are able to simultaneously monitor several situational dimensions. The monitoring process is a function of several factors that mainly rely on the reader's background knowledge, goals, and strategies, as well as the requirements of the task (Zwaan, Langston, & Graesser, 1995; Zwaan, Magliano, & Graesser, 1995; Zwaan & Radvansky, 1998; Zwaan, Radvansky, Hilliard, & Curiel, 1998). The Event-Indexing Model originally proposed that spatiality, causality, and temporality were involved in readers' mental representations of narratives (Zwaan, Magliano, & Graesser, 1995). Later, they increased the number of relevant dimensions by adding two other dimensions, that is, intentionality and protagonist (Zwaan, Langston, & Graesser, 1995). Those five dimensions have been shown to accurately represent the mental representations built by readers as they process narratives, and have proven to have a substantial impact on the level of coherence assigned to those representations. Earlier, I mentioned findings indicating that some dimensions are easily represented, whereas others are difficult to monitor. This being the case, it is crucial to determine how each dimension participates in the elaboration of a coherent representation, not only alone but also in interaction with other dimensions, while taking into consideration the respective weights of each dimension. Consistent with this argument, Albrecht and O'Brien (1993) showed that a physical characteristic of a protagonist (e.g., being a vegetarian) constitutes an inferential basis for the congruence of his or her intentions, as readers are capable of establishing a relationship between the protagonist's intentions and characteristics. If this is indeed the case, certain connections between other dimensions should also be evidenced, and it is likely that the monitoring of information relative to one dimension will affect (i.e., either facilitate or disrupt) the monitoring of another dimension. This assumption is reinforced if we agree with the dynamic view of the reading comprehension process. In this view, the representation of several situational dimensions should not only rely on the different phases of the reading comprehension process (i.e., construction and updating) but should also account for the foregrounding of the dimensions, depending on the portion of text being processed. As readers process a text, they may focus on some of the dimensions relative to the stable elements of the described events, including, for instance, the identity of the implied protagonists, their intentions, and the spatiotemporal framework. Once these elements are grounded, the reader's focus would shift to other dimensions. Thus, differential processing of situational dimensions should be observed, depending on whether readers build their foundations for the representation or enrich it.

Task requirements should also guide readers and cause them to allocate more or less attention to the dimensions implied by the situation. As stated earlier, seeing a map of the environment in which the story setting is described helped readers represent spatiality (Zwaan, Radvansky, Hilliard, & Curiel, 1998), whereas this dimension has been shown difficult to represent otherwise. In all likelihood, language-based tasks (e.g., summary tasks) may bring to the fore other situational dimensions that are more relevant to the protagonist, for instance. Thus, both the task's constraints and the reader's goals may influence the monitoring of situational dimensions, and as such, situational dimensions would not participate to an equal extent in the elaboration of the situation model. Further investigations should thus be conducted to shed light on this point.

A final but no less important argument that I also want to consider here pertains to the characterization of the situational dimensions of the types of text facing readers. The Event-Indexing Model (Zwaan Magliano, & Graesser, 1995; Zwaan, Langston, & Graesser, 1995) originally accounted for the monitoring of multiple dimensions, but only for a particular type of text, that is, stories. One question, then, is whether or not this model could be applied to other very different types of texts, such as science texts or argumentative or news texts. Zwaan and Radvansky (1998) considered this possibility for the protagonist dimension. According to these authors, the Event-Indexing Model could be more flexible, and could thus be adapted to any type of texts if the protagonist dimension was replaced by the "entity" dimension. This substitution would make the model's specifications more general, so it could be adapted to several types of texts. For example, the concept of "freedom" could be considered as an entity of a political discourse (Zwaan & Radvansky, 1998). By extension, a fact of society could be considered as an entity of a news text, and a protagonist as the core entity of a narrative. So far, however, the validity of this model has been demonstrated only for narratives, and its extension to other types of texts has yet to be tested. Nevertheless, it is likely that the relative weights attributed by readers to the various dimensions is a function of the type of text being processed. If the representation of the protagonist is central to stories, the monitoring of temporality should be crucial to history texts. But, it could also be the case that for one particular type of text (e.g., history text), and depending on the theme that is put into the foreground, readers focus more on one dimension (e.g., the protagonist's characteristics) than another (e.g., the temporal succession of events).

Throughout this section, I have stressed the crucial role of the reader's prior knowledge in the reading comprehension process. I showed that causality and emotions are two crucial dimensions that participate in the reader's construction of a situation model. The application of the principles of the Event-Indexing Model has also shown that it is important to account for the contribution of several dimensions in the reader's mental representation, and that there is unequal monitoring of these dimensions. This discrepancy between dimensions is a function of several factors, and once again the reader's prior knowledge is one of the most influential variables. An important challenge, therefore, is to deepen our knowledge of the characteristics of these dimensions, alone but also in interaction with each other, throughout the reading process. A better understanding of how each dimension and its relationships to the others affect the various cognitive mechanisms assumed to be involved when readers are engaged in a text comprehension process would necessarily contribute to a finer grained definition of comprehension.

Chapter 10

Toward a Definition
of Comprehension

My objective throughout this book has been to define the main characteristics of a reader's mental representations (i.e., situation models) during the reading comprehension process, by describing the various representational units used for modeling discourse entities and the mechanisms assumed to be involved in representation building. In particular, I have attempted to approach the definition of comprehension in a finer grained way, and to underline what kinds of information readers may call on as they elaborate their mental representations. I have focused on causality and emotion as two crucial dimensions in situation-model building, not only because representations of these two dimensions rely on world knowledge or on personal experiences but also because knowledge related to them is readily available. Finally, I have brought to the fore the notion of coherence, a core concept that allows readers to gradually incorporate ongoing information into their long-term memory representation. In doing this, I have been able to provide some answers to the following questions.

10.1. THE NATURE OF SITUATION MODELS

What are situation models made up of? Are some units considered "ideal" for building situation models?

Situation models are made up of entities, objects, and relationships between them. I have argued that the reader's situation model can be adequately built from various different types of entities, but those entities must be related to each other in a coherent way (see chapter 2). The way readers

189

represent discourse entities is closely tied to the way they envision real-world situations, and they assign coherence to these entities as they do in real-life situations. The role of several situational dimensions—including spatiality, causality, temporality, protagonist, and intentionality (chapter 9)—and the fact that causality and emotion (chapters 7 & 8, respectively) affect how these dimensions intervene both in situation-model construction and in inference making, provide strong arguments in favor of this analogous relationship between the represented and representing worlds. Causality is in the world, in such a way that two causally related events in the world should be causally related in the reader's situation model. I have presented several empirical findings showing that a reader's naive theory of causality is close to the causality assumed to be conveyed in texts (i.e., stories). In addition—and probably still insufficiently incorporated into our models of comprehension—the emotion dimension and the way it is represented by readers has much in common with how readers experience real-life situations. My argument that the semantic components of a particular emotion have behavioral features that are shared by several other emotions strengthens this idea (chapter 8). For example, no one would deny that crying is a common behavioral component of sadness and depression because everyone has probably seen individuals crying when they were in these particular moods (sad or depressed). The fact that readers are inclined to represent emotional information that is consistent with their own mood better than inconsistent information lends even more credit to this argument. Causality and emotion can therefore be conceived of as core dimensions in situation-model building during reading comprehension. Unlike causality, which has been widely studied over the past few years, emotion deserves more attention than it has been granted until now.

I have also emphasized the importance of investigating the factors responsible for the dominance or "better representation" of one dimension over the others (chapter 9). Some empirical findings presented in this book indicate, for example, that spatiality is one of the most difficult dimensions to monitor unless readers have received specific instructions to do so, which gives the reader's prior knowledge and task constraints a preponderant role. The difficulty readers encounter on this dimension is probably due to the fact that spatial models encode the situation described in the text from multiple perspectives, rather than from a single point of view (chapter 2). I have also stressed the need to deepen our knowledge of how a given dimension affects the influence of another dimension. The impact of emotional information on the activation strength of predictive causal inferences also contributes to validating this argument (chapter 7).

Assuming that situation models reflect the coherence assigned to the various dimensions of texts (which are close to the real world), the type of representational units (or objects) should help a reader establish coherence to a greater or lesser degree, depending on situational factors and the reader's prior knowledge. Most theories of knowledge representation, and in particular of comprehension, have posited certain crucial theoretical principles (evidenced by empirical findings) aimed at defining the most appropriate internal objects or units called on when readers are faced with a situation where they must try to understand a text. In my own studies, I assumed that readers call mainly on propositional units, in terms of a predicate and its arguments, to represent the text and knowledge networks at the textbase and situational levels (see Kintsch, 1988, 1998; Kintsch & van Dijk, 1978; van Dijk & Kintsch, 1983). Therefore, although I have discussed various other possible formats, I have demonstrated that propositions can adequately represent different types of reader knowledge, which reinforces their psychological relevance (see chapter 2). Consistent with this representational view, "predicates" reflect the various dimensions implied in the situation described by a text in accordance with the specific relationships they represent (see Kintsch, 1998). This view stresses the importance of the relationships between units.

Several other authors have argued that a full and satisfactory theory of knowledge involves representational systems other than the propositional system, mainly because of its arbitrariness and inability to account for the analogical nature of situation models (Barsalou, 1999; Johnson-Laird, 1983; Zwaan, 1999a). This view conceives of the internal structure of situation models as being closer to perception and action than do propositional systems, so they reduce the gap between the "fictitious" world readers have to represent and the way they experience similar real-life situations. Still other authors (Sanford & Garrod, 1981; 1998) define situation-model "entities" as being between the two extremes of what I would call a hypothetical "representational unit scale" for situation models, which make propositions the product of interpretation, not its precursor. Here, the reader's situation model is coherent because it first automatically activates knowledge in terms of scripts (i.e., scenarios), not because propositional units are interrelated (see chapter 2).

Despite this wide range of representational formats, a large consensus has been reached among researchers about the assumption that several processes are implemented by readers when they are processing a text. A greater weight is not granted to any one of the various types of unit readers activate throughout the reading process (chapter 3). The superiority of the functional aspects of situation models over their structural aspects has allowed researchers to go beyond the debate about the intrinsic nature of situation models. However, this casts no doubt on the idea that comprehension is a functional activity that gives a more crucial role to the relationships between units than to their intrinsic nature. In addition, and although most models of comprehension agree on the processes readers use to process a text, the time course of some of these processes and the question of whether they are underlain by automatic or strategic mechanisms are still under debate.

10.2. THE MAIN COGNITIVE PROCESSES INVOLVED IN SITUATION-MODEL BUILDING

What are the main processes involved in the elaboration of readers' mental representations?

Among the various cognitive processes I have described (see chapter 3), the construction process (Kintsch, 1988, 1998; Sanford & Garrod, 1981; Zwaan & Radvansky, 1998), also defined by Gernsbacher (1990) as the foundation-laying process for structures and substructures, has been widely regarded as the basis for defining situation-model building. Most researchers have assumed that this process allows readers to "activate" various meaningful units in memory as they process the text. This leads them to construct a rich representation, although some of the units and their interrelationships may be irrelevant or even contradictory. The activation mechanism has been defined as automatic, fast, and context-independent, and it is assumed to come into play as readers process text information. After this first phase, an integration process takes effect. It allows readers to attain a full and correct interpretation of the text. In order for the integration to take place, the information currently being processed has to be mapped to previously processed information. The mapping process may or not cause readers to update their representation, depending on whether coherence is established between the two kinds of information (i.e., currently being processed and already processed). However, unlike the construction process, the conditions under which the updating process occurs do not lead to a consensus (chapter 3).

I grant a central role to the updating process in my investigation of the reading comprehension process because studying it brings out several important issues. First, it stresses the importance of making the theoretical principles developed in memory research closer to those assumed by current theories of comprehension. The memory-based approach to text comprehension, particularly the main characteristics of the resonance process (see Myers & O'Brien, 1998), provide strong support for the idea that the underlying postulates of memory theories should be incorporated into a model of mechanisms specific to text comprehension. To gain an in-depth understanding of the various steps in the reading comprehension process, we can no longer dissociate the theoretical conceptions underlying the structural and functional properties of memory from those of comprehension, nor can we ignore the different views of whether readers access several sources of information in a strategic or automatic way. Ericsson and

Kintsch's (1995) view of memory, which involves the concepts of short-term working memory and long-term working memory, strengthens this argument (chapter 3). According to these authors, retrieval cues available in short-term working memory allow for fast retrieval of information in long-term working memory, and consequently, for the efficient integration of information across sentences. The four memory partitions proposed by Sanford and Garrod (1981, 1998) add further evidence to this argument: Occurrences that serve as tokens in explicit focus are used as relevant retrieval cues for information held in implicit focus (i.e., dynamic partitions), thereby allowing readers to readily access backgrounded information (i.e., static partitions) and thus to achieve a full interpretation of the text.

Access to backgrounded information has been conceptualized as a fast-acting, automatic process taking place in a bottom-up fashion (the resonance process: Myers & O'Brien, 1998). This view is consistent with Ericsson and Kintsch's (1995) framework. However, the process remains at a shallow level in the case of comprehension, and is more like a theory of activation than an integrated theory of comprehension. The empirical findings I presented earlier (chapter 4) on the importance of the nature of retrieval cues, and on how relevance is assigned to those cues (i.e., pointers), confirm the idea that there is a resonance process taking place during a first phase of reading. But it also highlights that, during a second phase, the mapping between the information currently being processed and the information already processed relies on relevance, allowing readers to build an integrated and coherent representation of the text (chapter 4). Situation models themselves may assign this relevance, and thereby serve as retrieval structures that are automatically activated. I have shown that they could override surface relationships between currently processed information and information to be reactivated (chapter 6). I have, therefore, underlined the crucial role played by the reader's knowledge and the activation of situational relationships that take precedence over textbase relations in the reader's attempt to establish a coherent representation. Thus, although updating requires passive resonance, it may not be sufficient because readers must take relevance and the nature of knowledge into account, and this constrains access to backgrounded information and integration.

A second important issue related to the updating process concerns the properties of the various intermediate mechanisms assumed to be based on a "good" fit between currently and previously processed information. For some authors, these mechanisms occur automatically and emerge in a bottom-up fashion (Ericsson & Kintsch, 1995; Kintsch, 1988, 1998; Myers & O'Brien, 1998; Sanford & Garrod, 1998). For a given reader, connections between these two types of information are either automatically reinforced (if related in a coherent way) or inhibited (in case of irrelevant or contradictory relations). Unlike this view, Gernsbacher's (1990) view argues that readers strategically "suppress" irrelevant information from their representation, based on the assumption that the suppression mechanism relies on linguistic coherence cues from various dimensions (e.g., spatiality, causality, etc.). This theoretical approach has been evidenced by a number of empirical findings showing that when current information and previous information are continuous along each of these dimensions, coherence is achieved and updating is successful (see also Zwaan & Radvansky, 1998). These two theoretical frameworks thus differ in their assumptions regarding how updating occurs. The former view (Kintsch, 1988, 1998; Sanford & Garrod, 1998) contends that coherence is established automatically and emerges from the combination of the textbase and knowledge networks. This is done in a dynamic way, with certain types of relationships between concepts being reinforced, whereas others are inhibited, namely those that cannot be maintained and co-occur in working memory because they are contextually inconsistent. The memory representation of irrelevant pieces of information will decay until it reaches a zero value and will therefore be eliminated (Kintsch, 1988). On the other hand, in line with Gernsbacher's (1990) theory, readers are assumed to constantly "search for coherence," each piece of text information being processed serving as a cue in this search.

10.3. THE ROLE OF READERS' PRIOR KNOWLEDGE AND TASK CONSTRAINTS IN SITUATION-MODEL BUILDING

What is the impact of the reader's prior knowledge and the task's constraints on situation-model building? Does comprehension emerge in a bottom-up fashion or is it constrained by the reader's expectations?

Unlike the processing of isolated sentences where readers only establish local coherence (between adjacent units), text processing requires building both local and global coherence. Global coherence involves mapping incoming information either with earlier text information held in long-term episodic memory, or with general knowledge, that is, information stored in long-term semantic memory. I have emphasized the dominance of the global approach to coherence over local approaches by demonstrating the importance of theories of causality (chapters 5 & 6) and of the reader's prior knowledge in situation-model building (chapters 3, 7, 8, & 9). From this, I have shown that readers are able to connect adjacent as well as distant units, and both local and global connections are established even when local connections are successful. In addition, by attributing a crucial role to the links between pieces of text information that are in and out of focus, including the reader's prior knowledge, I have attempted to show that the different weights assigned by readers to the relationships between these various sources of knowledge play a preponderant role that depends on the situation facing the reader and on the particular moment in the reading process. It follows from this that at each particular point in the reading process, not all relationships have the same importance level in the reader's mental representation, and the nature of the knowledge called on also depends on the type of information under focus at a specific time. This approach is consistent with a dynamic view of the reading comprehension process (Sanford & Garrod, 1998; Zwaan & Radvansky, 1998), and one of the crucial features of the computational models described in chapter 1 (Construction-Integration Model: Kintsch, 1988; Landscape Model: van den Broek et al., 1996) is precisely that they account for this dynamic process. For example, Kintsch's (1988) Construction-Integration Model relies on the online construction of the mental representation and provides us with a step-by-step description of situation-model building until the integration phase occurs, both across sentences and with the online contribution of the reader's prior knowledge. In the Landscape Model (van den Broek et al., 1996), the online activation of concepts itself triggers the reconstruction or reconfiguration of the entire representation, giving the relationships between the online and offline representations a crucial role (chapter 1). In other words, as each piece of information enters the cognitive system, the representation currently being built is updated and enriched through various sources of knowledge. This is what gives the situation-model representation all of its richness and complexity, it being the result of a dynamic interaction between several types of information. This is done dynamically, in a bottom-up and top-down fashion in such a way that readers can modify their representation when processing the text via fast access to backgrounded information, but also via anticipations and expectations about future events that lead readers to generate forward inferences. In this framework, then, the reader's representation depends on several levels of bottom-up and top-down constraints, all of which continuously call on coherence.

Throughout this book, I have also attempted to show that successful comprehension, that is, an adequate situation model, is the result of a "good" fit between object relations represented in the text and knowledge about those relations called on by readers. This idea is consistent with Sanford and Garrod's view of the reading comprehension process. According to these authors, when faced with a text, the reader first has to identify an appropriate reference domain (i.e., setting and situation) that loosely corresponds to what the text is about, and then has to use the identified domain to interpret the rest of the text. This approach is supported by evidence of automatic scenario matching (Sanford & Garrod, 1981), where knowledge of settings and situations constitutes the interpretational scenario for a text. In this approach, then, knowledge is automatically activated and mental representation coherence is achieved by prior knowledge activation. Relevance is no longer a synonym of strategy, here, but automatically constrains the possible candidates for establishing text coherence (and the coherence of the mental representation).

Finally, I have granted a crucial role to the reader's prior knowledge and task constraints in the inference-making process. I have mainly discussed predictive inferences because their generation is conditioned by several constraints, including the degree of causal constraint, the nature of contextual features, and the combined effect of immediately preceding information and contextual knowledge. I have also shown that situational knowledge is a determining factor in these inferences, whether or not it is combined with the immediately preceding event. However, to give an in-depth definition of comprehension, and to describe the main processes involved in the way readers call on specific or general knowledge during reading, one must take into account recent findings from related areas such as cognitive neuroscience or neuropsychology, which have shown that specific brain areas are involved in the construction of different levels of representation (textbase and situation model) and more specifically, in causal and emotional inference-making. These findings increase the "dimensional power" of causality and emotion because they provide another crucial level for interpreting readers' performance, one that is biologically relevant, not simply evidenced in classic cognitive psychology studies. For example, using a divided visual field methodology, Virtue, Linderholm, and van den Broek (2000) studied the influence of two levels of causal text constraints (high vs. low) on the generation of predictive inferences. The authors' assumption was based on Beeman's recent findings (Beeman, 1998; Beeman & Bowden, 2000) showing that the right hemisphere performs a coarse semantic coding compared to the left hemisphere, which allows for the selection of a precise meaning through a relatively fine semantic coding. Virtue et al. (2000) found that causal constraints differentially affect predictive inferences in the two hemispheres. In particular, they showed that although both hemispheres played a role in the generation of highly constrained predictive inferences, the right hemisphere appeared to be more efficient at producing predictive inferences that are less constrained by the text. Consistently, Beeman, Bowden, and Gernsbacher (2000) tested participants' ability to generate either predictive or coherence inferences and assessed inference-related activation in each hemisphere at different points in stories. Their main results showed that although both hemispheres were involved in inference-drawing, inference generation was affected by the processing specificities in the right and left hemispheres. The left hemisphere appears to play a greater role than the right hemisphere in selecting a coherence inference and incorporating it into the text representation, whereas information capable of supporting predictive inferences is more likely to be initially activated in the right hemisphere than in the left hemisphere. Fillon and I (Tapiero & Fillon, in press; Fillon & Tapiero, 2005) also used a split visual field methodology to test the differential processing of the two cerebral hemispheres, but on emotion inferences. In line with previous findings (Beeman, 1993; Davidson, 1995), the right hemisphere showed facilitation for both coherent and contradictory emotional information compared to the left hemisphere, thereby confirming the diffuse semantic coding of the right hemisphere and its dominance for multiple interpretations (see Beeman & Bowden, 2000; Beeman, Bowden, & Gernsbacher, 2000). These findings underline the crucial role of the right hemisphere in the construction of a coherent representation and show once again that emotion must be taken into account as a core dimension in readers' situation models. Although I have provided only a brief overview of the recent findings indicating differential processing of the two hemispheres during causal and emotional inference making, what I have presented here removes all doubts about the need for further investigations of how brain structures are related to the higher level processes involved in text comprehension. This should help us develop an integrated theory of comprehension that involves several research areas, so that different explanation levels of reading performance can converge to achieve an in-depth understanding of the situation models developed by readers.

10.4. THE VARIOUS CONSTRAINTS FOR A COHERENT SITUATION MODEL: AN INTEGRATED VIEW OF THE COMPREHENSION PROCESS

The three preceding questions and my attempts to answer them have made it quite plain that in order to propose a precise definition of readers' mental representations, it is necessary to take into account various levels of constraint that mutually interact in a bottom-up and top-down fashion and therefore affect the situation-model building. First, prior to text processing, the components of the situation itself—and the knowledge and expectations readers have about the situation, including the text genre (scientific, narrative, etc.), the task requirements (diagram, reading, questions, etc.), and the reader's goals and motivations—all work together in a top-down way influence to the reading comprehension process, and in some ways constrain the "initial" state of the mental representation when the reader begins the reading. Then, as the reader focuses on the first words in the text, other constraints that are more specific to the content proper of the text, and that rely on the reader's prior knowledge to get activated in relation to text information, modulate this representational state. This close-knit interplay between the different levels of constraints (i.e., situation, text, and reader's knowledge) as text information is being processed leads readers to achieve a greater or lesser degree of stability in the "state" of their representation, that is, a coherent situation model. Situation models would, in this case, be conceived of not as fixed structures but as "mental representation spaces" that would be flexible enough to allow for the dynamic interplay between the various constraints, becoming gradually modified and enriched through their interactions throughout the processing of the text. However, the focus on functional aspects of situation models (i.e., relations between units and processes) and on the idea that readers' mental representations should be analogous to how readers envision real-world situations converge and provide evidence of the need for other constraints, including biological ones, which would both provide and "authorize" a level of interpretation that would necessarily strengthen the explanatory power of any given theory. Recent findings on the relationship between language comprehension and motor programs, and the notion of comprehension as a simulation, are consistent with this argument (see Barsalou, 1999). In this view, if some regions of the brain are active when performing a particular task, the same regions should be activated when readers process text information dealing with that particular task.

If situation models are a kind of flexible mental space, comprehension could be defined as the gradual emergence of meaning, within such a space that would fluctuate constantly throughout the reading process. Comprehension attained by a specific reader in his or her mental representation space would emerge from the interaction between the various levels of constraint already stated and widely discussed in this book, namely the situation, the text, and the reader's knowledge. A valid theory of comprehension should therefore define the characteristics of each of these constraints, along with their interrelationships. Moreover, a full theory of comprehension requires incorporating, in a more interleaving way, the contributions of other disciplines like cognitive neuroscience. This will enable a finer grained approach, and most importantly, one that is biologically plausible, to the complexity and richness of this "mental state" that represents the level of comprehension the reader has reached.

References

Aaranson, D., & Ferres, S. (1984). The word-by-word reading paradigm: An experimental and theoretical approach. In D. Kieras & M. Just (Eds.), *New methods in reading comprehension research* (pp. 31–68). Hillsdale, NJ: Lawrence Erlbaum Associates.

Albrecht, J. E., & Myers, J. L. (1995). Role of context in accessing distant information during reading. *Journal of Experimental Psychology: Learning, Memory and Cognition, 21*, 1459–1468.

Albrecht, J. E., & Myers, J. L. (1998). Accessing distant text information during reading: Effects of contextual cues. *Discourse Processes, 26*, 87–107.

Albrecht, J. E., & O'Brien, E. J. (1993). Updating a mental model: Maintaining both local and global coherence. *Journal of Experimental Psychology: Learning, Memory & Cognition, 19*(5), 1061–1070.

Anderson, A., Garrod, S. C., & Sanford, A. J. (1983). The accessibility of pronominal antecedents as a function of episode shifts in narrative. *Quarterly Journal of Experimental Psychology, 35A*, 427–440.

Andler, D. (1991). *Introduction aux sciences cognitives* [Introduction to cognitive science]. Folio/Essais. Gallimard.

Arocha, J. F., & Patel, V. L. (1995). Construction-Integration Theory and clinical reasoning. In C. Weaver, S. Mannes, & R. C. Fletcher (Eds.), *Discourse comprehension: Essays in honor of Walter Kintsch* (pp. 359–381). Hillsdale, NJ: Lawrence Erlbaum Associates.

Aurouer, E. (2002). *Mise à jour d'un modèle de situation: Comment les lecteurs accèdent aux informations antérieures* [Updating a situation model: How readers access to backgrounded information]. Unpublished master's thesis, University of Lyon 2, Lyon, France.

Baddeley, A. D. (1986). *Working memory*. New York: Oxford University Press.

Baddeley, A. D., & Hitch, G. (1974). Working memory. In G. H. Bower (Ed.), *Recent advances in learning and motivation* (Vol. 8, pp. 47–89). New York: Academic Press.

Baker, L. (1979). Comprehension monitoring: Identifying and coping with text confusions. *Journal of Reading Behavior, 11*, 365–374.

199

Barsalou, L. W. (1993). Flexibility, structure, and linguistic vagary in concepts: Manifestations of a compositional system of perceptual symbols. In A. C. Collins, S. E. Gathercole, & M. A. Conway (Eds.), *Theories of memories* (pp. 29–101). London: Lawrence Erlbaum Associates.

Barsalou, L. W. (1999). Perceptual symbol systems. *Behavioral and Brain Sciences, 22,* 577–660.

Bartlett, F. C. (1932). *Remembering: A study in experimental and social psychology.* Cambridge, UK: Cambridge University Press.

Baudet, S. (1990). Représentation d'état, d'événement, d'action et de causation [State, event, action and causation representations]. In J. François & G. Denhière (Eds.), *Languages, 100,* pp. 45–64.

Beeman, M. (1993). Semantic processing in the right hemisphere may contribute to drawing inferences from discourse. *Brain and Language, 44,* 80–120.

Beeman, M. (1998). Coarse semantic coding and discourse comprehension. In M. Beeman & C. Chiarello (Eds.), *Getting it right: The cognitive neuroscience of right hemisphere language comprehension* (pp. 225–284). Mahwah, NJ: Lawrence Erlbaum Associates.

Beeman, M., & Bowden, E. M. (2000). The right hemisphere maintains solution-related activation for yet-to-be solved problems. *Memory and Cognition, 28*(7), 1231–1241.

Beeman, M., Bowden, E. M., & Gernsbacher, M. A. (2000). Right and left hemisphere cooperation for drawing predictive and coherence inferences during normal story comprehension. *Brain and Language, 71,* 310–336.

Black, J. B., & Bern, H. (1981). Causal coherence and memory for events in narratives. *Journal of Verbal Learning and Verbal Behavior, 20,* 267–275.

Black, J. B., & Bower, G. H. (1980). Story understanding as problem solving. *Poetics, 9,* 223–250.

Black, J. B., Turner, T. J., & Bower, G. H. (1979). Point of view in narrative comprehension, memory, and production. *Journal of Verbal Learning and Verbal Behavior, 18,* 187–198.

Blanc, N., Ducreux, A., & Tapiero, I. (2006). *Text comprehension: A relevant framework to study the relation between emotion and cognition.* Manuscript in preparation.

Blanc, N., & Tapiero, I. (2001). Updating a situation model: Effects of prior knowledge and task demands. *Discourse Processes, 31*(3), 241–262.

Blanc, N., & Tapiero, I. (2002). Construire une représentation mentale à partir d'un texte: Le rôle des illustrations et de la connotation des informations [Building a mental representation from text: The role of illustrations and connotation of information]. *Bulletin de Psychologie, 461,* 525–534.

Bloom, C. P., Fletcher, C. R., van den Broek, P. W., Reitz, L., & Shapiro, B. P. (1990). An online assessment of causal reasoning during comprehension. *Memory and Cognition, 18,* 65–71.

Bower, G. H. (1981). Mood and memory. *American Psychologist, 36,* 129–148.

Bower, G. H., Black, J. B., & Turner, T. J. (1979). Scripts in memory for text. *Cognitive Psychology, 11,* 177–220.

Bower, G. H., & Cohen, P. R. (1982). Emotional influences in memory and thinking: Data and theory. In S. Fiske & M. Clark (Eds.), *Affect and social cognition* (pp. 291–331). Hillsdale, NJ: Lawrence Erlbaum Associates.

Bower, G. H., Gilligan, S. G., & Monteiro, K. P. (1981). Selectivity of learning caused by affective states. *Journal of Experimental Psychology: General, 110,* 451–473.

Bower, G. H., & Mayer, J. D. (1985). Failure to replicate mood-dependent retrieval. *Bulletin of the Psychonomic Society, 23,* 39–42.

Bransford, J. D., Barclay, J. R., & Franks, J. J. (1972). Sentence memory: A constructive versus interpretive approach. *Cognitive Psychology, 3,* 193–209.

Bransford, J. D., & Johnson, M. K. (1972). Contextual prerequisites for understanding: Some investigations of comprehension and recall. *Journal of Verbal Learning and Verbal Behavior, 61*, 717–726.

Britton, B. K., & Tesser, A. (1982). Effects of prior knowledge on use of cognitive capacity in three complex cognitive tasks. *Journal of Verbal Learning and Verbal Behavior, 21*, 421–436.

Bryant, D. J., Tversky, B., & Franklin, N. (1992). Internal and external spatial frameworks for representing described scenes. *Journal of Memory and Language, 31*, 74–98.

Cailliès, S., & Tapiero, I. (1997). Structure textuelle et niveaux d'expertise [Textual structure and levels of expertise]. *L'Année Psychologique, 97*, 611–639.

Calvo, M. G., & Castillo, M. D. (1996). Predictive inferences occur on-line, but with delay: Convergence of naming and reading times. *Discourse Processes, 22*, 57–78.

Campanario, J. M., & van Oostendorp, H. (1996, September 4–6). Updating mental representation when reading scientific texts. In J. F. Rouet, J. Levonen, & A. Biardeau (Eds.), *Proceedings of the Using Complex Information Systems '96 Conference.* Poitiers, France: University of Poitiers.

Campion, N., & Rossi, J. P. (1999). Inférences et compréhension de texte [Inference and text comprehension]. *L'Année Psychologique, 99*, 493–527.

Carreiras, M., Gernsbacher, M. A., & Villa, V. (1995). The advantage of first mention in Spanish. *Psychonomic Bulletin & Review, 2*, 124–129.

Chase, W. G., & Simon, H. A. (1973). Perception in chess. *Cognitive Psychology, 1*, 55–81.

Chiesi, H. L., Spilich, G. J., & Voss, J. F. (1979). Acquisition of domain related information in relation to high and low domain knowledge. *Journal of Verbal Learning and Verbal Behavior, 18*, 257–273.

Cirilo, R. K. (1981). Referential coherence and text structure in story comprehension. *Journal of Verbal Learning and Verbal Behavior, 20*, 358–368.

Collins, A. M., Brown, J. S., & Larkin, K. M. (1980). Inferences in text understanding. In R. J. Spiro, B. C. Bruce, & W. F. Brewer (Eds.), *Theoretical issues in reading comprehension* (pp. 385–407). Hillsdale, NJ: Lawrence Erlbaum Associates.

Cook, A. O., Halleran, J. G., & O'Brien, E. J. (1998). What is readily available during reading? A memory-based view of text processing. *Discourse Processes, 26*, 109–129.

Cook, A. E., Limber, J. E., & O'Brien, E. J. (2001). Situation-based context and the availability of predictive inferences. *Journal of Memory and Language, 44*, 220–234.

Craik, K. (1943). *The nature of explanation.* Cambridge, England: Cambridge University Press.

Damasio, A. R. (1989). Time-locked multiregional retroactivation: A systems-level proposal for the neural substrates of recall and recognition. *Cognition, 33*, 25–62.

Daneman, M., & Carpenter, P. A. (1983). Individual differences in integrating information between and within sentences. *Journal of Experimental Psychology: Learning, Memory, & Cognition, 9*, 561–585.

Davidson, R. J. (1995). Cerebral asymmetry, emotion, and affective style. In R. J. Davidson & K. Hugdahl (Eds.), *Brain asymmetry* (pp. 361–387). Cambridge, MA: MIT Press.

Dell, G., McKoon, G., & Ratcliff, R. (1983). The activation of antecedent information during the processing of anaphoric reference in reading. *Journal of Verbal Learning and Verbal Behavior, 22*, 121–132.

Dellarosa, O. (1986). A computer simulation of children's arithmetic word problem solving. *Behavior Research Methods, Instruments, & Computers, 18*, 147–154.

de Vega, M. (1991). Change of character and change of perspective in narratives describing spatial environments. *European Colloquium on Mental Models.* Paris, France.

de Vega, M. (1995). Backward updating of mental models during continuous reading narratives. *Journal of Experimental Psychology: Learning, Memory and Cognition, 21*(2), 373–385.

de Vega, M., Diaz, J. M., & Leon, I. (1997). To know or not to know: Comprehending protagonists' beliefs ad their emotional consequences. *Discourse Processes, 23,* 169–192.

de Vega, M., Leon, I., & Diaz, J. M. (1996). The representation of changing emotions in reading comprehension. *Cognition and Emotion, 10*(3), 303–321.

Denhière, G. (1984). *Il était une fois …. Compréhension et souvenir de récits [Once upon a time … comprehension and stories remembering].* Lille, France: Presses Universitaires de Lille.

Denhière, G., & Baudet, S. (1992). *Lecture, compréhension de texte et science cognitive* [Reading, text comprehension and cognitive science]. Paris: Presses Universitaires de France.

Denhière, G., & Legros, D. (1983). Comprendre un texte: Construire quoi? Avec quoi? Comment? [Understanding a text: Building what? With what? How?]. *Revue Française de Pédagogie, 65,* 19–29.

Denis, M., & Cocude, M. (1992). Structural properties of visual images constructed from poorly or well-structured descriptions. *Memory and Cognition, 20*(5), 497–506.

Denis, M., & de Vega, M. (1993). Modèles mentaux et imagerie mentale [Mental models and mental imagery]. In M. F. Ehrlich, H. Tardieu, & M. Cavazza (Eds.), *Les modèles mentaux, approche cognitive des representations* [Mental models, cognitive approach of representations] (pp. 79–100). Paris: Masson.

Ducreux, A. (2001). *Influence des caractéristiques textuelles et des caractéristiques du lecteur sur la mise en place d'une représentation multi-niveaux* [Impact of text's properties and readers' characteristics on the elaboration of a multidimensional representation]. Unpublished master's thesis, University of Lyon 2, Lyon, France.

Ducreux, A., & Tapiero, I. (2001, September). *Effect of emotional information on a construction of a semantic representation.* Poster presented at the 12th meeting of the European Society for Cognitive Psychology, Edinburgh, Scotland.

Ehrlich, K., & Johnson-Laird, P. N. (1982). Spatial descriptions and referential continuity. *Journal of Verbal Learning and Verbal Behavior, 21,* 296–306.

Ericsson, K., & Kintsch, W. (1995). Long-term working memory. *Psychological Review, 102,* 211–245.

Fillon, V., & Tapiero, I. (2005, July). *Hemispheric dominance and inferences generation: Effect of the valence and relevance of emotional text information.* Oral presentation at the 15th Annual Meeting of the Society for Text and Discourse, Amsterdam, The Netherlands.

Fincher-Kiefer, R. (1995). Relative inhibition following the encoding of bridging and predictive inferences. *Journal of Experimental Psychology: Learning, Memory, and Cognition, 21,* 981–995.

Fincher-Kiefer, R. (1996). Encoding differences between bridging and predictive inferences. *Discourse Processes, 22,* 225–246.

Fischer, A. H. (1991). *Emotion scripts: A study of the social and cognitive facets of emotions.* Leiden: DSWO Press.

Fischer, B., & Glanzer, M. (1986). Short-term storage and the processing of cohesion during reading. *Quarterly Journal of Experimental Psychology, 38A,* 431–460.

Fletcher, C. R. (1994). Levels of representation in memory for discourse, In M. A. Gernsbacher (Ed.), *Handbook of psycholinguistics* (pp. 589–607). New York: Academic Press.

Fletcher, C. R., & Bloom, C. P. (1988). Causal reasoning in the comprehension of simple narrative texts. *Journal of Memory and Language, 27*, 235–244.

Fletcher, C. R., & Chrysler, S. T. (1990). Surface forms, textbases, and situation models: Recognition memory for three types of textual information. *Discourse Processes, 13*, 175–190.

Fletcher, C. R., van den Broek, P., & Arthur, E. J. (1996). A model of narrative comprehension and recall. In B. K. Britton & A. C. Graesser (Eds.), *Models of understanding text* (pp. 141–165). Hillsdale, NJ: Lawrence Erlbaum Associates.

Foltz, P. W. (1996). Latent Semantic Analysis for text-based research. *Behavior Research Methods, Instruments and Computers, 28*(2), 197–202.

François, J. (1991). La pertinence linguistique des représentations propositionnelles de la sémantique cognitive [The linguistic relevance of propositional representations from cognitive semantic]. *Sémiotiques, 1*, 69–80.

Franklin, N., & Tversky, B. (1990). Searching imagined environments. *Journal of Experimental Psychology: General, 119*, 63–76.

Frederiksen, C. H. (1987). Text comprehension in functional domains. In D. Bloom (Ed.), *Functional literacy activity in education: Cognitive and social approaches*. Norwood, NJ: Ablex.

Frederiksen, C. H., & Donin, J. (1991). Constructing multiple semantic representations in comprehending and producing discourse. In G. Denhière & J. P. Rossi (Eds.), *Text and text processing, 79*, 19–45. Amsterdam: North Holland.

Frijda, N. H. (1986). *The emotions*. Cambridge: Cambridge University Press.

Fridja, N. H. (1989). The different roles of cognitive variables in emotion. In A. F. Bennet & K. M. McConkey (Eds.), *Cognition in individual and social contexts* (pp. 325–337). Amsterdam: Elsevier Science.

Galletti, S. (2004). *Influence de la nature des informations contextuelles et de la force des contraintes textuelles sur la production d'inférences causales et émotionnelles* [Impact of the nature of contextual information and strength of texts' constraint on the generation of causal and emotional inferences]. Unpublished master's thesis, University of Lyon 2, Lyon, France.

Galletti, S., & Tapiero, I. (2004, November). *Effects of contextual information on the strength of predictive inferences generation*. Oral presentation at the 45th Annual Meeting of the Psychonomic Society, Minneapolis, MN.

Garrod, S. C. (1995). Distinguishing between explicit and implicit focus during text comprehension. In G. Rickheit & C. Habel (Eds.), *Focus and coherence in discourse processing* (pp. 3–17). Berlin, Germany: de Gruyter.

Garrod, S. C., O'Brien, E. J., Morris, R. K., & Rayner, K. (1990). Elaborative inferencing as an active or passive process. *Journal of Experimental Psychology, 16*, 250–247.

Garrod, S. C., & Sanford, A. J. (1988). Thematic subjecthood and cognitive constraints on discourse structure. *Journal of Pragmatics, 12*, 519–534.

Garrod, S. C., & Sanford, A. J. (1990). Referential processes during reading: Focusing on role of individuals. In D. A. Balota, G. B. Flores d'Arcais, & K. Rayner (Eds.), *Comprehension processes in reading* (pp. 465–485). Hillsdale, NJ: Lawrence Erlbaum Associates.

Gernsbacher, M. A. (1989). Mechanisms that improve referential access. *Cognition, 32*, 99–156.

Gernsbacher, M. A. (1990). *Language comprehension as structure building*. Hillsdale, NJ: Lawrence Erlbaum Associates.

Gernsbacher, M. A. (1991). Comprehending conceptual anaphors. *Language and Cognitive Processes, 6*, 81–105.

Gernsbacher, M. A. (1996). Coherence cues mapping during comprehension. In J. Costermans & M. Fayol (Eds.), *Processing interclausal relationships in the production and comprehension of text* (pp. 3–21). Mahwah, NJ: Lawrence Erlbaum Associates.

Gernsbacher, M. A., & Faust, M. (1991). The role of suppression in sentence comprehension. In G. B. Simpson (Ed.), *Understanding word and sentence* (pp. 97–128). Amsterdam: North Holland.

Gernsbacher, M. A., Goldsmith, H. H., & Robertson, R. W. (1992). Do readers mentally represent character's emotional states? *Cognition and Emotion, 6*(2), 89–111.

Gernsbacher, M. A., Hallada, B. M., & Robertson, R. R. W. (1998). How automatically do readers infer fictional character's emotional states? *Scientific Studies of Reading, 2*(3), 271–300.

Gernsbacher, M. A., & Hargreaves, D. (1988). Accessing sentence participants: The advantage of first mention. *Journal of Memory and Language, 27*, 699–717.

Gernsbacher, M. A., & Hargreaves, D. (1992). The privilege of primacy: Experimental data and cognitive explanations. In D. L. Payne (Ed.), *Pragmatics of word order flexibility* (pp. 83–116). Philadelphia: John Benjamins.

Gernsbacher, M. A., & Robertson, R. R. W. (1992). Knowledge activation versus sentence mapping when representing fictional characters' emotional states. *Language and Cognitive Processes, 7*(3/4), 353–371.

Gillund, G., & Shiffrin, R. M. (1984). A retrieval model for both recognition and recall. *Psychological Review, 91*, 1–67.

Glanzer, M., Dorfman, D., & Kaplan, B. (1981). Short-term storage in the processing of text. *Journal of Verbal Learning and Verbal Behavior, 20*, 656–670.

Glanzer, M., Fischer, B., & Dorfman, D. (1984). Short-term storage in reading. *Journal of Verbal Learning and Verbal Behavior, 23*, 467–486.

Glenberg, A. M. (1997). What memory is for. *Behavioral and Brain Sciences, 20*, 1–55.

Glenberg, A. M., & Langston, W. E. (1992). Comprehension of illustrated text: Pictures help to build mental models. *Journal of Memory and Language, 31*, 129–151.

Glenberg, A. M., Meyer, M., & Lindem, K. (1987). Mental models contribute to foregrounding during text comprehension. *Journal of Memory and Language, 26*, 69–83.

Glenberg, A. M., & Robertson, D. A. (2000). Symbol grounding and meaning: A comparison of high-dimensional and embodied theories of meaning. *Journal of Memory and Language, 43*(3), 379–401.

Goetz, E. T., Anderson, R. C., & Schallert, D. L. (1981). The representation of sentences in memory. *Journal of Verbal Learning and Verbal Behavior, 20*, 369–385.

Goldman, S. R., & Varma, S. (1995). Capping the Construction-Integration model of discourse comprehension. In C. A. Weaver, S. Mannes, & C. R. Fletcher (Eds.), *Discourse comprehension: Essays in honor of Walter Kintsch* (pp. 337–358). Hillsdale, NJ: Lawrence Erlbaum Associates.

Graesser, A. C., & Clark, L. F. (1985). *The structures and procedures of implicit knowledge.* Norwood, NJ: Ablex.

Graesser, A. C., Millis, K. K., & Zwaan, R. A. (1997). Discourse comprehension. *Annual Review of Psychology, 48*, 163–189.

Graesser, A. C., Robertson, S. P., Lovelace, E. R., & Swinehart, D. M. (1980). Answers to why questions about story plot and predict recall of actions. *Journal of Verbal Learning and Verbal Behaviour, 19*, 110–119.

Graesser, A. C., Singer, M., & Trabasso, T. (1994). Constructing inferences during narrative text comprehension. *Psychological Review, 3*, 371–395.

Graesser, A. C., & Zwaan, R. A. (1995). Inference generation and the construction of situation models. In C. A. Weaver, S. Mannes, & C. R. Fletcher (Eds.), *Discourse comprehension: Strategies and processing revisited* (pp. 117–139). Hillsdale, NJ: Lawrence Erlbaum Associates.

Gray-Wilson, S., Rinck, M., McNamara, T. P., Bower, G. H., & Morrow, D. G. (1993). Mental models and narrative comprehension: Some qualifications. *Journal of Memory and Language, 32,* 141–154.

Groen, G. J., & Patel, V. L. (1988). The relationship between comprehension and reasoning in medical expertise. In M. Chi, R. Glaser, & M. J. Farr (Eds.), *The nature of expertise* (pp. 287–310). Hillsdale, NJ: Lawrence Erlbaum Associates.

Guéraud, S., Blanc, N., & Tapiero, I. (2001). *Inhibition et suppression: Mise en evidence de l'existence de ces deux* mécanismes *en comprehension de texte* [Inhibition and suppression: Existence of these two mechanisms in text comprehension]. Poster presented at the 100th Congress of the French Society of Psychology, Paris, France.

Guéraud, S., Tapiero, I., & O'Brien, E. J. (2005). *Predictive inferences: The interacting influence of context and general world knowledge.* Manuscript submitted for publication.

Gygax, P., Garnham, A., & Oakhill, J. (2004). Understanding emotions in text: Readers do not represent specific emotions. *Language and Cognitive Processes, 19*(5), 613–638.

Gygax, P., Oakhill, J., & Garnham, A. (2003). The representation of characters' emotional responses: Do readers infer specific emotions? *Cognition and Emotion, 17*(3), 413–428.

Gygax, P., Tapiero, I., & Carruzzo, E. (in press). Emotion inferences during reading comprehension: What evidence can the self-pace reading paradigm provide? *Discourse Processes.*

Haberlandt, K., & Bingham, G. (1978). Verbs contribute to the coherence of brief narratives: Reading related and unrelated sentence triplets. *Journal of Verbal Learning and Verbal Behavior, 17,* 419–425.

Haberlandt, K. D., & Graesser, A. C. (1985). Component processes in text comprehension and some of their interactions. *Journal of Experimental Psychology: General, 114,* 357–374.

Haenggi, D., Gernsbacher, M. A., & Bolliger, C. M. (1994). Individual inferences in situation-based inferencing during narrative text comprehension. In H. van Oostendorp & R. A. Zwaan (Eds.), *Naturalistic text comprehension* (pp. 79–96). Norwood, NJ: Ablex.

Haenggi, D., Kintsch, W., & Gernsbacher, M. A. (1995). Spatial situation models and text comprehension. *Discourse Processes, 19,* 173–199.

Halliday, M. A. K., & Hasan, R. (1976). *Cohesion in English.* London: Longmans.

Hasher, L., & Zacks, R. T. (1988). Working memory, comprehension and aging: A review and a new view. In G. H. Bower (Ed.), *The psychology of learning and motivation* (p. 22). New York: Academic Press.

Haviland, S. E., & Clark, H. H. (1974). What's new? Acquiring new information as a process in comprehension. *Journal of Verbal Learning and Verbal Behavior, 13,* 512–521.

Hayward, W. G., & Tarr, M. J. (1995). Spatial language and spatial representation. *Cognition, 55,* 39–84.

Hintzman, D. L. (1986). "Schema abstraction" in a multiple-trace memory model. *Psychological Review, 93,* 411–428.

Huitema, J. S., Dopkins, S., Klin, C. M., & Myers, J. L. (1993). Connecting goals and actions during reading. *Journal of Experimental Psychology: Learning, Memory and Cognition, 19*(5), 1053–1060.

Johnson, H. M., & Seifert, C. (1994). Sources of the continued influence effect: When misinformation in memory affects later inferences. *Journal of Experimental Psychology: Learning, Memory, and Cognition, 20*(6), 1420–1436.

Johnson, H. M., & Seifert, C. M. (1993). Correcting causal explanations in memory. *Proceedings of the 15th Annual Conference of the Cognitive Science Society*. Hillsdale, NJ: Lawrence Erlbaum Associates.

Johnson-Laird, P. N. (1983). *Mental models*. Cambridge, MA: Cambridge University Press.

Just, M. A., & Carpenter, P. A. (1987). *The psychology of reading and language comprehension*. Boston: Allyn & Bacon.

Keefe, D. E., & McDaniel, M. A. (1993). The time course and durability of predictive inferences. *Journal of Memory and Language, 32,* 446–463.

Keenan, J. M., Baillet, S. D., & Brown, P. (1984). The effects of causal cohesion on comprehension and memory. *Journal of Verbal Learning and Verbal Behavior, 23,* 115–126.

Keenan, J. M., Potts, G. R., Golding, J. M., & Jennings, T. M. (1990). Which elaborative inferences are drawn during reading? A question of methodologies. In D. A. Balota, G. B. Flores d'Arcois, & K. Rayner (Eds.), *Comprehension processes in reading* (pp. 377–402). Hillsdale, NJ: Lawrence Erlbaum Associates.

Kintsch, W. (1974). *The representation of meaning in memory*. Hillsdale, NJ: Lawrence Erlbaum Associates.

Kintsch, W. (1988). The role of knowledge in discourse comprehension: A construction-integration model. *Psychological Review, 95,* 163–182.

Kintsch, W. (1998). *Comprehension: A paradigm for cognition*. New York: Cambridge University Press.

Kintsch, W., & Greeno, J. G. (1985). Understanding and solving word arithmetic problems. *Psychological Review, 85*(1), 109–129.

Kintsch, W., & Keenan, J. M. (1973). Reading rate and retention as a function of the number of propositions in the base structure of sentences. *Cognitive Psychology, 5,* 257–274.

Kintsch, E., & Kintsch, W. (1995). Strategies to promote active learning from text: Individual differences in background knowledge. *Swiss Journal of Psychology, 54*(2), 141–151.

Kintsch, W., Mandel, T. S., & Kozminsky, E. (1977). Summarizing scrambled stories. *Memory and Cognition, 5,* 547–552.

Kintsch, W., & Mross, E. F. (1985). Context effects in word identification. *Journal of Memory and Language, 24,* 336–349.

Kintsch, W., & van Dijk, T. A. (1978). Toward a model of text comprehension and production. *Psychological Review, 85,* 363–394.

Kintsch, W., & Welsch, D. M. (1991). The construction-integration model: A framework for studying memory for text. In W. E. Hockley & S. Lewandowsky (Eds.), *Relating theory and data: Essays on human memory* (pp. 363–367). Hillsdale, NJ: Lawrence Erlbaum Associates.

Kintsch, W., Welsch, D. M., Schmalhofer, F., & Zimny, S. (1990). Sentence memory: A theoretical analysis. *Journal of Memory and Language, 29,* 133–159.

Klin, C. M., Guzmàn, A. E., & Levine, W. H. (1999). Prevalence and persistence of predictive inferences. *Journal of Memory and Language, 40,* 593–604.

Klin, C. M., Murray, J. D., Levine, W. H., & Guzman, A. E. (1999). Forward inferences: From activation to long-term memory. *Discourse Processes, 27,* 241–260.

Klin, C. M., & Myers, J. (1993). Reinstatement of causal information during reading. *Journal of Experimental Psychology: Learning, Memory, and Cognition, 19,* 554–560.

Kneepkens, E. W. E. M., & Zwaan, R. A. (1994). Emotions and literary text comprehension. *Poetics, 23,* 125–138.

Landauer, T. K., & Dumais, S. T. (1997). A solution to Plato's problem: The latent semantic analysis theory of acquisition, induction and representation of knowledge. *Psychological Review, 104,* 211–420.

Langston, W., Kramer, D. C., & Glenberg, A. M. (1998). The representation of space in mental models derived from text. *Memory and Cognition, 26,* 247–262.

Langston, W., & Trabasso, T. (1999). Modeling causal integration and availability of information during comprehension of narratives. In H. van Oostendorp & S. Goldman (Eds.), *The construction of mental representations during reading* (pp. 29–69). Mahwah, NJ: Lawrence Erlbaum Associates.

Lazarus, R. S. (1982). Thoughts on the relations between emotion and cognition. *American Psychologist, 37,* 1019–1024.

Legros, D. (1989). Etude de l'effet d'un procédé de dramatisation sur la mémorisation d'un récit: Implications pour l'élaboration de matériels de diagnostic cognitive [Impact of the effect of drama on stories recall: Implications for the elaboration of test for a cognitive diagnosis]. *Questions de Logopédie, 21,* 93–103.

Le Ny, J. F. (1979). *La sémantique psychologique* [The psychological semantics]. Paris: Presses Universitaires de France.

Levelt, W. J. M. (1984). Some perceptual limitations on talking about space. In A. J. van Doorn, W. A. van de Grind, & J. J. Koenderink (Eds.), *Limits in perception.* Utrecht, Netherlands: VNU Science Press.

Linderholm, T., Virtue, S., Tzeng, Y., & van den Broek, P. (2004). Fluctuations in the availability of information during reading: Capturing cognitive processes using the Landscape Model. *Discourse Processes, 37,* 165–186.

Lorch, R. F. (1998). Memory-based text processing: Assumptions and issues. *Discourse Processes, 26*(2,3), 213–221.

Mackie, J. L. (1980). *The cement of the universe: A study of causation.* Oxford, UK: Clarendon Press.

Magharo, J., Trabasso, T., & Langston, M. (1995, November). *Cohesion and coherence in sentence and story understanding.* Paper presented at the meetings of the Psychonomic Society, Los Angeles, CA.

Magliano, J. P. (1999). Revealing inference processes during text comprehension. In S. R. Goldman, A. C. Graesser, & P. van Den Broek (Eds.), *Narrative comprehension, causality, and coherence: Essays in honor of Tom Trabasso* (pp. 55–75). Mahwah, NJ: Lawrence Erlbaum Associates.

Magliano, J. P., Baggett, W. B., Johnson, B. K., & Graesser, A. C. (1993). The time course of generating causal antecedent and causal consequence inferences. *Discourse Processes, 16,* 35–53.

Magliano, J. P., Zwaan, R. A., & Graesser, A. C. (1999). The role of situational continuity in narrative understanding. In H. van Oostendorp & S. R. Goldman (Eds.), *The construction of mental representation during reading* (pp. 219–245). Mahwah, NJ: Lawrence Erlbaum Associates.

Mandler, G. (1975). *Mind and emotion.* New York: Wiley. (Reprinted 1982 by Krieger, Melbourne, Florida)

Mandler, J. M. (1986). On the comprehension of temporal order. *Language and Cognitive Processes, 1,* 309–320.

Mandler, J. M., & Johnson, N. S. (1977). Remembrance of things parsed: Story structure and recall. *Cognitive Psychology, 9,* 111–151.

Mann, W. C., & Thompson, S. A. (1986). Relational propositions in discourse. *Discourse Processes, 9,* 57–90.

Mannes, S. M., & Kintsch, W. (1987). Knowledge organization and text organization. *Cognition and Instruction, 4*(2), 91–115.

Martins, D. (1982). Influence of affect in comprehension of a text. *Text, 2,* 141–154.

Martins, D., & Le Bouédec, B. (1998). La production d'inférences lors de la compréhension de textes chez des adultes: Une analyse de la literature [Inference generation in text comprehension with adults: A review of the literature]. *L'Année Psychologique, 98,* 511–543.

McClelland, J. L., & Elman, J. L. (1986). The TRACE Model of Speech Perception. *Cognitive Psychology, 18,* 1–86.

McKoon, G., Gerrig, R. J., & Greene, S. B. (1996). Pronouns resolution without pronouns: Some consequences of memory-based text processing. *Journal of Experimental Psychology: Learning, Memory, and Cognition, 22*(4), 919–932.

McKoon, G., & Ratcliff, R. (1986). Inferences about predictable events. *Journal of Experimental Psychology: Learning, Memory, and Cognition, 12,* 82–91.

McKoon, G., & Ratcliff, R. (1990). Textual inferences: Models and measures. In D. A. Balota, G. B. Flores d'Arcais, & K. Rayner (Eds.), *Comprehension processes in reading* (pp. 403–421). Hillsdale, NJ: Lawrence Erlbaum Associates.

McKoon, G., & Ratcliff, R. (1992). Inference during reading. *Psychological Review, 99,* 440–466.

Miall, D. S. (1989). Beyond the schema given: Affective comprehension of literary narratives. *Cognition and Emotion, 3,* 55–78.

Miller, G. A., & Johnson-Laird, P. N. (1976). *Language and perception.* Cambridge, MA: Harvard University Press.

Miller, J. R., & Kintsch, W. (1981). Readability and recall of short prose passages: A theoretical analysis. *Journal of Experimental Psychology: Human Learning and Memory, 6,* 335–354.

Minsky, M. A. (1975). A framework for representing knowledge. In P. Winston (Ed.), *The psychology of computer vision* (pp. 211–277). New York: McGraw-Hill.

Molinari, G., & Tapiero, I. (2000, July). *Integration of domain knowledge from an outline and a target text: Effects of expertise, and semantic information.* Oral presentation at the 10th Annual Meeting of the Society for Text and Discourse, Lyon, France.

Molinari, G., & Tapiero, I. (2005). Différences "Novices–Experts" dans l'apprentissage de domaines spécifiques par la lecture: Effet de la structure textuelle et des catégories sémantiques [Novice–expert differences in learning a specific domain throughout reading: Effect of textual structure and semantic categories]. In D. Alamargot, P. Terrier, & J.-M. Cellier (Eds.), *Production, compréhension et usages des ecrits techniques au travail.* Octarès Press.

Molinari, G., & Tapiero, I. (in press). Integration of new domain-related states and events from texts and illustrations by subjects with high and low prior knowledge. *Learning and Instruction.*

Morrow, D. G., Bower, G. H., & Greenspan, S. L. (1989). Updating situation models during narrative comprehension. *Journal of Memory and Language, 28,* 292–312.

Morrow, D. G., Greenspan, S. L., & Bower, G. H. (1987). Accessibility and situation models in narrative comprehension. *Journal of Memory and Language, 26,* 165–187.

Mross, E., & Roberts, J. (1992). *The Construction-Integration Model: A program and manual* (Tech. Rep. No. 92–14). Boulder: University of Colorado, Institute of Cognitive Science.

Murray, J. D., Klin, C. M., & Myers, J. L. (1993). Forward inferences in narrative text. *Journal of Memory and Language, 32,* 464–473.

Myers, J. L., & O'Brien, E. J. (1998). Accessing the discourse representation during reading. *Discourse Processes, 26,* 131–157.

Myers, J. L., Shinjo, M., & Duffy, S. A. (1987). The role of causal relatedness and memory. *Journal of Memory and Language, 4,* 453–465.

Nezworski, T., Stein, N. L., & Trabasso, T. (1982). Story structure versus content in children's recall. *Journal of Verbal Learning and Verbal Behavior, 21,* 196–206.

Oakhill, J. V., & Garnham, A. (1996). *Mental models in cognitive science: Essays in honor of P. Johnson-Laird.* Hove, East Sussex, UK: Psychology Press.

O'Brien, E. J., & Albrecht, J. E. (1991). The role of context in accessing antecedents in text. *Journal of Experimental Psychology: Learning, Memory, and Cognition, 17*(1), 94–102.

O'Brien, E. J., & Albrecht, J. E. (1992). Comprehension strategies in the development of mental model. *Journal of Experimental Psychology: Learning, Memory, and Cognition, 18*(4), 777–784.

O'Brien, E. J., Albrecht, J. E., Hakala, C. M., & Rizzella, M. L. (1995). Activation and suppression of antecedents during reinstatement. *Journal of Experimental Psychology: Learning, Memory, and Cognition, 21*(3), 626–634.

O'Brien, E. J., Duffy, S. A., & Myers, J. L. (1986). Anaphoric inference during reading. *Journal of Experimental Psychology: Learning, Memory, and Cognition, 12*, 346–352.

O'Brien, E. J., & Myers, J. L. (1987). The role of causal connections in the retrieval of text. *Memory and Cognition, 15*, 419–427.

O'Brien, E. J., & Myers, J. L. (1999). Text comprehension: A view from the bottom up. In S. R. Goldman, A. C. Graesser, & P. van den Broek (Eds.), *Narrative comprehension, causality, and coherence: Essays in honor of Tom Trabasso* (pp. 36–53). Mahwah, NJ: Lawrence Erlbaum Associates.

O'Brien, E. J., Plewes, S., & Albrecht, J. E. (1990). Antecedent retrieval processes. *Journal of Experimental Psychology: Learning, Memory, and Cognition, 16*, 241–249.

Ohtsuka, K., & Brewer, W. F. (1992). Discourse organization in the comprehension of temporal order in narrative texts. *Discourse Processes, 15*, 317–336.

Omanson, R. C. (1982). The relation between centrality and story category variation. *Journal of Verbal Learning and Verbal Behavior, 21*, 326–337.

Ortony, A., Clore, G. L., & Collins, A. (1988). *The cognitive structure of emotions*. Cambridge, UK: Cambridge University Press.

Otero, J., & Campanario, J. M. (1990). Comprehension evaluation and regulation in learning from science texts. *Journal of Research in Science Teaching, 27*, 447–460.

Otero, J., & Kintsch, W. (1992). Failures to detect contradictions in a text: What readers believe versus what they read. *Psychological Science, 3*(4), 229–235.

Patel, V. L., & Groen, G. J. (1991). The general and specific nature of medical expertise: A critical look. In K. A. Ericsson & J. Smith (Eds.), *Toward a general theory of expertise* (pp. 93–125). New York: Cambridge University Press.

Peeck, J. (1994). The perspective inducing function of text illustration. In H. van Oostendorp & R. A. Zwaan (Eds.), *Naturalistic text comprehension* (pp. 135–148). Norwood, NJ: Ablex.

Peracchi, K. A., & O'Brien, E. J. (2004). Character profiles and the activation of predictive inferences. *Memory and Cognition, 32*, 1044–1052.

Perrig, W., & Kintsch, W. (1985). Propositional and situational representations of text. *Journal of Memory and Language, 24*, 503–518.

Perrig, W. J., & Perrig, P. (1988). Mood and memory: Mood-congruity effects in absence of mood. *Memory and Cognition, 16*(2), 102–109.

Potts, G. R., & Peterson, S. B. (1985). Incorporation versus compartmentalization in memory for discourse. *Journal of Memory and Language, 24*, 107–118.

Potts, G. R., St. John, M. F., & Kirson, D. (1989). Incorporating new information into existing world knowledge. *Cognitive Psychology, 21*, 303–333.

Quintana, M. P. (1994). *La représentation en mémoire des relations causales dans le traitement de textes narratifs* [Representation in memory of causal relations in stories processing]. Unpublished master's thesis, University of Lyon 2, Lyon, France.

Quintana, M. P. (1996). *Nature de la représentation en mémoire de textes narratifs: Réseau via médiations versus réseau direct* [Nature of memory representation in stories: Network via mediations versus direct]. Unpublished master's thesis, University of Lyon 2, Lyon, France.

Rapp, D. N., Gerrig, R. J., & Prentice, D. A. (2001). Readers' trait-based models of characters in narrative comprehension. *Journal of Memory and Language, 45*, 737–750.

Ratcliff, R., & McKoon, G. (1978). Priming in item recognition: Evidence for the propositional structure of sentences. *Journal of Verbal Learning and Verbal Behavior, 17*, 403–417.

Rinck, M., Glowalla, U., & Schneider, K. (1992). Mood-congruent and mood-incongruent learning. *Memory and Cognition, 20*, 29–39.

Rizzella, M. L., & O'Brien, E. J. (1996). Accessing global causes during reading. *Journal of Experimental Psychology: Learning, Memory and Cognition, 22*(5), 1208–1218.

Rossetti, C. (2005). *Pointeurs du discours et processus de resonance en comprehension de textes* [Discourse pointers and resonance process in text comprehension]. Unpublished master's thesis, University of Lyon 2, Lyon, France.

Rossi, J. P., & Bert-Erboul, A. (1991). Sélection des informations importantes et compréhension de texts [Important information selection and text comprehension]. *Psychologie Française, 36–2*, 135–143.

Rumelhart, D. E., McClelland, J. L., & The PDP Research Group. (1986). *Parallel distributed processing* (Vols. 1 & 2). Cambridge, MA: MIT Press.

Rumelhart, D. E., & Norman, D. A. (1978). Accretion, tuning and restructuring: Three modes of learning. In J. W. Cottin & R. Klatzky (Eds.), *Semantic factors in cognition*. Hillsdale, NJ: Lawrence Erlbaum Associates.

Rumelhart, D. E., & Norman, D. A. (1988). Representation in memory. In R. C. Atkinson, R. J. Herrnstein, G. Lindzey, & R. Duncan Luce (Eds.), *Steven's handbook of experimental psychology* (pp. 511–587). New York: Wiley.

Sachs, J. S. (1967). Recognition memory for syntactic and semantic aspects of connected discourse. *Perception and Psychophysics, 2*, 437–442.

Sanford, A. J. (1987). *The mind of man: Models of human understanding*. Brighton, UK: Yale University Press.

Sanford, A. J., & Garrod, S. C. (1981). *Understanding written language: Explorations in comprehension beyond the sentence*. New York: Wiley.

Sanford, A. J., & Garrod, S. C. (1998). The role of scenario mapping in text comprehension. *Discourse Processes, 26*(2&3), 159–190.

Schank, R. (1975). The structure of episodes in memory. In D. G. Bobrow & A. M. Collins (Eds.), *Representation and understanding: Studies in cognitive science*. New York: Academic Press.

Schank, R. (1986). *Explanation patterns: Understanding mechanically and creatively*. Hillsdale, NJ: Lawrence Erlbaum Associates.

Schank, R. C., & Abelson, R. (1977). *Scripts, plans, goals and understanding: An inquiry into human knowledge structures*. Hillsdale, NJ: Lawrence Erlbaum Associates.

Scherer, K. (1982). Emotion as a process: Function, origin and regulation. *Social Science Information, 21*(4/5), 555–570.

Schmalhofer, F., & Glavanov, D. (1986). Three components of understanding a programmer's manual: Verbatim, propositional, and situational representations. *Journal of Memory and Language, 25*, 279–294.

Schmalhofer, F., McDaniel, M. A., & Keefe, D. (2002). A unified model for predictive and bridging inferences. *Discourse Processes, 33*(2), 105–132.

Schmidt, H. G., & Boshuizen, H. P. A. (1993). On the origin of intermediates effects in clinical case recall. *Memory and Cognition, 21*(3), 338–351.

Shapiro, B. P., van den Broek, P., & Fletcher, C. R. (1995). Using story-based causal diagrams to analyse disagreemants about complex events. *Discourse Processes, 20*, 51–77.

Spilich, G. J., Vesonder, G. T., Chiesi, H. L., & Voss, J. F. (1979). Text processing of domain-related information for individuals with high and low domain knowledge. *Journal of Verbal Learning and Verbal Behavior, 18*, 275–290.

Stanfield, R. A., & Zwaan, R. A. (2001). The effect of implied orientation derived from verbal context on picture recognition. *Psychological Science, 12*, 153–156.

Stein, N. L., & Glenn, C. G. (1979). An analysis of story comprehension in elementary school children. In R. O. Freedle (Ed.), *New directions in discourse processing* (pp. 53–120). Hillsdale, NJ: Lawrence Erlbaum Associates.

Stevenson, R. J. (1986). *The time course of pronoun comprehension.* Proceedings of the 8th Annual Conference of Cognitive Science Society (pp. 102–109). Hillsdale, NJ: Lawrence Erlbaum Associates.

Suh, S., & Trabasso, T. (1993). Inferences during reading: Converging evidence from discourse analysis, talk-aloud protocols, and recognition priming. *Journal of Memory and Language, 32*, 279–300.

Swinney, D. A. (1979). Lexical access during sentence comprehension: Reconsideration of some context effects. *Journal of Verbal Learning and Verbal Behavior, 18*, 645–659.

Tan, S. (1994). Story processing as an emotion episode. In H. van Oostendorp & R. A. Zwaan (Eds.), *Naturalistic text comprehension* (pp. 165–188). Norwood, NJ: Ablex.

Tapiero, I. (1991). Acquisition et transfert de connaissances à l'aide de textes [Learning and knowledge transfer from texts]. *Psychologie Française, Tome 36–2*, 177–187.

Tapiero, I. (1992). *Traitement cognitif du texte narratif et expositif et connexionnisme: Expérimentations et simulations* [Cognitive processing of stories and expository texts and connectionism: Experimentations and simulations]. Unpublished doctoral dissertation, University of Paris 8, Paris, France.

Tapiero, I. (2000). *Construire une représentation mentale cohérente: Structures, relations et connaissances* [Building a coherent mental representation: Structures, relations and knowledge]. Postdoctoral thesis for the "Habilitation á diriger des recherches," University of Lyon 2, Lyon, France.

Tapiero, I. (2003). Text structure and expertise: The use of the Construction-Integration Model. *Cognitive Science Quarterly, 3*(1), 5–25.

Tapiero, I., & Blanc, N. (2001). Aspect multidimensional des representations mentales construites à partir de testes narratifs: De l'approache thénique aux apports emporiques [Multidimensional aspect of mental representation build from narratives: From a theoretical perspective to empirical contributions]. *L'Ammée Psychologique, 101*, 655–682.

Tapiero, I., & Cailliès, S. (1995). The learning of a functional system: Level of expertise and semantic textual coherence. *Proceedings of the American Educational Research Association, San Francisco, CA.*

Tapiero, I., & Denhière, G. (1995). Simulating recall and recognition by using Kintsch's Construction-Integration Model. In C. A. Weaver, S. Mannes, & C. R. Fletcher (Eds), *Discourse comprehension: Essays in honor of Walter Kintsch* (pp. 211–232). Hillsdale, NJ: Lawrence Erlbaum Associates.

Tapiero, I., & Fillon, V. (in press). Hemisphere differences in the processing of negative and positive emotional inferences. In F. Schmalhofer & C. A. Perfetti (Eds.), *Higher level language processes in the brain: Inference and comprehension processes.* Mahwah, NJ: Lawrence Erlbaum Associates.

Tapiero, I., & Otero, J. (1999). Distinguishing between textbase and situation model in the processing of inconsistent information: Elaboration versus tagging. In H. van Oostendorp & S. R. Goldman (Eds.), *The construction of mental representation during reading* (pp. 341–365). Mahwah, NJ: Lawrence Erlbaum Associates.

Tapiero, I., & Otero, J. (2002). Situation models as retrieval structures: Effects on the global coherence of science texts. In A. C. Graesser, J. A. Leon, & J. Otero (Eds.), *Psychology of science text comprehension* (pp. 179–198). Mahwah, NJ: Lawrence Erlbaum Associates.

Tapiero, I., van den Broek, P., & Quintana, M.-P. (2002). The mental representation of narrative texts as networks: The role of necessity and sufficiency on the detection of four types of causal textual relations. *Discourse Processes, 34*(3), 237–258.

Taylor, H. A., & Tversky, B. (1992). Spatial mental models derived from survey and route descriptions. *Journal of Memory and Language, 31*, 262–292.

Taylor, H. A., & Tversky, B. (1996). Perspective in spatial descriptions. *Journal of Memory and Language, 35*, 371–391.

Thorndyke, P. W. (1977). Cognitive structures in comprehension and memory of narrative discourse. *Cognitive Psychology, 9*, 77–110.

Till, R. E., Mross, E. F., & Kintsch, W. (1988). Time course of priming for associate and inference words in a discourse context. *Memory and Cognition, 16*, 283–299.

Trabasso, T. (1991). The development of coherence of narratives by understanding international action. In G. Denhière & J. P. Rossi (Eds.), *Text and text processing* (Vol. 79, pp. 297–317). Amsterdam: North Holland.

Trabasso, T., Secco, T., & van den Broek, P. (1984). Causal cohesion and story coherence. In H. Mandl, N. L. Stein, & T. Trabasso (Eds.), *Learning and comprehension of text*. Hillsdale, NJ: Lawrence Erlbaum Associates.

Trabasso, T., & Sperry, L. (1985). Causal relatedness and importance of story events. *Journal of Memory and Language, 24*, 595–611.

Trabasso, T., & van den Broek, P. (1985). Causal thinking and representations of narrative events. *Journal of Memory and Language, 24*, 612–630.

Trabasso, T., van den Broek, P. W., & Suh, S. Y. (1989). Logical necessity and transitivity of causal relations in stories. *Discourse Processes, 12*, 1–25.

Tversky, B. (1991). Spatial mental models. In G. H. Bower (Ed.), *The psychology of learning and motivation: Advances in research and theory* (Vol. 27, pp. 109–145). New York: Academic Press.

van den Broek, P. W. (1990a). The causal inference maker: Toward a process model of inference generation in text comprehension. In D. A. Balota, G. B. Flores d'Arcais, & K. Rayner (Eds.), *Comprehension processes in reading* (pp. 423–445). Hillsdale, NJ: Lawrence Erlbaum Associates.

van den Broek, P. W. (1990b). Causal inferences and the comprehension of narrative texts. In A. C. Graesser & G. H. Bower (Eds.), *Psychology of learning and motivation: Inferences and text comprehension* (pp. 175–196). San Diego, CA: Academic Press.

van den Broek, P. W., Bauer, P. J., & Bourg, T. (1997). *Developmental spans in event comprehension and representation: Bridging fictional and actual events.* Mahwah, NJ: Lawrence Erlbaum Associates.

van den Broek, P. W., Fletcher, C. R., & Risden, K. (1993). Investigations of inferential processes in reading: A theoretical and methological integration. *Discourse Processes, 16*, 169–180.

van den Broek, P. W., & Gustafson, M. (1999). Comprehension and memory for texts: Three generations of reading research. In S. R. Goldman, A. Graesser, & P. W. van den Broek (Eds.), *Narrative comprehension, causality, and coherence* (pp. 15–34). Mahwah, NJ: Lawrence Erlbaum Associates.

van den Broek, P. W., & Lorch, R. F. (1993). Network representations of causal relations in memory for narrative texts: Evidence from primed recognition. *Discourse Processes, 16*, 75–98.

van den Broek, P. W., Rapp, D. N., & Kendeou, P. (2005). Integrating memory-based and constructionist processes in accounts of reading comprehension. *Discourse Processes, 39*(2&3), 299–316.

van den Broek, P. W., Risden, K., Fletcher, C. R., & Thurlow, R. (1996). A "landscape" view of reading: Fluctuating patterns of activation and the construction of a stable memory representation. In B. K. Britton & A. C. Graesser (Eds.), *Models of understanding text* (pp. 165–187). Hillsdale, NJ: Lawrence Erlbaum Associates.

van den Broek, P. W., Risden, K., & Husebye-Hartman, E. (1995). The role of readers' standards for coherence in the generation of inferences during reading. In R.

F. Lorch, Jr. & E. J. O'Brien (Eds.), *Sources of coherence in reading* (pp. 353–373). Hillsdale, NJ: Lawrence Erlbaum Associates.

van den Broek, P. W., Trabasso, T., & Thurlow, R. (1990). *The effects of story structure on children's and adults' ability to summarize stories.* Paper presented at the Annual Meeting of the American Educational Research Association. Boston, MA.

van den Broek, P. W., Virtue, S., Everson, M., Tzeng, Y., & Sung, Y. C. (2002). Comprehension and memory of science texts: Inferential processes and the construction of a mental representation. In J. Otero, J. A. Leon, & A. C. Graesser (Eds.), *The psychology of science text comprehension* (pp. 131–154). Mahwah, NJ: Lawrence Erlbaum Associates.

van den Broek, P. W., Young, M., Tzeng, Y., & Linderholm, T. (1999). The landscape model of reading: Inferences and the online construction of memory representation. In H. van Oostendorp & S. R. Goldman (Eds.), *The construction of mental representation during reading* (pp. 71–99). Mahwah, NJ: Lawrence Erlbaum Associates.

van Dijk, T. A. (1972). *Some aspects of text grammars: A study in theoretical poetics and linguistics.* The Hague: Mouton.

van Dijk, T. A. (1977). *Text and context.* London: Longman.

van Dijk, T. A. (1995). On macrostructures, mental models and other inventions: A brief personal story of the Kintsch–van Dijk Theory. In C. A. Weaver, S. Mannes, & C. R. Fletcher (Eds.), *Discourse comprehension: Essays in honor of Walter Kintsch* (pp. 383–410). Hillsdale, NJ: Lawrence Erlbaum Associates.

van Dijk, T. A., & Kintsch, W. (1983). *Strategies of discourse comprehension.* New York: Academic Press.

van Oostendorp, H. (1996). Updating situation models derived from newspaper articles. *Medienpsychologie, 8,* 21–33.

van Oostendorp, H., & Bonebakker, C. (1996). Het vasthouden aan incorrecte informatie bij het verwerken van nieuwsberichten [Holding on to misinformation during processing news reports]. *Tijdschrift voor communicativetenschap, 24*(1), 57–74.

Virtue, S., Linderholm, T., & van den Broek, P. (2000, July). *Hemisphere differences in the processing of high and low constraint predictive inferences.* Poster presented at the 10th Annual Meeting of the Society of Text and Discourse, Lyon, France.

Warren, W. H., Nicolas, D. W., & Trabasso, T. (1979). Event chain and inferences in understanding narratives. In R. O. Freedle (Eds.), *New directions in discourse processing.* Hillsdale, NJ: Lawrence Erlbaum Associates.

Weingartner, K. M., Guzman, A. E., Levine, W. H., & Klin, C. M. (2003). When throwing a vase has multiple consequences: Minimal encoding of predictive inferences. *Discourse Processes, 36*(2), 131–146.

Wilkes, A. L., & Leatherbarrow, M. (1988). Editing episodic memory following the identification of error. *Quarterly Journal of Experimental Psychology, 40A,* 361–387.

Zwaan, R. A. (1996). Processing narrative time shifts. *Journal of Experimental Psychology: Learning, Memory and Cognition, 22*(5), 1196–1207.

Zwaan, R. A. (1999a). Embodied cognition, perceptual symbols, and situation models. *Discourse Processes, 28*(1), 81–88.

Zwaan, R. A. (1999b). Situation models: The mental leap into imagined worlds. *Current Directions in Psychological Science, 8*(1), 15–18.

Zwaan, R. A. (2004). The immersed experiencer: Toward an embodied theory of language comprehension. In B. H. Ross (Ed.), *The psychology of learning and motivation* (Vol. 44, pp. 35–62). New York: Academic Press.

Zwaan, R. A., & Graesser, A. C. (1993). Reading goals and situation models: A commentary on Glenberg and Matthew. *Psychology,* 415.

Zwaan, R. A., Langston, M. C., & Graesser, A. C. (1995). The construction of situation models in narrative comprehension: An event-indexing model. *Psychological Science, 6*(5), 292–297.

Zwaan, R. A., Madden, C. J., & Whitten, S. N. (2000). The presence of an event in the narrated situation affects its availability to the comprehender. *Memory and Cognition, 28*(6), 1022–1028.

Zwaan, R. A., Magliano, J. P., & Graesser, A. C. (1995). Dimensions of situation models construction in narrative comprehension. *Journal of Experimental Psychology: Learning, Memory, and Cognition, 21*(2), 386–397.

Zwaan, R. A., & Radvansky, G. A. (1998). Situation models in language comprehension and memory. *Psychological Bulletin, 12*, 162–185.

Zwaan, R. A., Radvansky, G. A., Hilliard, A. E., & Curiel, J. M. (1998). Constructing multidimensional situation models during reading. *Scientific Studies of Reading, 2*(3), 199–220.

Zwaan, R. A., & Rapp, D. N. (in press). Discourse comprehension. In M. A. Gernsbacher & M. J. Traxler (Eds.), *The handbook of psycholinguistics*. San Diego, CA: Elsevier.

Zwaan, R. A., & van Oostendorp, H. (1993). Do readers construct spatial representations in naturalistic story comprehension? *Discourse Processes, 16*, 125–143.

Zwaan, R. A., & van Oostendorp, H. (1994). Spatial information and naturalistic story comprehension. In H. van Oostendorp & R. A. Zwaan (Eds.), *Naturalistic text comprehension* (pp. 97–114). Norwood, NJ: Ablex.

Author Index

Subject Index

A

Action, situation model element, 40–42
Activated knowledge structure, linguistic input, automatic mapping between, 42–46
Amodal structures, 46–47
Analogical mapping, between symbols, referents, situation models as, 47–53

B

Backward hypothesis, online
new textual information, 68–75
updating, 68–75

C

Causal coherence, 3–31
Causal inference maker model, 152–155
Causal inferences, reading comprehension process, 151–167
Causal network model, 123–136
readers' naive theories of causality, 123–136
Causal test response time, by type of contextual elaboration, degree of sufficiency, 166

Causality theories, naive, readers', 119–136
Cognitive mechanisms, situation model elaboration, 55–113
coherence, 85–113
mental-representation building by reader, 57–84
theories of comprehension, 57–84
theories of text comprehension, 85–113
Coherence, 85–113, 137–148
causal, 3–31
as component of comprehension, 86–91
construction, updating, 91–94
as dynamic component of comprehension, 86–91
global, 115–148
local, 119–123
referential, 3–31
relevance, 94–112
situational continuity, 91–94
text comprehension, 85–113
updating, 91–94
Comprehension, defined, 189–198
Comprehension theories, 57–113
Construction-integration model, 14–26
experts situation model, 23
"ideal" situation model, 22–23
intermediates situation model, 23–24
novices situation model, 24–26